Dear Betty,

From one communicator to another, it has been an honor and a priviledge to lead this transformation from traditional to social with you.

Best,

Erin

SOCIAL MARKETING *to the* BUSINESS CUSTOMER

LISTEN TO YOUR B2B MARKET,
GENERATE MAJOR ACCOUNT LEADS,
AND BUILD CLIENT RELATIONSHIPS

PAUL GILLIN
ERIC SCHWARTZMAN

John Wiley & Sons, Inc.

Published by John Wiley & Sons, Inc., Hoboken, New Jersey.
Published simultaneously in Canada.

For general information on our other products and services or for technical support, please contact our Customer Care Department within the United States at (800) 762-2974, outside the United States at (317) 572-3993 or fax (317) 572-4002.

Wiley also publishes its books in a variety of electronic formats. Some content that appears in print may not be available in electronic books. For more information about Wiley products, visit our web site at www.wiley.com.

Library of Congress Cataloging-in-Publication Data:

Gillin, Paul.
Social marketing to the business customer : listen to your B2B market, generate major account leads, and build client relationships / Paul Gillin, Eric Schwartzman.
p. cm.
Includes index.
ISBN 978-0-470-63933-7 (hardback); ISBN 978-0-470-93972-7 (ebk); 978-0-470-93973-4 (ebk)
1. Internet marketing. 2. Marketing—Social aspects. 3. Social media. I. Schwartzman, Eric. II. Title.
HF5415.1265.G554 2011
658.8'72—dc22

2010031874

Printed in the United States of America

10 9 8 7 6 5 4 3 2 1

To my grandfathers, Morton and Phillip,
for teaching me the value of a buck.
—Eric

To Patrick J. McGovern,
a brilliant mind and my personal hero.
—Paul

CONTENTS

Part Three: Going to Market

FOREWORD

If you're reading this book, you are probably interested in understanding how social marketing can enhance your brand, grow your business, and increase customer loyalty. The authors of this book make the important point that B2B relationships are defined by value, and social marketing has the power to dramatically increase the value that companies can provide to their customers.

Dell is, at our core, a B2B company and has been since Michael founded Dell in 1984 when he started out selling computers to businesses and universities. He had an idea that direct relationships with customers would allow more people access to technology so they could reach their full potential, and that is still very much a guiding principle for us today. Today, sales to commercial and public customers account for approximately 80 percent of revenue—and there's nothing more direct than using the input we get from social media to help our customers solve their most complex challenges.

Why Social?

Many companies talk about the importance of customers, but when it comes to embracing the principles of openness and interaction that social marketing enables, they may hesitate. After all, there may be just as much unfavorable feedback as there is favorable feedback out there. However, it's the combination of both the positive and the negative that can truly empower organizations to make meaningful changes to better serve customers and build loyalty. Social media certainly make listening easier, but it's the actions that organizations take from their conversations that build enduring relationships with customers that last long after a single transaction.

When I'm meeting with customers or speaking at conferences, I'm often asked why Dell has embraced social media with such enthusiasm. Our commitment to blogs, social networks, and customer forums seems particularly striking in light of the fact that just four years ago we were the target of some vocal criticism in those same places. Here's why we embrace social media. It's because these social communities are where we get honest, candid feedback from our customers that we incorporate into solutions that better meet their needs. Our early conversations with online critics were actually a blessing. They reminded us of the importance of how direct customer interaction drives our business strategy and growth. Dell is mentioned in thousands of online conversations, and on any given day, comments about Dell on Twitter can reach as many as 10 million people. Each of these discussions is an opportunity for us to enhance or build a customer relationship, and to act on what we hear. Social media provide simply another way that we can listen to and engage with our customers—and a powerful way for us to learn what we need to do to help our customers succeed.

At Dell, we believe that team members are our most valuable assets, and they should be the ones to interact with our customers. If a customer has a technical issue, he or she will chat with someone from our product or engineering team. If it's a service issue, that customer will interact with our support team. We provide the foundation that our global team members need to use social media as part of their jobs through our Social Media and Communities University.

This scale of interaction may sound a bit scary at first, but it doesn't have to be when you align people around a common purpose so that when they speak to customers, they're working toward the same goal. For Dell, that purpose is to provide technology that gives our customers the power to do more—to grow, to thrive.

Why Social Marketing for B2B?

B2B relationships are fundamentally not about companies but about people. At Dell, we encourage team members to use their blogs and Twitter accounts to talk about their families, vacations, and passions, if that's information they want to share. These glimpses into the personal lives of professional colleagues are essential to building strong relationships. Think of it: When you speak to a trusted business partner at a meeting or on the phone, you typically spend several minutes chatting about events that go on outside the office. The better you know people professionally, the better you get to know them personally.

B2B relationships are also about being helpful, and here is where social media have opened some amazing new opportunities for us. A great example is our Social Media for Small Business page on Facebook. Those business owners look to us for advice on how to leverage social channels for their businesses, and we're excited to share what we have learned. We take great care not to make this resource a sales pitch. These days, the best marketing is the kind that helps people to be successful.

The authors give one example of how we support our customers in Chapter 1, where they tell the story of Dell TechCenter, an online support resource for customers who purchase Dell solutions for their businesses. TechCenter exemplifies the value of personal engagement in a business context. Our TechCenter staffers have gotten to know many of our customers personally as a result of their technical support interactions. These relationships are enhanced through dinners and meet-ups at conferences or even at Dell's offices, where customers often request meetings with the TechCenter experts.

Preparing for What's Next

The information technology ecosystem is constantly transforming itself, but even more impactful is how people are using technology to create innovations that will change our world. A few years ago, customers primarily used Dell.com to buy products. Today, it's the focal point for a variety of social platforms where they learn from each other as well as from us. Tomorrow, the boundaries between online and offline may entirely disappear as "digital" and "virtual" just become ingrained in how we all communicate.

However, the one constant that will remain is the value that organizations of all sizes can realize from social marketing. Does social marketing enable a business to get closer to its customers? Does it provide feedback that can be used to improve the customer experience? Does it help grow the business and build the brand? The answer in all cases is *yes*. Embracing social marketing and finding a way to integrate it into the fabric of doing business can help B2B companies truly provide more value to the people they serve and create loyal customers for life.

—KAREN QUINTOS
Senior Vice President and
Chief Marketing Officer, Dell Inc.

ACKNOWLEDGMENTS

Much of what I've learned about business-to-business (B2B) social marketing has resulted from the generosity of Ellis Booker, former editor-in-chief of *BtoB* magazine. It was Ellis who gave me writing assignments and eventually a monthly column when I was striking out in this territory in 2006. *BtoB* publisher Bob Felsenthal has also been generous in allowing me to further my education in this area as a representative of his fine publication. Many of the case studies in this book began as *BtoB* assignments.

Dell is often held up as an icon of B2B social media excellence. Richard Binhammer has helped me understand how that innovative company has transformed itself. He's also been a great source of contacts.

Jen McClure and her nonprofit Society for New Communications Research deliver unrivaled insight through their publications and conferences. She has made it possible for me to meet so many people who have influenced my life that I can never thank her enough.

Shel Holtz and Neville Hobson have recorded an incredible 553 episodes of their "For Immediate Release" podcast as of this writing. I never miss a program. They've pointed me to people and research that was invaluable in preparing this book.

Several people gave generously of their time in helping me understand the issues in B2B social marketing, including Alan Belniak (PTC); Barbara Bix, Chris Boudreaux (SocialMediaGovernance.com); Jim Cahill (Emerson); Bobbie Carlton, Ron Casalotti (Bloomberg);

Brian Casey (AuntMinnie); Nick Fishman (EmployeeScreen); Christian Gunning (Boingo); Jay Halberg (Spiceworks); Scott Hanson (Dell); Sumaya Kazi (YoProCo); Christina Kerley, Wyatt Kilmartin (RIDGID); Joseph Manna (Infusionsoft); James Mathewson (IBM); Debbie McGrath (HR.com); Michelle Murray (Cree); Bill Robb (Cisco); Danny Schaeffler, Allan Schoenberg (CME); Rick Short (Indium); Dwayne Spradlin (InnoCentive); David van Toor (NoPlanB.com); Deirdre Walsh (National Instruments); and Scott Wurtele (IdeaConnection). I'm sure I've missed a few, and I apologize for that.

My wife and soul mate, Dana, has stuck with me through four books in four years, which qualifies her for sainthood. She has carefully copyedited and proofread each one. I don't know what I would do without her, and I hope I never find out.

—Paul Gillin

Above all, I thank my wife, Celia, for her love and support, and my son, William, for continuously renewing my spirit and perspective.

Many have contributed to my professional growth and understanding of the social media world. They include (in alphabetical order) Elizabeth Albrycht, David Almy, Robin Antin, Lauren Bartlett, Major Carrie Batson, Kimberlee Beers, Pete Blackshaw, Paul Bloch, Henri Bollinger, Tim Bourquin, Michael Butler, David Carr, CC Chapman, Major Danny Chung, Craig Comeau, Christopher Degnan, Andree Deissenberg, Joe DeMattos, Major Christian Devine, Scott DeYager, Steve Doctorow, John Elsasser, Michael Furtney, Steve Garfield, John Gerstner, Tammy Lynn Gilmore, Lisa S. Gleason, Billie Gross, Captain Dustin Hart, John Hatfield, Liza Henshaw, Neville Hobson, Harlan Hogan, Shel Holtz, Captain Kymberly Jurado, Greg Jarboe, Dominic Jones, Beth Kanter, Sulosana Karthigasu, Joanne Killeen, Lieutenant Colonel Daniel King, Erica Klein, Bruce P. Kleiner, Stacey Knott, Michael Kroll, Kaiser Kuo, Dany Levy, Marsha Lindsay, Michael Liskin, Lawrence Lokman, Krista Loretto, Matthew Lussenhop, William Lutz, Mary Matalobos, John Matel, Jennifer McClure, Barbara McDonald, Julie McDonald, Thomas S. Miller, Bull Murray, Michael Netzley, Major David Nevers,

Karen North, Gunnery Sergeant Chanin Nuntavong, Leysia Palen, Christopher Penn, Jeremy Pepper, Andy Perez, Steve Perlman, Bryan Person, Jeremy Rawitch, Lieutenant Colonel Gregory Reeder, Sean Riley, Kevin Roderick, Steve Rubel, Colonel Brian Salas, Rob Scheidlinger, Colleen Seaver, Tony Selznick, Fay Shapiro, Helene Silber, Jim Sinkinson, Tom Smith, Brain Solis, Don Spetner, Sarah Spitz, Mark Story, Tom Tardio, Captain Eric Tausch, Laurel Touby, Judy Voss, and John Wall.

To everyone else who has shared their experience, strength and hope, I am forever grateful.

—Eric Schwartzman

HOW TO USE THIS BOOK

Social marketing is about tools, people, and organization. To get the greatest impact, you need to introduce the technology to a receptive audience and then apply it for business value. We've organized this book into three parts to step you through the process.

Part 1 (Chapters 1 through 5) sets the table for the introduction of tools. These chapters tell you how social marketing is revolutionizing customer relationships and offer seven business case scenarios for applying tools. We then offer advice on how to sell social marketing to skeptical bosses, build an organization that listens and responds constantly to its constituents, and create guidelines and policies for appropriate behavior. The framework for building a policy is covered in Appendix A.

Part 2 (Chapters 6 through 9) is about technology. We tell you how to build a listening dashboard, which is an essential first step to applying new technology. Chapter 7 guides you through the intricacies of search and keywords; these are essential concepts to know when building online visibility. We then look at the major public social media platforms, such as LinkedIn and Twitter, and offer some context for the value of each. Finally, we tell you how to build your own community platform.

Part 3 (Chapters 10 through 15) is about putting social marketing to work. We start with a series of short case studies that spotlight B2B companies that are achieving results with various tools. The next few chapters step you through the process of identifying good opportunities for social marketing, generating leads, and putting communities to work. We include plenty of examples of how others are achieving success. We wrap up with an explanation of how to calculate return on investment (ROI). Contrary to popular perception, we believe you *can* figure out the ROI of social marketing if you have the right historical data in place.

PREFACE

The idea for this book was hatched in October 2009 at the Inbound Marketing Summit in Foxboro, Massachusetts. More than 70 speakers packed a terrific two-day agenda, relating stories of how they sold everything from cameras to Cabernet Sauvignon using the new tools of social media.

On the afternoon of the first day, an attendee raised her hand and asked how a speaker's advice could be applied to business-to-business (B2B) marketing. The speaker (we can't remember who it was) asked which members of the audience worked for B2B companies. More than half the hands in a room packed with 450 marketers went up.

Paul watched the scene with interest. He had been a journalist and executive at B2B publishers in the technology field for more than 20 years before making the switch to social media consulting in 2005. It had never occurred to him how different the needs are between a company that sells clothing and one that sells uniforms. A quick check on Amazon revealed that of the 50+ social media marketing books that had been published in the prior year, not one specifically addressed the needs of the B2B marketer.

We began to ask questions of event organizers and social media publishers. Why was it that consumer success stories like Zappos and Blendtec continued to dominate conference agendas and research reports when B2B companies had been such early and enthusiastic adopters of social tools? The answer we got back most often—that similar principles applied to both types of businesses—seemed insufficient.

We love it when the two guys from EepyBird.com drop Mentos into bottles of Diet Coke, but we couldn't see how that example would apply to a marketer at ConAgra.

The two of us were already planning to collaborate on a book based on Eric's archive of On the Record . . . Online podcasts. We quickly switched gears and spent the next 6 months delving into the intricacies of the business buying decision. We learned how very different the two business types really are.

Changing Channels

B2B marketing has been conducted pretty much the same way for decades. Direct sales forces followed up on leads generated by trade print advertising, trade show exhibitions, direct-mail campaigns, and telemarketing. These channels were always expensive and have become less effective than they once were. As this Penril modem ad from an early 1980s issue of *Computerworld* demonstrates (Figure P.1), the limitations of traditional, intrusion-based advertising sometimes forced B2B marketers to use extreme tactics to attract attention.

Consider the corporate technology executive, who was the target for this ad. Until about 10 years ago, the typical information technology (IT) manager's mailbox bulged with print trade magazines. It was not unusual for IT executives to have a stack of unread magazines in the corner of their offices and to take piles of them on plane trips for rapid processing. Paul remembers with a chuckle the IT manager who referred to his weekly trade magazine deliveries in a metric he called "stack feet."

This was a highly wasteful system. Technology companies could pay as much as $30,000 for a full-page advertisement that might be seen by only a tiny percentage of the magazine's readers in any given week. Of those who noticed the ad, an even smaller percentage were in a position to make a purchase at that time. It was impossible to communicate the value of a product in this format; advertisers mainly relied on quick slogans borrowed from the consumer sector that they hoped would spur a phone call. Lead quality was poor, and sales cycles were long and arduous.

Figure P.1 Old Computer Ad.

It's not surprising that the technology sector was one of the first to discard print advertising. Today, only a handful of technology magazines still exist in the United States, and their average size has shrunk from hundreds of pages a week to a few dozen. In 2009, the trade publishing sector was the single largest declining print market, with ad pages contracting 28 percent on top of years of previous declines.

The collapse of that industry was dramatized in November 2008, when *PC Magazine,* which once generated more than $100 million in annual revenues, announced it was exiting the print business and going fully online.

What explains this dramatic turnaround? Quite simply: choice. Business buyers are looking to make decisions as quickly and as intelligently as possible. Searching for solutions online is more efficient than relying on the serendipity of encountering an ad in a magazine or seeing a flyer in a mailbox. Americans older than age 15 conducted 131 billion searches in December 2009,[1] according to comScore. Marketo reported that 93 percent of B2B buyers use search to begin the buying process,[2] and Forbes Insight reported that 74 percent of C-level executives call the Internet "very valuable," and 53 percent said they prefer to locate information themselves.[3] Nor is it shocking that direct-mail spending is expected to decline nearly 40 percent by 2014. Buyers' information discovery habits have changed forever thanks to search engines.

But it isn't just search. Business buyers have been saying for many years that their most important source of information is each other. Research in early 2010 by Genius.com and DemandGen Report found that 59 percent of B2B buyers engaged with peers before making a buying decision, 48 percent followed industry conversations, and 44 percent conducted anonymous research among a select group of vendors. Forrester Research reported that more than 8 in 10 IT decision makers said word-of-mouth recommendations are their most important source when making buying decisions.[4] Countless other surveys, stretching back more than 30 years, have reached the same conclusions. Business buyers actively seek out others like them because they believe they will get the most direct, untarnished advice.

Marketers have many more options for reaching business buyers than they did just five years ago. All of the traditional channels are still available, and many new ones have also emerged. Marketing today is a lot more complex than it used to be, but the opportunities are also greater for marketers who can figure out the right combination of dials to turn.

Social media empowers individuals to share their experiences directly with one another and without the filters of corporate public relations (PR) departments and lawyers. People are more honest and direct when speaking with their peers, which is one reason why feedback from social networks is more compelling than packaged case studies. As the number of channels multiplies and more participants come online, the quality of information improves, a phenomenon knows as the "network effect."

Today, prospective buyers have other options beyond search. They can ask questions directly of one another via Twitter, Facebook, and LinkedIn. Response is nearly instantaneous and, because each message is tied back to an individual profile, participants have a high degree of confidence in the quality of the information.

"If a customer in the chemicals industry is having a challenge and wants to know best practices for distribution of chemicals through a supply chain, he or she can turn to another chemicals customer in our ecosystem through our [online] communities and learn," says Mark Yolton, senior vice president of the 2-million-member SAP Community Network.

Andrew McAfee, principal research scientist at the MIT Sloan School and author of *Enterprise 2.0,* has gone so far as to suggest that a new kind of search is emerging based on the ask-and-answer metaphor. So now, not only can we search the web for others' experiences, but we can ask questions directly of an anonymous or semi-anonymous group and get back experiential advice. Those "stack feet" of printed magazines have been replaced by a vast network of people who freely share their firsthand experiences for no reason other than to help others make better decisions.

For many B2B companies, these new information-gathering metaphors will ripple across every function in the organization. Customers, suppliers, and investors will demand that businesses become more open and responsive. They will grant attention to companies that deliver useful information and shun those that simply deliver sales pitches. "People want to buy, but they don't want to be sold to," says Benjamin Ellis, a serial entrepreneur based in the United Kingdom who now specializes in social marketing.

Find Your Own Path

There's an inherent risk in generalizing about the needs of companies that run the gamut from high-volume office supply retailers like Staples to highly focused firms like American Biltrite, whose Autowrap division is so specialized that executives already know everyone who could possibly do business with them. In some ways, these two kinds of B2B companies couldn't be more different, but there are also a surprising number of common threads to their experiences: their markets are value-driven and relationship-based. There are no impulse purchases and no fashion statements. Word of mouth is a powerful source of influence. Reputations and even careers ride on buying decisions.

Any company that sees virtue in better connecting the people who build and sell its products with the people who buy them can find opportunities to apply the new tools of social marketing. In the following pages, we'll introduce you to dozens that already have. We'll also continue to tell stories on our blogs: paulgillin.com, spinfluencer.com, and ontherecordpodcast.com. We hope you'll contribute yours to the conversation.

Paul Gillin
paul@gillin.com
twitter.com/pgillin

Eric Schwartzman
eric@ericschwartzman.com
twitter.com/ericschwartzman

Part One

Setting the Table

CHAPTER ONE

The Changing Rules of B2B Marketing

Friends know Scott Hanson as an affable native Texan with a penchant for computers, cars, and poker. But to thousands of technology professionals around the world, Hanson is a celebrity. By day, he and three other technologists at Dell manage the Dell TechCenter, an online community that helps enterprise information technology (IT) professionals unravel the thorniest problems that occur when trying to integrate technology from multiple vendors.

Dell conceived of the community in 2007 as a way to enhance loyalty among its largest customers. Members share advice and ask questions of Hanson and the other engineers, who dispense it for free. The community is open and fully searchable, although only registered members can submit articles and comments. In 2008, about 100 people visited the site every day. By early 2010, that number was over 5,000.

Hanson and colleagues Jeff Sullivan, Kong Yang, and Dennis Smith are celebrities of sorts in the community of enterprise customers, who frequently seek them out for meetings at trade shows and during visits to the company's executive briefing center. Their celebrity has paid off handsomely for Dell: Hanson won't provide specifics, but Dell has estimated that the TechCenter is indirectly responsible for many millions of dollars in sales each year.

That's despite the fact that Dell TechCenter isn't charged with selling anything. The site is free of advertising, and the member list may never be used for promotions. "The last thing IT people want when they come to a technical resource is an ad asking them to buy a laptop," Hanson says.

Those sales are generated by the affinity that the staff has developed with these key corporate customers. It's a camaraderie that is nurtured by personal contact. In the early days of Twitter, the Dell TechCenter staff had set up a common Twitter account as a secondary channel of communication. But it turned out that customers wanted to speak to people, not brands. The Twitter initiative really gained traction when Hanson became @DellServerGeek and Sullivan became @SANPenguin. Suddenly the discussion became more personal and the people behind Dell TechCenter more real to their constituents.

Welcome to the new world of business-to-business (B2B) communications. Dell TechCenter and other initiatives like it are microcosms of the changes that are sweeping across the corporate world as a consequence of the rapid growth of social media tools like blogs, communities, and user-generated multimedia.

Companies like Dell, which does 80 percent of its sales volume with corporate customers, are ideally positioned to take advantage of these new channels. In fact, B2B companies were among the earliest adopters of social media. Technology leaders such as Microsoft, IBM, and Cisco had hundreds of thousands of employees blogging as early as 2005, and those same companies are now expanding their footprint into social networks like Facebook, YouTube, and, overwhelmingly, Twitter. Microsoft has featured interviews with thousands of its own employees in video programs on its Channel 9 web site. The company wanted to expose its human side to a market that saw it as closed and secretive.

B2B technology companies have also been among the most creative users of social channels to reach the highly skilled people they need to hire in competitive labor markets. Recruiters have found that social channels are far more effective in identifying prospective employees than recruitment advertising sources, and that prospects came into the hiring cycle with a better understanding and more enthusiasm about the company they were hoping to work for.

Yet B2B applications of social media get remarkably little attention. Perhaps that's because their focused communities of buyers pale in size to the millions who flock to Facebook Official Pages for Coca-Cola and Nike. Perhaps it's because glitzy video contests and games don't resonate with the time-challenged professional audience. It doesn't really matter. Few B2B companies seek the consumer spotlight, and their audiences, which may spend millions of dollars with them, are more interested in substance than in style. Fortunately, B2B social media is all about substance.

The B2B Difference

Why are B2B companies different, and why do they justify a social media book just for them? For one thing, B2B marketers quietly spend about $80 billion per year, some $3 billion of that online. Spending on B2B Internet marketing is expected to grow at a compound rate of 12 percent through 2013, with social media spending showing a 21 percent compound annual growth rate.[1]

B2B marketers are far more entrenched in social channels than they are given credit for. Business.com reported in late 2009 that 81 percent of B2B companies maintain company-related accounts or profiles on social media sites, versus 67 percent of business-to-consumer (B2C) companies.[2] The same study also found that three out of four B2B companies have a presence on Twitter, compared with half of B2C companies. Research by *BtoB* magazine and the Association of National Advertisers in early 2010 found that 57 percent of B2B marketers were using social media channels, compared with 66 percent of all marketers and up from just 15 percent in 2007. A study of social network usage by employees of major corporations conducted by NetProspex in May, 2009 found that 12 of the top 20 most active employee populations were at companies that sell primarily to other businesses.

There are big differences between selling to organizations and selling to individuals (Figure 1.1). Let's look at a few:

B2B marketing is much more likely to focus on value than experience. This distinction isn't absolute, of course; makers of automobiles and dishwashing detergent also figure value into the equation. But in nearly all B2B decisions, value is the driving force. Value can be expressed in many ways, including price/performance, the fit with the customer's business objective, flexibility, and compatibility with existing systems. The point is that the "Wow!" factor that is so important to many consumer buying decisions rarely means much in business engagements. In fact, flash obfuscates the clarity that business buyers need.

B2B buying decisions are usually made by groups, whereas consumer buying decisions are made by individuals. This has huge implications for marketing. B2B marketing programs must influence multiple people at multiple stages of the buying process, and each of those individuals has different priorities. The chief financial officer (CFO), for example, is focused on return, whereas the product manager may be thinking more about user experience or lead generation. "In B2B marketing, your end consumer is often not the same

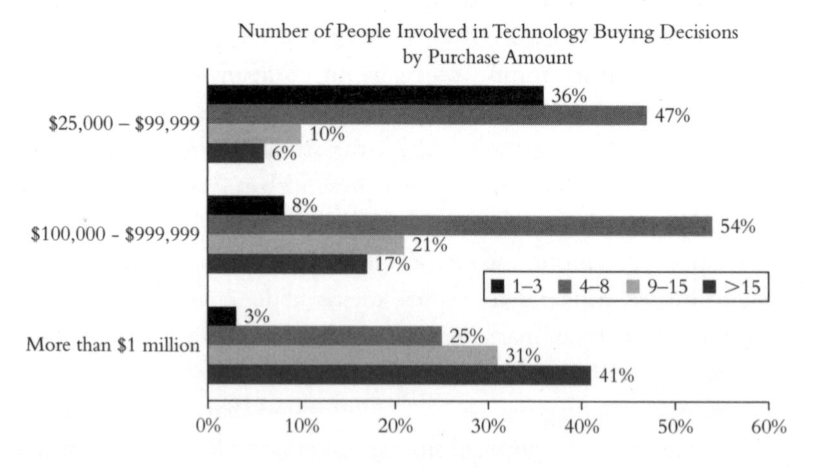

Figure 1.1 People involved in buying decision.
Source: Marketing Sherpha/TechWeb.

person as the purchaser," says Alan Belniak, social media director at enterprise software maker PTC.

Interestingly, the opportunities for individual engagement are changing the group-buying dynamic in some cases. Salesforce.com, an enormously successful B2B software provider, gained a foothold in large corporations by pitching its service directly to individual sales representatives. By building a groundswell of enthusiasm, Salesforce was able to unseat major enterprise competitors who sold from the top down. However, even with this influence inversion, a company-wide commitment to Salesforce remains a group decision.

For this and other reasons, **business buying cycles are longer than consumer buying cycles**. This is primarily because more dollars are at stake and more people are involved in the decision. The choice of packaging machinery for a manufacturing plant, for example, affects that company's ability to deliver its product to the marketplace, which in turn affects its sales and stock value. With so much at stake, decisions often involve many rounds of meetings and may take a year or longer to conclude.

Business buying decisions are more likely to be a commitment than consumer buying decisions. Products like enterprise e-mail systems or aircraft engines live with the customer for a very long time. Issues such as the viability of the manufacturer, its quality of support, and its future product road maps have significant influence on these decisions. Once the sale is made, buyer and seller are bound together in an ongoing dialog. Businesses do business with those they trust.

Relationships play a more important role in B2B than in B2C decisions. In some cases, business buyers bet their careers on the choices they make. They need to feel confident that their supplier will validate the soundness of their judgment. Smart B2B marketers realize that their job is as much about ensuring the success of the buyer as it is about selling the product.

Service and support are essential decision factors. Business customers won't wait 20 minutes on hold to speak to a support technician, particularly if their assembly line is down. They expect their problems to be solved when they need them solved.

- **B2B sales have lots of moving parts.** At the high end in particular, contracts are often custom bid and may include bundled services, special discounts, and detailed price schedules. This process involves extensive communication between the parties and direct contact between different departments of both organizations.
- **Channel relationships are complicating factors in the marketing equation.** B2B marketers constantly struggle to strike a balance between selling to channel partners such as resellers and distributors and selling directly to customers. Channel partners ultimately sign the check for many B2B transactions and see themselves as owning the relationship with the customer. However, customer pull is a significant influence on sales, regardless of the channel. This is a perpetual quandary for many B2B companies, which must market to both constituencies without muddling the message or creating conflict.

Social media are well suited to addressing many of the unique issues noted so far. They're particularly effective at connecting customers with the people behind the products they buy. This barely matters in consumer markets, but in high-dollar transactions that may affect the fate of the buying company, the ability to communicate directly with designers, engineers, and support personnel can make all the difference. This is why we recommend that B2B companies that undertake social initiatives apply them broadly across the organization. The more you open up your company, the more credibility and trust you earn from your prospects and customers.

Buyers want their suppliers to use these channels. Cone Inc.'s 2009 Social Media in Business study found that 93 percent of business buyers believe all companies should have a presence in social media and 85 percent believe social media should be used to interact and become more engaged with them.

"The value of social is in building stronger, more connected relationships that extend beyond the traditional face-to-face kind," says Adam Christensen, manager of social media at IBM. "It's now more of a continuing conversation, so that when two people do actually get together again . . . the relationship is better."

Engagement won't work if it's limited to traditional marketing and sales; to be effective, social media must be adopted broadly throughout the company. Some executives will find much to fear in these developments. They have been trained to believe that employees are not fit to speak for the company and that disaster ensues when the message is not tightly controlled. For large companies in particular, an image of invincibility is a treasured corporate asset. That makes their inevitable pratfalls all the more embarrassing.

This isn't to say that fears of loss of control are invalid. Adobe Systems found out the hard way in early 2010 that even unbridled employee enthusiasm can have undesirable side effects. An Adobe Platform Evangelist named Lee Brimelow posted a series of screenshots on Adobe's Flash blog that were intended to show how bleak the online world would look without Adobe's Flash video display technology. In a subtle attempt at humor, Brimelow included a screenshot of a pornography site in his gallery (see Figure 1.2). Adobe was not amused when the gaffe exploded into a firestorm of mockery and anger.

Figure 1.2 Lee Brimelow's screen shot.

Nevertheless, we are confident Adobe will recover from this incident and may actually benefit from it. Brimelow's halfhearted apology had a kind of "lighten up" tone to it that reminded his audience that no lives had been lost. And the furor gave him another chance to state his passion for Flash and for Apple, whose omission of Flash from the iPad computer had sparked the blog entry in the first place. The fact that Adobe didn't fire or publicly rebuke its evangelist actually burnished its image as a tolerant and forgiving employer.

On the other hand, the upside of spreading social tools throughout the organization can be enormous, particularly for companies that have enthusiastic customers and passionate employees. Consider the once popular "case study," an essential B2B marketing document that has become a rat's nest of approvals and legal concerns. All you have to do is scan the web sites of a few B2B technology vendors to realize how sterilized and empty most case studies have become. By the time gatekeepers have had a chance to purge them of any hint of negativity or implied endorsements, the average case study has become little more than an extended sound bite. In fact, many companies now no longer submit to case studies at all out of the fear that endorsing one vendor could ruffle feathers of another. What are these companies afraid of? Aren't they the ones with the market leverage?

Contrast that with the blog entry written by the customer or the active discussion group on a technical forum. It turns out that when customers can speak to one another without submitting to some kind of marketing filtration system, they have interesting things to say. And no one is getting in trouble for this. Better yet, marketers can listen for free.

Social media marketing is a way to humanize the business, to turn frailties into endearing qualities that encourage experimentation, loyalty, and forgiveness. Today's most admired social media marketers—Dell, Cisco, Starbucks, Google, Ford, Procter & Gamble, and Wal-Mart, to name just a few—have adopted a philosophy of open experimentation layered upon a culture of risk tolerance. But one thing they all share in common is that they all had the good fortune of making high-profile, public mistakes, which compelled their upper management to update their communications strategy.

"Apathy is one of the biggest challenges to social media implementation. When things are going well, people are less inclined to allocate budget. But when the brand gets slapped around publicly, or there's a recall or a crisis of some kind, that's an opportunity," says Pete Blackshaw, executive vice president of Nielsen Online Digital Strategic Services. "Negative conversations that go viral are a wakeup call to management." In many cases, at today's risk-averse companies, it may take a crisis to bring about cultural change. We hope that's not the case for you.

To Err Is Human

In her book *Open Leadership,* Charlene Li tells how Cisco chief executive officer (CEO) John Chambers challenges prospective employees. "I ask [them] to tell me about [their] failures," he says. ". . . it's surprising how many people say, 'Well, I can't think of one.' That person immediately loses credibility with me." Businesses are just like people. When they pretend to be infallible, they come off as dishonest because nobody's perfect.

In this book, we will argue that social marketing isn't a task to be delegated exclusively to the marketing department and that replacing traditional media channels with social ones will achieve only marginal benefits, if it achieves anything at all. To tap into the true power of these new channels, businesses need to rethink their culture and value systems. They need to reject the concept that all company information is a proprietary asset to be shrouded in secrecy. They need to reject the veneer of infallibility as an operating principle. Those were appropriate strategies in the information-starved world that existed prior to 2000, but marketing in the age of the web is about giving and participating and being as omnipresent as a company can be. In social marketing, developing solid interpersonal relationships is, generally speaking, much more important than showmanship.

Fallibility is endearing. When a notable politician or sports figure goes on *Saturday Night Live* and submits to the cast's mockery with a good-natured grin, we instinctively like him. In fact, willingness to accept shortcomings actually demonstrates confidence. Dell is the poster child for corporate humility. The company was twice a very public victim of social media savagery: once at the hands of disgruntled blogger Jeff Jarvis in 2006, and again two years later, when it denied overheating problems with its laptop batteries. Instead of walling itself off from its public, Dell did the opposite. It embraced social channels with a fervor few companies could match. In 2009, Jarvis himself traveled to Round Rock, Texas, on assignment for *BusinessWeek* to document Dell's remarkable change of heart. "Dell has leapt from worst to first," he wrote in the lead paragraph of his feature story, which was titled "Dell Learns to Listen." One of the reasons Dell is considered such a thought leader in social media today is because it stumbled so publicly in the past, learned from its mistakes, and championed culture change.

We don't mean to suggest that this transformation is easy. Large corporations in particular have enormous institutional impediments to change. One is middle management. Although we've seen many examples of middle managers championing change, people in that role can also see open communication as a threat to their control. They rarely derail an initiative entirely, but they can greatly slow its progress.

A more serious impediment, particularly in B2B companies, is long-serving senior managers who simply see no reason to do business any differently. In some cases, they're right. We've worked with B2B companies whose markets were so focused that the sales organization already had personal relationships with every customer in the market. At these companies, social marketing isn't an imperative, but today's global business world changes so quickly that it seems shortsighted not to be acquainted with the tools that can open up opportunities in new markets. In Chapter 3 we look at how to sell social marketing to tough customers.

Much to Gain

We assert that B2B companies actually have more to gain from social marketing than their consumer counterparts because social tools address so many factors that are unique to their market:

- **Group decision making** is enhanced when everyone involved in the decision has access to the resources that the vendor is bringing to the table. This benefits small B2B suppliers in particular, because they can more easily expose their expertise and experience to prospective customers.

- **Business buying cycles** are shortened when buyers don't have to navigate through intermediaries to answer questions. Social media makes it easy to reach the source directly.
- Similarly, it's easier for buyers to make a **commitment** to a vendor when they know the people behind the brand. This awareness even provides an additional layer of comfort for **service and support**. If a vendor were to go bankrupt, for example, buyers would still have a way to find the people who built the products.
- **Relationships** can now be forged at every level. Although this may present a threat to the sales organization, it improves the chance that the buyer and seller will find touch points elsewhere in the organization. For example, product developers may be more effective than marketers at establishing trusted relationships with influencers in customer organizations.
- Complicated sales are made less complex when all parties have **open channels of communication**. This reduces finger-pointing and improves customer satisfaction. For the selling company, it also creates ways to identify new business and upsell opportunities.
- **Channel relationships** are smoother when all parties are clued into what each other is doing and can take advantage of opportunities for joint promotion and co-op marketing.

In short, social media can affect B2B relationships at nearly every level, but these benefits don't come without risk. Preparing a company to speak openly to constituents such as customers, regulators, and government agencies requires vision, commitment, and a tolerance for error. Not all companies have the culture or fortitude to make the shift. They are better off piloting initiatives through smaller projects designed to demonstrate business value internally or waiting until customer demand requires a culture change. And some companies, particularly at the high end of the market, may find that social media has little or no apparent value. This book is for them as well.

We wrote this book not to evangelize social media as a panacea, although we clearly believe that it has value in many areas. We believe that some organizations are better suited to embrace the principles we describe herein than others. If they decide that social marketing is not for them, at least at this time, that's fine. However, everyone needs to be aware of the dynamics that are reshaping markets of all kinds. Even if they don't affect your industry at the moment, chances are they will as the Facebook generation moves into the boardroom.

We hope that you can learn from the advice and examples that follow on how to apply these new principles, and also where to avoid them entirely. The important thing is that you strike out on a course that makes sense for your business.

CHAPTER TWO

Seven Ways You Can Use Social Media

Social tools can be applied to many areas of the business, ranging from product development to sales to customer support. We cover lead generation, the Holy Grail for business-to-business (B2B) companies, in Chapter 12. Here are seven other ideas.

Market Intelligence

By now, nearly everybody knows how to set up a Google Alert, but that's only one way to listen to conversations. Google's coverage is vast, but it isn't total. For example, the search engine indexes almost none of Twitter and very little of what goes on in gated social networks. Search engines are also structurally limited in their ability to understand images, audio and video. A variety of tools are available, ranging in price from free to thousands of dollars per month, that listen to, quantify, analyze, and even attempt to translate the vagaries of language into customer sentiment.

The bigger opportunity in market intelligence is developing a holistic picture of your competitive environment and your market. Searching for mentions of your own brand is a start, but you'll learn much more if you expand your criteria. The information you get back is only as good as the keywords you search. Among the search phrases to consider are:

- Competitors
- Customers
- Channel partners
- Regulatory agencies and commissioners
- Legislators
- Influential authors, journalists, and bloggers
- Individuals within the organizations mentioned at the start of this list
- Topics relevant to your market

In addition, there are many more sources to track today than just a couple of years ago. These include:

- Blogs
- Twitter and other microblogs
- Video and audio
- Photo-sharing sites
- Regulatory filings
- Facebook, LinkedIn, and vertical social networks
- Wikipedia
- Discussion forums
- Social bookmarking sites

A good practice is to set up a social media dashboard, which you can do with services like My Yahoo!, iGoogle, and Pageflakes. Another free online service called Google Reader allows news, blog and other search results to be tracked via RSS feeds, which can be monitored, shared, and stored indefinitely online through the service. When you refresh the dashboard, the latest search results are displayed. This feature is particularly useful with Twitter, which indexes only a few days of conversations in its search engine. However, when saved as an RSS feed, messages are available until deleted. In Chapter 6, we walk you through the process of building a social media monitoring dashboard with Google Reader to catch almost anything that moves online about your company, your competitors and your business segment. In addition, there are other services that search Twitter history, including Google and Microsoft Bing.

Market intelligence dashboards have value across the company and can be a useful way to demonstrate the effectiveness of social media as a barometer of customer opinion, as well as an early warning of changes in the market or competitive activity. We recommend you always follow your competitors and your largest customers on Twitter. In both cases, you want to keep up with what's on their minds.

Identify Opportunities

Dashboards can also help you scope out opportunities to expand existing business or find new markets. For example, many business opportunities are now aggregated through Twitter hashtags, which are unique identifiers like #RFP or #jobs that can be used to group conversations. You can also learn a lot about changes at current customers or companies you're pitching to. For example, the web site Listorious.com lists hundreds of chief financial officers who use Twitter. Mine these lists for people to follow at companies that matter to you. If you can answer one of their questions, you can often get their attention in ways that would be difficult or impossible to do by more traditional means of communication.

LinkedIn can be a fantastic resource for finding influential people. This business networking site looks at companies from the bottom up by listing the people who work there. Much of LinkedIn is public, so it can be a useful way to get past the traditional gatekeeper departments like sales, support, and public relations, who often try to restrict access to decision makers. You can use LinkedIn company profiles to find people with connections to your own network or simply as a starting place for more detailed research. One of the more useful features of profiles is that they link to groups to which the member belongs. You can use this information to scope out issues that are of interest to them, creating additional opportunities to connect.

You can also use social networks to identify new product opportunities. These days, even B2B customers express their frustrations in public venues, creating opportunities for savvy listeners to identify solutions. The no-nonsense professional groups on LinkedIn are a great place to find out what professionals are talking about. Small business networks like Startups.com, Anita Campbell's Small Business Trends and Biznik.com can clue you into new businesses that are emerging to address opportunities that others have identified. These can be sources of inspiration, partnership, or acquisition.

Twitter is also a great place to go fishing, because people often express needs or vent frustration to their followers. In this case, you'll want to listen for keywords that indicate need. For example, if you sell accounting software, search for that term in the context of other words like "does anyone know?" or "can anyone recommend?"

You can also use the web to "crowdsource" solutions to business problems. This rapidly growing phenomenon has launched more than 50 companies that farm out projects to networks of individual specialists.[1] Several specialize in solving the kinds of very complex problems that commonly bedevil B2B companies. We discuss this topic in more detail in Chapter 13. Many common business problems can be solved by searching message boards or inviting feedback from Twitter followers. These results can then be used to convince internal skeptics of the value of participating in online communities.

Build Thought Leadership Through Blogging

One of the fastest ways to score points with prospective and existing customers via social media, and to build visibility within your company, is to create a blog around an area of expertise. Blogs are quick to set up, relatively easy to use, and perform well in search engines. For those who excel at written communications, blogs quickly communicate news and updates to the market and demonstrate thought leadership.

Choose a topic about which you have considerable interest and knowledge in a niche where there is little competition. Don't be frustrated by the large number of blogs that may already exist. Many people experiment with blogs and then abandon them. Others tend them only lightly. A blog that hasn't been updated in a year is as good as invisible, so you can gain ground quickly by simply maintaining an active posting schedule.

Blogging for thought leadership isn't the same as blogging to update your customers. Take off your marketing hat and think like an editor or analyst. Concentrate on the issues that interest others in your field, such as developments in technology, new research, or interesting insights from others. You can even interview other thought leaders and include an audio or text transcript. Remember, your goal is to educate and inform, not to sell. Believe us, the sales will come as people researching your market find your thought-leading insight at the top of their Google search results.

For some regulated businesses, blogs about public policy issues such as nutrition, health, infrastructure, and science are a way to speak to important business issues without drawing scrutiny from overseers. But for publicly traded companies, be forewarned that allowing people to comment on a blog your company maintains obligates you to set the record straight whenever information that could affect the trading value of your stock is posted there. Brian Lane, a former director of corporate finance at the Securities and Exchange Commission, describes how selective responses can backfire. "The company denied [the allegation] when it was false. They didn't deny it this time. Therefore it's true. And the stock gets hammered," he says. "If you're going to engage, you can't engage for just one day; you have to be engaged every minute."

These days, you can use a free tool like Twitterfeed to automatically convert your blog headlines into tweets. You can also use applications like Seesmic, Ping.fm, Posterous, TweetDeck, TubeMogul, blip.tv, FriendFeed, and Google Buzz to move messages from one social media network to another.

Reuse content whenever you can, angling it for different audiences or markets. "A white paper can become several blog posts that can each be promoted through Twitter," says Deirdre Walsh, community and social media manager at National Instruments, a test and measurement firm.

You can also syndicate content through other industry blogs and publishing web sites, often by doing little more than filling out a short form. Popular syndication sites like Alltop grab RSS feeds and organize them by topic. This is bonus visibility with zero additional work. The more outlets you use, the faster your online presence grows. If the content is original and useful, the calls from reporters and speaking invitations soon follow.

Be specific. Writing about big issues like the environment will throw you into the stew with established competitors and make it more difficult for you to gain visibility. Instead, write about environmental issues in your market niche. You won't get as much traffic as TreeHugger.com, but that isn't the point. The more specific you are, the better you will perform on keywords that matter to you and the people you want to reach. Although the search volume for those keywords may not be large, the probability of those clicks turning into leads is greater if you own the keywords. (See Chapter 7 for details.)

If several people will be contributing to the blog, identify authors who are eager to participate. Create Twitter accounts for each contributor and be sure everyone who contributes to the blog also tweets about new entries. Use your business Twitter account to tweet entries, too.

In Hard Focus is a blog by San Francisco entrepreneur Stephen Russell. He uses it to educate and evangelize about advances in video surveillance. Russell's topics include essays on new technologies that improve facial recognition or that tap into armies of smart phone users to identify public threats. He often gets on the phone with academic researchers, asks smart questions, and shares their insight with his audience as blog entries.

It happens that Russell is also the founder of 3VR, a company that sells a line of video search tools for use by security professionals. You wouldn't know that from Russell's blog, however, where he identifies himself simply as "editor" and mentions his company affiliation only in passing. The purpose of In Hard Focus isn't to sell products, but to position the chief executive officer (CEO) as a visionary.

And it works.

With more than 1,000 daily visitors, the blog has established Russell as a thought leader in an industry he very much wants to influence.

The 3VR web site has its own company blog that refers visitors to Russell's latest insights. However, Russell intentionally keeps In Hard Focus on its own domain so that his role as visionary is kept at arm's length from his role as CEO. It turns out that thought leadership is very good for business. "I talk to prominent security directors, city planners and government officials all the time, and I'm always amazed at how many have read our blogs," Russell says.

Danny Schaeffler is an expert on sheet metal formability, which is the capacity for different kind of sheet metal to be molded into shapes. There are dozens of different grades of steel that are used to make everything from fenders to railroad tracks. Choosing the right kind for the job is critical to getting the proper result.

Schaeffler started blogging in 2006, shortly after setting up shop as a formability consultant. About one quarter of his business now comes from people searching terms like "sheet metal stress analysis." In an international marketplace, "if companies don't know that you're out there, you never get the opportunity to be considered," he says. He spends 5 to 10 hours each week blogging, mostly in half-hour increments. He uses Twitter to solicit questions from his audience and has built a newsletter list compiled from visitors to the blog.

The community of people who care about sheet metal formability isn't large, he says, but social media has brought those experts together. "It's surprising how many of us end up knowing each other," he says.

Market Research

Why would anyone would want to do focus groups anymore when such a treasure trove of market insight exists for free online? We've sat behind the glass wall munching on M&M's more times than we can count and have always been struck by the artificiality of paying people to share opinions in group settings. People are easily influenced, and in our experience, a focus group quickly comes to reflect the opinions of its most vocal members. At best, it's only the opinions of a few people.

The easiest way to use social media for market research is simply to start listening. Build a Google Reader dashboard like the one outlined earlier in this chapter and described in detail in Chapter 6 and start looking for trends in your market. Monitor positive and negative mentions of your company, as well as your competitors, and track changes over time. Pay particular attention to new products and to common customer gripes, for they yield the best opportunities. Many services are now available that monitor customer conversations; these services range in price from less than $100 per month up to $10,000 or more. Our advice is to start by building a dashboard of your own and seeing what value you derive from it. B2B companies that serve small markets may find that they can do a perfectly good job of listening to markets without spending money on a commercial service because the volume of content is relatively low.

You can gain even more insight by participating in conversations as a group leader or by asking questions of your Facebook friends or Twitter followers. CME Group, the big Chicago-based futures and options exchange, has accumulated an impressive 750,000 followers on Twitter. Corporate Communications Director Allan Schoenberg says customer feedback is one of the most valuable benefits of having a Twitter presence. "We can track what the competition is doing, monitor key messages and identify key themes," he says.

The company also maintains a handful of private LinkedIn groups for professional traders and customers. "I look at these as private focus groups," Schoenberg says. "The groups are all less than 200 people, and they're all customers. You can ask these people anything and get a reaction." LinkedIn is particularly useful from a B2B perspective because members of the group can be identified through their professional profiles. There's none of the anonymous rabble-rousing that goes on in public discussion forums.

Vico Software requires each of its sales representatives to set up or join LinkedIn groups related to commercial construction in their geographic territories. The purpose isn't to sell the company's suite of construction management software but rather to become involved in the local community and build relationships. "There are 108 LinkedIn groups devoted to construction; we participate in 39 of them," says marketing vice president Holly Allison.

For regionally focused monitoring, Twitter advanced search or third-party apps like Twittervision allow you to specify a radius around a city or zip code. This feature lets you monitor broader, categorical B2B keywords such as "machine shop" or "labor attorney." If your business relies on physical proximity, this is a terrific opportunity to find prospective customers. One of our favorite examples of this is the auto repair shop owner who monitors Twitter for keywords such as "crash" or "accident" within a 50-mile radius. People who tweet about their auto mishaps get a tweet from him that links to a Web page with advice about how to choose a repair shop. Not surprisingly, the owner's shop meets all the recommended criteria.

You can take research to the next level by signing on with a professional community management firm like Communispace or LiveWorld, which bring professional moderation and audience development to the process. The costs are quite a bit steeper than running your own LinkedIn group, but these services add value in managing the community and delivering results that match your needs. The Ford Motor Company uses a combination of both, outsourcing content creation to agency partners and relying on their own staff for day-to-day community management.

Support Customers

Businesses are using Twitter to respond to customer inquiries and complaints. Comcast pioneered this tactic with @ComcastCares, a Twitter presence created in 2007 by Frank Eliason, who joined Citicorp in mid-2010. At the time, Comcast's customer service reputation was so low that a Google search on "Comcast customer service" returned as many negative results as positive ones. Eliason conceived of a new approach to customer care: search for online complaints on Twitter and resolve problems publicly so that every resolved issue becomes a public relations opportunity. In choosing Twitter as the primary channel for the experiment, Eliason made a bet that openness and speed would be a differentiator. By responding with a calm and helpful demeanor, Comcast was able to capture media attention and make rapid progress in its efforts to improve its image.

Comcast had no illusions about transforming its customer service operation with Twitter. Although the company had more than 40 representatives tweeting at the time of this writing, the total number of customer issues that they address is a drop in the bucket compared with the overall volume of service calls the company handles. What's important is that these are Comcast's most *vocal* customers. They are the ones who are most likely to make noise and attract attention. That's why rapid response is so effective. Vocal customers typically constitute about 1 percent of a company's overall customer base, but they can do a lot of damage. They can also do a lot of good. The brilliance of Comcast Cares was that it measurably improved the *perception* of the company's customer service without requiring a structural overhaul or massive retraining. "The folks that man the phones and monitor e-mail feedback tend to have the best skills at managing volatile customers," says Pete Blackshaw, author of *Satisfied Customers Tell Three Friends, Angry Customers Tell 3000.* "That skill set is transferrable to Twitter and Facebook."

Many companies are now following Comcast's example, including B2B companies that serve large customer bases in time-dependent situations. Twitter can be a godsend to these companies because it provides an alternative communication channel when primary channels are unavailable. E-mail marketing service provider iContact of Raleigh, North Carolina, turned to Twitter when it was hit by a major denial-of-service attack in 2009. The company was offline for almost 2 days, but was able to tap into its Twitter followers to deliver updates on recovery efforts. Those people told others, and word quickly spread that iContact was on the case. For an e-mail company to go dark for that long could be a cataclysmic failure, but iContact was able to stay engaged with its customers even while its web site was unavailable.

Although using Twitter for public troubleshooting clearly works for some companies, we have some reservations about buying in fully to this strategy. For one thing, Twitter is not a good medium for dealing with complex problems. For another, we question the advisability of rewarding customers for complaining in public. The approach we recommend is to use Twitter to listen and respond but to ultimately drive the conversation back to private channels such as e-mail and the call center if necessary. Although some complainers want to use the crowd to their advantage, most just want to get their problem resolved.

B2B companies may also get equal or better results by using long-form channels like blogs or video for customer support. That's because business customers often require more customized or detailed support than users of a commodity service. One of the great values of blogs is that they bring subject matter experts into direct contact with those who advise on and purchase their products and services. These experts can use direct communications to support early users and large accounts to improve quality and generate new ideas.

Crisis Management

We don't wish a crisis on you, but it's a smart idea to have a social media plan in place in case one develops. Consider what happened to Boingo Wireless.

Boingo sells Internet access worldwide to a customer base that is about 80 percent business travelers. These time-pressed people frequently need to get online in the few minutes they have between airport connections, so availability is critical. Boingo learned early that Twitter was an effective early warning system to identify problems with its access points, as travelers frequently used their handheld devices to consult each other before calling customer support. About one quarter of the company's support requests come in over Twitter.

That early warning system came in handy in April 2010, when a test e-mail message meant for just a few people was inadvertently sent to all Boingo customers. Recipients were told that their subscriptions were being canceled and they were being shifted to a pay-as-you-go plan. Worse was that about 20 percent of Boingo customers got more than one copy of the message. Even though the e-mail was identified as a test, panicked and angry customers took to Twitter to vent.

Fortunately, Boingo had social media manager Baochi Nguyen. She's online all the time, and she picked up the first complaints a little more than an hour after the errant e-mail went out. Nguyen immediately alerted the company's e-mail manager, who shut down transmission before further damage could be done. Corporate communications director Christian Gunning was quickly brought into the process to assuage customers, some of whom were already speculating about devious company motives. The response team answered as many tweets as they could, aware that because Twitter is a public medium, Boingo customers could easily tap into the conversations.

Within four hours after the e-mail was sent, nearly a dozen Boingo employees were involved in crisis containment. "We didn't hide or wait till we could circle our wagons; we just started talking to customers," says Gunning. "You could literally see the tide change from 'Why the hell are you spamming me?' to 'We all make mistakes.'" A follow-up blog post with the tongue-in-cheek title, "A Big Fat Apology" explained the mistake in more detail.

It's impossible to quantify the payback of Boingo's rapid response, but it's likely that the team headed off a far worse situation.

Many companies first recognize the value of social channels during a crisis, when time is of the essence. It's a good practice to start a corporate Twitter account, even if it's only used lightly, because it may be an asset when conventional communication channels are slow or unavailable.

After a winter storm that left two thirds of the state without any power in late 2008, Public Service of New Hampshire (PSNH) realized the benefits of social media for crisis management in the trenches. Luckily, prior to the outage, PSNH spokesperson Martin Murray had already established a presence on Twitter, Flickr, and Facebook. PSNH was able to communicate status updates to consumer and business customers, many of whom had no working electronic devices other than the mobile phones they charged at work.

Since these services all support mobile posting, Murray, who also had no power in his home, was still able to monitor communications after hours. In a crisis of scale, PSNH leveraged social media to maintain communication with its community under truly dreadful circumstances.

At the very least, make sure you own your company name and variants thereof on popular social networks before the cyber-squatters do. You never know when you will need them. BP was publicly humiliated by a critic on Twitter who registered the name @BPGlobalPR and was using it to savage the company over its response to the oil spill in the Gulf of Mexico. There was little BP could do but watch in embarrassment. The company launched its own official, verified Twitter account. But the @BPGlobalPR Twitter account quickly amassed more than 10 times the number of followers.

Solicit Feedback

Business customers spontaneously form special interest groups around products or topics that matter to them. Use the search function in Facebook, LinkedIn, or niche social networks in your market, and you'll probably find your company's name, or at the very least a topic around the market you serve. Why not tap into these groups for advice?

Many B2B companies use customer advisory councils for this purpose, but the process can work informally online as well. LinkedIn is a particularly strong platform for customer feedback because the community is focused and professional. Start by joining relevant groups and just listening to the conversations for a couple of weeks. It's best if you get your product people involved and let marketing serve as a coach. Professional customers prefer to engage with the people who build the products they use.

When engaging on LinkedIn or other professional communities, be aware of the ground rules. LinkedIn groups have a designated administrator and some require prospective members to apply for admission. In all cases, it's a good idea to introduce yourself to the administrator and explain why you're there. Some groups expressly prohibit vendors from participating. Don't try to argue your way into the conversation in this case. Chances are there are other groups that would be happy to have you.

You don't have to reveal secrets to play. Simply asking for feedback on your products or seeking input on common challenges can spark a useful conversation. Do not, under any circumstances, try to sell to people in these communities. That's a fast track to banishment. Be curious, respectful, and deferential to their opinions. Only a minority of them will want to share, but a core of 10 to 20 percent will be eager to engage.

You need a strong stomach to do this. If members of the community have problems with your product, they will be open about that. Don't respond defensively, but promise to route complaints to the appropriate people and then follow up. If possible, take contentious conversations to a private channel such as e-mail for resolution.

Some companies with strong engineering cultures encounter resistance to these feedback channels from developers who believe that they know best what customers need. In that case, it's better to adopt guerrilla tactics such as listening to existing conversations and forwarding useful information to people on the product side. Engineers, after all, are rewarded based on the success of their products. If they see opportunities to make customers happier, it's in their best interests to respond.

The process of soliciting feedback can range from simply listening to conversations to actively participating in online discussions to building branded communities around companies and products. One useful tactic is to set up surveys and invite members to fill them out. Low-cost survey services like SurveyMonkey are quite flexible and cost just a few dollars a month. There are even free alternatives like FreeOnlineSurveys.com, SurveyPirate, and Kwik Surveys. Another good free option is Google Forms, which permits you to build quick, functional feedback forms at no cost. No-cost services are limited in capability, so if you want to use advanced features like demographic segmentation or conditional branching, you're better off paying a few dollars for a professional tool.

If your budget permits it, consider creating your own branded community. SAP Networks uses customer feedback on its e-commerce site to improve product performance. Low ratings provide incentive for product managers to either improve product performance or encourage happy customers to share positive opinions. If ratings are low across the board, it's probably an indication that the product needs work. The public nature of the online store becomes an extra incentive to fix the problem.

There are literally hundreds of options for customizing a branded social network, ranging from enterprise software suites like Oracle Beehive and Telligent to open-source community platforms like

Drupal to hosted communities offered by Jive, SocialText, Lithium, and Awareness Networks, among others. In Chapter 9 we talk about how to narrow down the possibilities to the software category that's right for you. Chapter 13 tells how to administer your own communities. You can gain tremendous insight this way, but be prepared to staff your effort appropriately. You'll need at least one full-time equivalent to manage an active community.

We'll explore many of these opportunities in more detail in later chapters. But first let's get the basics in place: selling the value of social marketing to the skeptics.

CHAPTER THREE

Winning Buy-In and Resources

The good news is that selling social marketing programs is easier today than it's ever been. A compelling body of case evidence has emerged over the past couple of years[1] and the mainstream popularity of services like LinkedIn and Facebook have made social networks at least understandable to skeptics. In the same way that America Online drove business adoption of the Internet 15 years ago, consumer applications are creating business awareness today.

But this doesn't necessarily make social marketing an easy sell, in part because many business leaders still aren't sure if social media is an opportunity or a productivity drain. More than half of the chief information officers (CIOs) interviewed by Robert Half Technology in early 2010 said their firms do not allow employees to visit social networking sites for any reason while at work, primarily because of productivity concerns.[2] In business-to-business (B2B) companies, which tend to be more conservative than their business-to-consumer (B2C) counterparts, resistance to change is even more pronounced. A 2010 survey of 104 B2B marketers by digital marketing agency White Horse found that 36 percent were frustrated by low executive interest in social marketing, compared with just 9 percent for B2C marketers. Nearly half the respondents also reported that lack of organizational knowledge, preference for traditional marketing, and the perceived irrelevance of social marketing to their field were obstacles to change.

B2B companies often have long-term customer relationships and see little value in adding social media to the mix. Many are small, family-owned operations that focus on a niche and don't aspire to be much bigger than they already are. In some cases, their markets are so small that executives believe they already know all their prospects. Those companies may see little need for social marketing outside of customer support.

Tradition-minded executives also see peril in the fact that online conversations can't be controlled. Their nightmare scenario is that critics lambaste the brand on its own web site or Facebook page. The fact that thought leaders like Dell, Microsoft, Southwest Airlines, and Google came to terms with this risk years ago and have learned to embrace customer feedback matters little. Traditional marketing says that which can't be controlled should be avoided.

FINDING ALLIES ONLINE

Perhaps you don't know who your potential allies are. In that case, start searching. Look up your company name on LinkedIn and analyze the profiles you find to see just how engaged they are. How many connections do they have? How many recommendations? To which groups do they belong? Are they active?

Use Twitter's "find people" feature to see if any of your LinkedIn prospects are there. Or just Google "First_Name Last_Name on Twitter." When you find prospects, see how active they are by looking at the date and time stamps on their tweets. Are their tweets all social all the time, or do they tweet about work-related subjects, too?

Check out who's following them. Are they connected to any of your suppliers, customers, industry trade media, or regulatory agencies? If so, there's a high likelihood their messages will be passed along to targeted audiences.

Do they reference their employer in their bio? What's the ratio of people they're following to people following them? If it's 2:1 following:followers, they're still getting started. If it's the opposite, they're influencers who are already enjoying success.

And then there's the overriding question of return on investment, which even enthusiasts will tell you is a tricky proposition for initiatives that may not pay off for a year or more. See Chapter 14 for more on that.

Caveats

We asked many successful practitioners and experts how they sell social programs, and this chapter is a summary of their advice. We want to restate one caveat at the outset: **Social marketing is not for every company**. Some businesses are so specialized or their markets so focused that they already know who all their customers and prospects are. These companies are probably better off working their face-to-face channels than starting a blog. There may be opportunities to influence the market through media coverage or customer service, but the rewards are harder to find.

Culture may also be a significant barrier. Businesses with a rigid top-down management style may be incompatible with the free flow of information that social marketing involves. This doesn't mean they can't benefit from using the tools, but the payoff will be modest because the real potential of social marketing is realized when a company trusts its people to communicate with external audiences without strict oversight.

Finally, businesses that operate in controversial markets or that have been the target of legal or regulatory action may be better off sticking with conventional channels for communications. A very real concern for regulated industries is the lack of audit trails on public networks. Most of today's popular social networking channels do not maintain records long enough to satisfy government regulators or won't make that information readily available. At the time of this writing, the only way around this limitation was to actually save your social media communications yourself. Cloud-based customer relationship management (CRM) provider Salesforce.com has implemented a set of features for attaching tweets and Facebook status updates to customer records, but for most services, the onus is on the user to keep audit trails.

We assume these limitations don't describe your company; otherwise, you probably wouldn't be reading this book. More likely, you're one of the many marketers who is dealing with resistance at some or all levels of the organization (see Figure 3.1). Here's the advice we gathered.

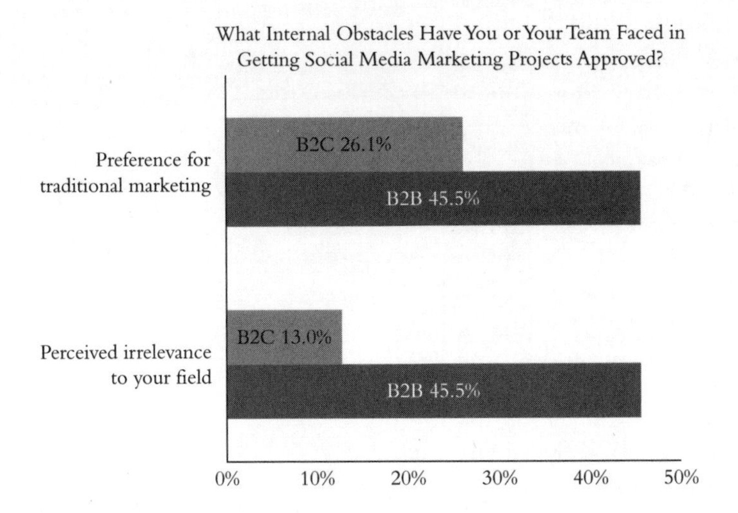

Figure 3.1 Internal Obstacles.
Source: White Horse survey of 104 B2B and B2C marketers.

Sell the Concept

If you want to get the chief executive officer (CEO) or board of directors behind the initiative, talk about trends, your market, and/or your specific customers. The statistics are pretty hard to ignore. Grab the videos "Social Media Revolution 2" (http://socialnomics.net) and "Did You Know 2.0," which you can easily find with a search engine, and show people stats like these:

- Facebook gets more weekly visits in the United States than Google and has a population larger than all but two countries.
- The Internet took four years to reach 50 million users; In contrast, Facebook added 200 million users in less than a year.
- There were 1 billion iPod applications sold in the first 9 months of availability.
- Eighty percent of companies use social media for recruitment.
- Studies show that Wikipedia is as accurate as the Encyclopedia Britannica.
- Seventy-eight percent of consumers trust peer recommendations online; only 14 percent trust advertisements.

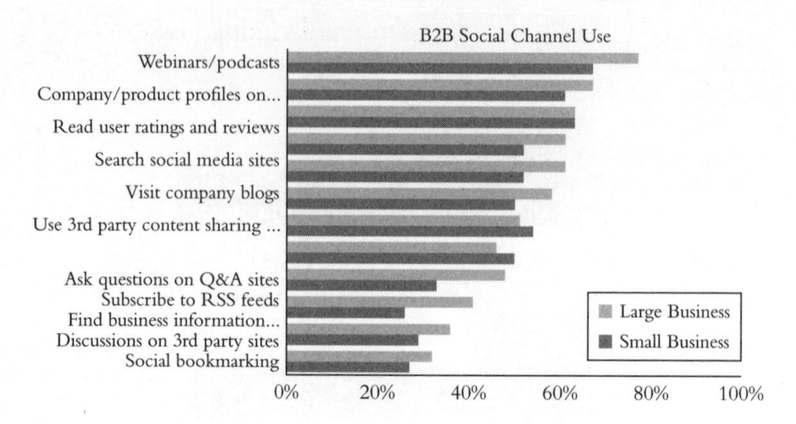

Figure 3.2 B2B Social Channel Use.
Source: Business.com.

- Only 18 percent of TV advertising campaigns generate positive return on investment.
- Revenues of the U.S. newspaper industry have fallen by nearly half since 2006.

Business.com's 2009 B2B Social Media Benchmarking Study shows that some social channels are already firmly embedded in buyer behavior (see Figure 3.2). Today, you almost need a good reason *not* to use these media.

Forrester Research segments social technology use into profiles it calls Social Technographics, which are fully explained in the book *Groundswell* by Bernoff and Li. There's a calculator at Forrester.com/Empowered that shows the usage characteristics of B2B companies.

There's also a growing body of industry-wide data, much of which is freely available. We like Tekrati, which tracks analyst reports and can quickly notify subscribers of new research. Research about B2B marketing trends can be found at eMarketer, MarketingSherpa, MarketingProfs, MarketingCharts, Marketo and Social Media B2B, or just by searching.

The main objective of conducting such research is to demonstrate that the way businesses and their customers relate to one another is changing, and the onus is on businesses to adapt. Conversations will happen with or without you. Can you really afford not to engage in the channels your market is already using?

You can also let your customers make the argument for you. Use a low-cost research tool like SurveyMonkey or Zoomerang to conduct a quick customer survey. Ask customers how they go about researching products and companies. Chances are you'll find that search and online peer relationships are pretty popular. There is no more compelling message to your management than to show that customers are someplace your company isn't.

Start monitoring online sources for mentions of your company and your competitors and bring examples to management. This usually gets their attention quickly, particularly if customers are complaining about you or praising your competitors.

"When we sit down with B2B companies for the first time, we often do a light social monitoring audit for executives to show what's being said out there," says Eric Anderson, vice president of marketing at White Horse. "Their perception is that social media is consumer-focused, with people sharing information about what they had for lunch. They're really gobsmacked to see how much conversation is going on about their industry."

Conversation monitoring often makes the decision for you about where and how to engage. If the action is on Twitter, go there. If bloggers are talking about you, engage them through public relations (PR) channels or consider starting a blog of your own. Effective social marketing relies on your ability to identify, remember, and connect with your prospects through their preferred networking channels, which you discover by listening.

Another effective approach is to position social marketing as an extension of existing PR activities. Demonstrate how social media can help expand communication channels and make them more efficient, recommends Nielsen online digital strategic services executive vice president Pete Blackshaw.

For example, more than 200 reporters at the *New York Times* have Twitter accounts. Media relations firm Cision reported that 89 percent of journalists use blogs for conducting online research.[3]

"Convincing a PR or customer service executive that they need an apparatus to listen to reporters and customers is the path of least resistance because it extends the reach of what they're doing already," says Blackshaw.

Biotech giant Monsanto took this approach in early 2009, when it launched a blog[4] called "Monsanto According to Monsanto." With environmental and food activists bent on spurring legislation to require labeling of all genetically modified foods, Monsanto wanted a public place to tell its story. Rather than having to respond to individual queries from reporters, Monsanto linked to its argument against the need for labeling. These are called sneeze posts, and they can be written up and search optimized for every frequently asked question your company receives. The time savings can be impressive.

You can also win buy-in by finding places where social media could be a superior alternative to existing processes. For example, foregoing the cost of one focus group and investing that money into a one-year license of a conversation monitoring platform is a modest experiment without much downside.

If you want to show what other businesses are doing, you can find good case study collections at:

- The Word of Mouth Marketing Association Case Study Library (WOMMA.org/casestudy)
- Business.com (Blogs.Business.com/b2b-online-marketing)
- The Society for New Communications Research (SNCR.org)
- Forrester Groundswell Awards (http://bit.ly/B2BAwards)
- The Association Social Media Wiki (AssociationSocialMedia.com)
- The New PR Wiki (TheNewPR.com)

Live research is also useful, particularly when incorporated into a presentation. For example, if you want to make the argument that your company should leverage Twitter because there are conversations going on there about your business sector, use Twitterfall to show real time activity or mark relevant tweets as favorites to show your management.

Just Do It

If management isn't likely to be convinced by your persuasive powers, and if you're willing to take the risk of bending the rules, consider guerilla tactics. Choose a small project that can demonstrate social marketing's benefits and try a pilot campaign. Choose something that's likely to show a payoff with a minimum of time investment, such as a Twitter account for a product or a public blog about your market that isn't specifically affiliated with your company.

Figure 3.3 was adapted from MarketingSherpa's 2010 Social Media Marketing Benchmark Report. It shows the popularity of B2B marketers' social marketing objectives contrasted with their actual effectiveness. Note the areas of mismatch. This doesn't mean big goals such as revenue growth aren't attainable, but they are not the place to start. Social marketing works best in the areas where marketing has traditionally focused. Increasing attendance at a seminar series is one example.

Catapult Systems, based in Austin, Texas, is a Microsoft-focused information technology (IT) consulting firm with about 250 employees. It used Twitter and LinkedIn to complement conventional marketing channels when it staged a multicity tour anchored by three of the company's internal Windows 7 experts. Each employee was given

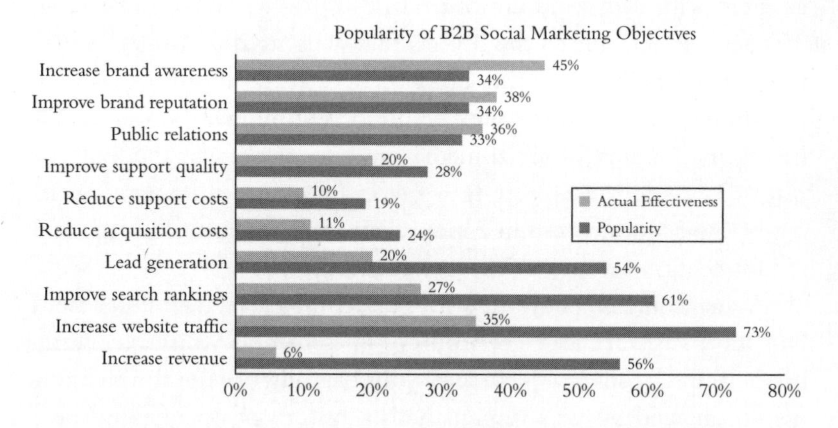

Figure 3.3 Popularity of B2B Social Marketing Objectives.
Source: Marketing Sherpa.

a consistent message and URL to add to e-mail signature lines. Those on Twitter were asked to regularly post invitations to the seminars.

Catapult also created LinkedIn groups for each of its regional events and invited its top 25 prospects in each city to join. Prospects were invited to submit questions for the experts to answer, which hundreds did.

Catapult didn't try to reinvent marketing with this campaign. It simply piggybacked employee promotion on top of its traditional channels to maximize visibility. E-mail forwards and retweets complemented direct mail and advertising. The company also staged a monthly series of 45-minute webcasts and a small group event for prospects who indicated readiness to buy. The seminars on the road-show tour were packed, with each of the more than 700 total attendees having been introduced to Catapult as an authority on Windows 7.

Choose projects that are already successful or that fly under the corporate radar. In either case, success provides a platform for growing your initiative, and failure is less likely to attract executive attention.

American Express OPEN Forum, a social network for small business owners, was originally conceived to support an existing conference series. It later blossomed into a valuable channel for Amex to connect with a coveted customer base. OPEN Forum traffic grew 350 percent annually in the 3 years following its 2007 launch, and it passed the 1 million monthly unique visitor mark in early 2010. The community was the first Amex brand to venture into Twitter, and it has been a foundry of social media experimentation for the financial giant. By tying the project to a successful existing program, social marketing advocates within Amex minimized downside risk and laid the foundation for further experimentation.

When launching new initiatives under the radar, **seek allies who can lend support and credibility**. These people won't necessarily be social media advocates. In fact, your best ally may be the technology challenged 30-year veteran with a history of openness to new ideas. Or the person may just be a gadget fiend who's always the first to adopt the latest consumer electronics.

If your ally owns a product line or department, you're in luck because you have the opportunity to make a visible impact on the business. But even if the person is an individual contributor, you have options. Perhaps your ally could start a LinkedIn group or Twitter account around the market in which your company competes. It's important that allies be positive about the potential for social marketing and in a position to make something happen, even on a small scale.

Choose projects with a low risk of entry and a low likelihood of failure. Twitter is an excellent starting point. The cost of joining is zero. Launching a Twitter account to support a new business initiative is unlikely to embarrass anyone. In the early stages, the point is to show results you can build on, not to try for the big score.

If you're a professional communicator, you have a built-in advantage. PR and marketing communications pros are already entrusted with the authority to speak for the organization and are natural choices to lead social marketing forays. PR leads marketing in the management and oversight of social media communications at most organizations, according to a study Eric did with the Public Relations Society of America, Korn Ferry International, and United Kingdom–based market research firm Trendstream. If you're not a professional communicator, seek support from your marketing or PR team. They're likely to be well aware of the changes that are going on in the media landscape and eager to contribute.

Executives at Emerson Process Management were skeptical about launching a blog in 2005, but they trusted 15-year veteran communicator Jim Cahill. His subsequent success at building search awareness and generating leads prompted Emerson to expand to other social platforms and to promote Cahill to the position of social media manager.

At CME Group, the corporate communications department spearheaded the company's move into Twitter and later other social platforms because of the trust they already enjoyed with executive management and the legal department. "We were already speaking publicly so it made sense for us to speak for the exchange [in social venues]," says Allan Schoenberg, director of corporate communications.

Schoenberg and his colleagues had already forged strong relationships with the company's legal team, which is critical in a heavily regulated industry. That trust gave them the political capital they needed to experiment with new channels.

Lawyers can kill a social marketing initiative before it ever leaves the ground. **Don't try to go around the legal department; educate them instead**. If case study evidence doesn't work, look up advice from some prominent law bloggers, such as those mentioned later in this chapter. Always be careful about choosing people to dispense legal advice, of course. Just because a law firm has a blog doesn't make it proficient in social media law.

Answering Common Objections

1. There's no return on investment.

If you pitched a program backed by research that's likely to deliver even modest gains with minimal risk, you've answered this question already. The return is calculated by subtracting the cost of the marketing pilot, the cost of goods sold, and operating expenses from revenue generated. But long-term intangible benefits are more difficult to quantify.

"What's the ROI of a golf club membership or a round of golf with a customer?" asks Mark Story, new media director at the U.S. Securities and Exchange Commission when he's challenged to justify the ROI of social media. These are emerging communications channels. When they're used for business, they lead to stronger relationships, and relationships are valuable in business.

There's no direct ROI for telephones, holiday parties, or company cars. Telephones make it easier for people to communicate, but with the exception of phone orders, there's no way to come up with a hard number for the ROI of a phone system. Holiday parties contribute to a more joyful work environment, but there's no way to calculate the ROI for happiness in the workplace. The ROI and business case arguments are often used as stalling tactics to justify inaction.

The reality is that you *can* calculate social media ROI. If you have a few basic metrics in place and a rigorous approach to understanding activity on your website, ROI is actually not hard to measure. In Chapter 14, we show you how to figure the ROI of social media, as long as you have good base data. However, our hope is that you don't have to resort to excruciating analysis to justify your plans. In conversations with scores of successful marketers, we have yet to find one who applies a rigorous ROI analysis to social marketing. Their companies do it because they believe investments in customer relationships are worthwhile.

2. We don't have the resources.

Investments in social marketing programs can be difficult to estimate because there's no set formula for engagement. Solis suggests a "cost per interaction" equation that estimates the time it takes to find relevant conversations, engage the people behind them, monitor response and follow up. He estimates roughly 25 minutes per interaction, which means one person at 80 percent utilization can engage with 14 customers per day. Determine where your organization has the most to gain by engaging in conversations and estimate how many people you'll be able to touch with the resources you have.

Think small. Launch a group on LinkedIn or a vertical network around a topic that's relevant to your market. Build an audience and then decide if it makes sense to move to a branded community. In most cases, you can get a foothold with an investment of no more than an hour a day. Figure 3.4 shows the amount of time spent on Twitter each day by a group of 73 B2B marketers who have generated sales from Twitter. The majority spent less than 60 minutes.

3. We can't control what people say about us.

True, but you no longer have a choice. Searching for conversations about your company can turn up some pretty compelling evidence that you need to be part of online conversations because they happen with or without you. If you can't find mentions of your company, look for competitors. Chances are there are conversations under way

Figure 3.4 Daily Time Spent Managing Twitter.
Source: BtoB Magazine.

that are already influencing purchasing decisions. You have nothing to lose by getting involved. At least that way you're in the game.

Successful social marketers take an entirely different view of this issue. They see lack of control as an opportunity to *take* control. Once you know how customers perceive your brand, you can make more intelligent decisions about your own positioning. Negative comments are an early warning of a problem that could get bigger if not addressed. Misperceptions are more containable if corrected early rather than being allowed to grow out of control. Detractors can quickly be identified and an effort can be made to convert them into supporters if you listen to them.

4. *We'll lose brand consistency.*

"If we trust our employees to get on a plane, fly to a conference, make a presentation and answer questions in public—or even just answer a company phone or corporate email account—the horse is out of the barn already," says Rick Short, marcom director at Indium Corporation, an electronic assembly materials company that's using social marketing. The only difference with social marketing is scale.

You need to educate employees who speak in public about the brand, the mission, and the company values. This can be done with an internal training program, but it's usually best to start with just a few people who are clear on these talking points, such as the communications department and people who are already on the speaking circuit. Blogger training isn't much different than speaker training. Before launching its corporate blog, Johnson & Johnson first experimented behind the firewall, giving management the chance to practice in a safe, controlled environment.

Brand consistency is mainly a matter of good internal communication practices. Social media doesn't change that.

5. We'll be exposed to legal risk.

This is a legitimate concern, particularly for companies in regulated industries. Showing that other companies in your industry are using social media is a good starting point, but perhaps your company is a first mover. You need to have your legal team on board as described earlier. If the answer is still no, you're probably out of luck. Regulators are not people to be toyed with. But you shouldn't give up hope. The Federal Trade Commission issued guidelines on social media practices in 2009, the Financial Industry Regulatory Authority (FINRA) followed in early 2010, and the Food and Drug Administration was set to follow as we finished writing this book. Some of the early rules from these agencies have been derided as heavy-handed and unenforceable, but at least they are the beginning of a process that will evolve rapidly with experience. Nearly every regulatory agency is grappling with this issue right now, so keep your ear to the ground.

Some resources we suggest, all easily searchable:

- Tom Goldstein at Akin Gump publishes the SCOTUS blog, which covers U.S. Supreme Court developments.
- Denise Howell hosts "The Week in Law," an hour-long podcast about legal matters affecting social media and technology.

- Kevin O'Keefe runs LexBlog, which supports and hosts blogs for 3,000 attorneys who are using social media to develop their professional practices.
- Santa Clara University associate professor of law Eric Goldman blogs on cyberlaw and intellectual property issues at EricGoldman.org.

Embracing Disruption

In the prologue to the book *The Living Company*, Arie de Geus profiles a study he commissioned at Shell Oil about the traits of Fortune 500 companies with extraordinary longevity.

> *Long-lived companies were sensitive to their environment. Whether they had built their fortunes on knowledge or on natural resources they remained in harmony with the world around them. As wars, depressions, technologies, and political changes surged and ebbed around them, they always seemed to excel at keeping their feelers out, tuned to whatever was going on around them.*[5]

Successful companies learn to embrace disruption, but that kind of culture is difficult to create. Social marketing is disruptive. It changes the way businesses work. People don't like change.

These days, however, few of us have a choice. As we noted in the opening chapter, today's great businesses are those that adapt most readily to the conditions around them. Companies that embrace social marketing must prepare for an environment that will be in a constant state of turmoil. "Every time you think you have your plan down, the landscape changes," says Carlos Dominguez, a Cisco senior vice president. Fortunately, many senior executives can buy into the idea that creating a culture of experimentation is a good thing. Position social marketing as a step toward that goal.

CHAPTER FOUR

Creating a Social Organization

Cisco Systems is a survivor. Founded in 1984, the company is today a $35 billion giant in the hotly competitive computer networking industry. As hundreds of rivals have come and gone, Cisco has persevered, maintaining premium pricing and an uncanny ability to anticipate shifts in its market. The information technology market is brutal, and Cisco has endured its fair share of ups and downs, but today it enjoys a dominant position in enterprise accounts who buy networking equipment by the truckload.

John Chambers has guided Cisco since 1995. That's an unusually long tenure for an executive at a high-tech firm. One reason Chambers enjoys such strong support from Cisco's board of directors is that he continually shifts the company's business strategy to accommodate changes in the market. For example, Cisco grew through acquisition for many years and, in the process, built a corporate culture that assimilated new people and ideas with remarkable efficiency. However, that required a rigorous methodology that left little tolerance for variation. As the volume of acquisitions has declined in recent years, Chambers has focused on abandoning the command-and-control management style that served the company well for two decades. His new mission is to push decision making out to the edges of the organization.

In a 2009 interview with the *New York Times,* Chambers said this transition hasn't been easy for him or his staff:

> *I'm a command-and-control person. I like being able to say turn right, and we truly have 67,000 people turn right. But that's the style of the past. That was great when you were a single product, when the market was moving slower and one executive or an executive team could run the whole company.*
>
> *Today's world requires a different leadership style—moving more into a collaboration and teamwork, including learning how to use Web 2.0 technologies. If you had told me I'd be video blogging and blogging, I would have said, no way. And yet our 20-somethings in the company really pushed me to use that more.*

Chambers has it right. The fast-moving world of business no longer accommodates institutional bottlenecks. There are too many competitors ready to steal your business while you agonize over the "right" decision.

This new approach to business won't go over well with some of your people. The management philosophies that have served us since the Industrial Revolution are based on the idea that line-level employees are basically stupid, incapable of making important decisions for themselves, and in need of rigid rules and constant oversight to make sure they don't screw up.

Command-and-control management worked well at a time when spheres of influence were limited to people's family and close friends. Today, though, the people on the front lines are every bit as visible as executives, sometimes even more so. Customer service issues are among the most common complaints on Twitter, and companies that have chopped and outsourced their support organizations over the last decade are feeling the consequences of those cutbacks in the form of public customer backlash.

In his book *Grapevine,* BzzAgent founder Dave Balter asserts that the main cause of customer dissatisfaction is service, not products. Customers understand that not all products or companies are perfect, and they have remarkable tolerance for failures if vendors quickly rectify problems. In a world of commoditized products, customer service has become the great differentiator. One of the major reasons tech companies like IBM, Hewlett-Packard, EMC, and Microsoft are able to charge premium prices for their products is that they go to extremes to ensure customer satisfaction, even if it means dispatching technicians in the corporate jet in the middle of the night to rescue a failed server. Think of the last time you complained to your peers about a company you do business with. Chances are your gripe wasn't about the product, but rather about the uncaring attitude the company showed when you complained.

The social organization takes a completely different approach to customer service. In effect, everyone in the company is deputized to solve customer problems. When Boingo misfired the test e-mail to all of its customers as described in Chapter 2, every available employee was pulled in to respond to complaints. What could have been an embarrassing crisis actually turned into a public relations coup because the issue was addressed so quickly. Within a week, Boingo was fielding calls from media wanting to hear about its customer service heroics. When was the last time you turned crisis into opportunity?

The option of remaining closed and insular is less and less practical in an era of open communication, so businesses need to evaluate their approach to engaging with communities in a practice that some people are calling social customer relationship management (CRM). Traditional CRM involves tracking customer behavior and contacts to identify opportunities for additional business. Social CRM builds social interactions into the mix so that tweets, blog comments, and even face-to-face contacts are woven into the profile of each customer. To make social CRM work, all employees must become ambassadors who project a common message and document their contacts for inclusion in customer profiles. This is easier said than done.

The Openness Challenge

Experience has shown that truly successful companies permit their people to cross departmental lines fluidly and even breach traditional lines of command in the quest to provide the best possible customer experience and to respond to opportunities whenever they arise. B2B companies have an advantage in this respect because they serve a smaller number of customers than their B2C peers and their interactions tend to demand a higher level of domain expertise. When employees at all levels are empowered to make decisions—and when customers are involved at appropriate levels—the opportunities multiply. A few notable firms like Dell and Zappos have managed to enable this at a large scale. However, they are the exceptions. Most businesses need to implement social CRM gradually.

In her 2010 book *Open Leadership,* Charlene Li tells of SolarWinds, a network management software provider whose 25,000-member community of network administrators handles most of their own support needs. Not only is the community efficient (SolarWinds has just two full-time customer support people), it is considered a competitive advantage.

"When the company went public in May 2009, they dedicated a part of their precious investor presentation time to explaining the value of their user community," Li wrote. "'[O]ur community is in many ways the key long-term competitive advantage that we have,' said Kenny Van Zandt, SolarWinds's senior vice president."

Li defines the new breed of progressive leaders as being those who are willing to give up on the "need to be *personally* involved in the decision making process." The pace of change no longer permits a few executives to be bottlenecks. And research has consistently demonstrated that the wisdom of crowds works. What's different today is that the tools to capture that wisdom are far better than they've ever been.

Effective leaders are learning to delegate decisions to the crowd when their input adds little or no value. Li quotes Chis Conde, chief executive officer (CEO) of business continuity service provider SunGard: "It is very arrogant to think you can make better decisions than the thousands of people below you." Instead, Condi sees his job as being to "make painful decisions that no one else can make and maintain a collaboration system that can handle all the other decisions that the organization needs to make."

There is no one way to go about creating a social organization. Each business must proceed at its own pace within the boundaries of its own culture. Altimeter Group's Owyang has identified five models of social organizations:

- **Centralized**—This model preserves most of the control that hierarchical organizations have traditionally valued, but it interweaves a layer of social media expertise, often in the form of a dedicated manager or organization. The company can take advantage of social channels without giving up on lines of authority. A centralized model is most appropriate to large manufacturing organizations that have many line workers or union members who wouldn't necessarily represent the best line of customer contact.
- **Coordinated**—This federated approach extends some control to individual departments or business units while concentrating expertise in a central organization. Local managers have some latitude but still must work within centrally administered guidelines. The advantage is that frontline innovation can be rewarded but central management authority isn't challenged.
- **Dandelion**—This metaphor refers to a dandelion's sprawling network of seeds, each of which is loosely related to the others but all of which function more or less independently. Centers of excellence, if there are any, are maintained informally or with a dotted-line responsibility to a central group. This model is best suited for large organizations such as consulting or accounting firms, where there are many business units, each of which serves specialized, high-value markets. It requires complete executive buy-in because a considerable amount of authority is decentralized.
- **Organic**—Let a hundred flowers bloom. Each individual makes his or her own decisions about whether and how to participate in social activities. There is little formal coordination, and best practices are shared between participants. This approach works best in small, entrepreneurial companies where

individual expression is rewarded. However, the model scales badly and can lead to chaos if not monitored.

- **Honeycomb**—This is the rarest of social governance models and also the most sophisticated. All employees are encouraged to think of themselves as customer service representatives and to use whatever means they consider appropriate to deliver customer value. Corporate policies govern behavior, but individuals have considerable latitude to make decisions, even if they sometimes cross lines of authority. This model requires support from the highest levels of the company. Dell and Zappos are two notable examples of this sophisticated approach.

We don't want to suggest that any of these governance models is the best one for you. You need to choose an approach that harmonizes with your markets, your business structure, and your company culture. The honeycomb approach may sound appealing, but if you try to implement it in a command-and-control culture, the initiative will fail and you'll be further behind than when you started. Keep an eye on your competitors. The more distributed models enhance speed and responsiveness and can give a fast company an advantage against a slow one. If your competitors are responding to customer comments in near-real time and achieving results, then you have to consider whether your entire culture needs to change.

Infectious Growth

In Chapter 3 we advised you to sell social initiatives gradually to reluctant stakeholders. One nice characteristic of successful social projects is that their success prompts skeptics to jump on board.

RIDGID Branding, a unit of Emerson Electric Co. that makes tools for professional tradespeople, launched its community under the radar in mid-2000, when no one was talking about social media. In fact, RidgidForum was actually managed by an intern. The forum was conceived as a simple and inexpensive experiment to see if professional tradespeople wanted to interact in an online venue. Uptake was slow at first, but by 2003, the membership topped 3,000. "That's when things really started to take off," says Wyatt Kilmartin, director of RIDGID Branding.

"It took three years to get to 3,000 members, three more to get to 10,000 and just two more to get to 20,000," Kilmartin remembers. "We never promoted it other than to mention it in press releases. There wasn't a lot of cost involved." Today, RidgidForum encompasses more than 300,000 posts and has become an invaluable source of everything from customer feedback to product ideas. It's a magnet for search engines, which draws leads to RIDGID's web site, and the community's value to members has had measurable benefits in customer loyalty.

Watching an online professional community reach a tipping point is a beautiful thing. It takes time, but when members begin to sustain an active discussion, the effect on the host company can be transformative. Developers and product managers begin to tune into the conversations and design product enhancements based on guidance from the community. Marketers start looking to customers to help them with positioning and to seek help evangelizing the company to others. Active communities literally change companies from the ground up.

Sumaya Kazi was named senior social media manager at Sun Microsystems in 2007, when the computer company was first experimenting with using new channels to communicate with customers. Sun already had more than 4,300 public bloggers at the time, but the idea of an overarching social media strategy "was so foreign," says Kazi, who is now CEO of YoProCo, a social network for young professionals.

Sun executives knew that there were benefits to social media across the organization, but they couldn't predict where the opportunities lay. Kazi quickly realized "you can't push social media on any one. It has to be something that people are comfortable with."

Her approach was to educate and evangelize. Among her tactics:

- Starting a private Facebook group for employees to provide weekly facts and tips on how to use social media. Sun Facebook Fridays eventually grew to more than 2,000 members.
- Launching a monthly seminar that was presented live in a Sun conference facility and streamed to employees globally. Content

included how-to advice, case studies, and guest speakers such as Naked Conversations co-author Shel Israel. "That was amazing for us," Kazi says.
- Hosting a weekly Internet radio program called "Socially Speaking." Every Tuesday afternoon, Kazi brought in guests who were active in social media to talk about what worked.

As awareness of social media applications grew, employees began to come up with their own ideas. Photos of kids and family vacations began to sprout on Sun's internal network, and membership in a Facebook group for employees grew to more than 12,000. "Being able to connect with employees outside of a work environment fostered a lot more teamwork on the job," Kazi says. "We had no problem getting buy-in over time."

Ron Casalotti was closely involved in the launch of Business Exchange, a professional networking community run by *BusinessWeek* magazine. Business Exchange breaks the traditional publishing model by enabling members of the community to define the organization and content of the site. Members can even choose to curate their own topical areas, thereby becoming visible experts on the subject.

This idea took some selling at *BusinessWeek*. Journalists are notoriously territorial and conservative, so the idea of permitting community members to become self-declared experts in the same areas they covered struck some of them as wrong. But as the site has grown and prospered (it was registering 1.5 million page views per day in mid-2010), it has emerged as a valuable resource to the editorial staff. Journalists may be conservative, but they're also feedback junkies. The ability to test story ideas and get instant commentary from the community proved addictive. "It spurred people who weren't sure what this social media thing meant," Casalotti says.

Working at Internet Speed

Social organizations function differently from hierarchical ones. For one thing, they become more customer-focused. Employees learn to appreciate that conversations are going on in real time, and the faster they respond, the more satisfied the customer. This means that organizational walls start to tumble. It also means that social organizations become more nimble, responsive, and service-oriented. This not only makes them leaner, but also faster.

Open collaboration is creating new styles of doing business. No one exemplifies the style better than Google, a consumer-focused company that derives the vast majority of its nearly $25 billion in annual revenue from business customers. Google produces an amazing array of products, ranging from mapping software to computer-aided design (CAD) to medical records organizers. It develops them in a process that includes customer feedback at every stage.

Google rarely holds press conferences and eschews secrecy about its product plans. "If we never had to do another press release, we'd be thrilled," says Google Director of Global Marketing and Public Affairs Gabriel Stricker. "Sometimes, we have to do them, but we'd almost always rather just blog it."

Google shares its ideas openly in public "labs" and often announces them in low-key style via blogs. Rather than agonize over getting everything perfect, they test their products by releasing them, and reiterate over time. Its developers and product managers work the long tail of publicity through one-on-one interviews and frequent speaking engagements. Some of its products have been in public "beta test" for as long as 5 years. The company uses every social media outlet it can, and never relies on the mainstream media spotlight.

Google does this by design because it believes that businesses that build products behind closed doors take too long to get their products out and risk becoming invisible because no one talks about them. On the other hand, a public process not only results in better products but also forms the foundation for a word-of-mouth marketing force.

As any good political advertising specialist will tell you, if you want people to talk about your campaign ads, you have to be willing to get something wrong. You have to be willing to drop a shoe, so others have the opportunity to pick it up. If you're too perfect, there's really not much to talk about, because you've worked everything out internally by having a conversation with yourself already that we weren't privy too.

Google's approach has some downsides. It makes mistakes in public and endures some ridicule as a result. It is also quick to pull products out of public test for reasons it doesn't always fully divulge. Customers seem willing to tolerate this, however, because they believe they get good value, and because most of their products can be used for free.

Contrast Google's strategy to that of its neighbor a few miles to the north, Apple Computer. Apple takes a much more traditional approach to product development. It holds its plans close to the vest and reveals them with fanfare at elaborate press conferences that generate months of media speculation. The company may only hold a couple of press conferences a year, but they're always memorable.

Apple not only doesn't use social media, it has actively litigated against bloggers who have revealed sensitive information. However, Apple is every bit as good a social marketer as Google. The difference is that Apple's rabid base of fans provides plenty of word-of-mouth speculative frenzy without the vendor's direct involvement. Apple may not actively promote this adoration, but it doesn't discourage it, either.

Is your company more like Apple or Google? Most businesses model themselves on the Apple example. They shroud their plans in secrecy in hopes of entering the market with a splash. Unfortunately, few companies are Apple. In today's crowded, noisy market, companies that choose not to talk to their constituents are quickly forgotten. "One of my personal irritations in interacting with brands is when you interact and they don't interact back," says Allan Schoenberg, director of corporate communications at CME Group, which uses an assortment of social channels. There are other risks as well. Releasing a product that is wrongly positioned or that customers don't want can be an expensive and embarrassing mistake. Why not take advantage of all the advice that's out there for free?

In the new world of information surplus, the winners are those who do the best job of talking about their innovations before they reach the market. Prospective customers want to be involved in the process, and they punish those businesses that don't indulge them.

This doesn't mean every company should embrace open collaboration. Secrets do have value, and customers aren't always good at articulating what they want. The easiest way to start down the path toward a social organization is to start listening to online conversations and selectively sharing the insights that you learn. Find your allies in the organization, come up with small projects that have a high likelihood of success, and publicize your results. Don't set your expectations too high if your company is conservative, highly regulated, or heavily unionized. The objective isn't to be the most open company in the world, but to take better advantage of customer engagement than your competitors do. Once people start tuning into their customers on an ongoing basis, they never want to go back.

CHAPTER FIVE

Creating and Enforcing Social Media Policies

On January 14, 2009, James Andrews was flying into Memphis to make a presentation to the worldwide communications group at Federal Express on behalf of his employer, public relations agency Ketchum Inc. Upon his arrival at the airport, he had what he called "a run-in with an intolerant individual." The encounter prompted him to send this Twitter message: "True confession but I'm in one of those towns where I scratch my head and say 'I would die if I had to live here!'"

Many of us have had similar thoughts about places we've visited, but in the days before social media, we mostly kept our opinions to ourselves. Twitter, which is the most immediate of social media tools, presents a sometimes irresistible opportunity to share impulsive thoughts with our friends. Only Twitter isn't e-mail; it's more like a party line. Andrews found this out to his chagrin the next morning when he was confronted by a group of indignant FedEx employees, many of them Memphis natives, who had already read and discussed his tweet. The message made it up the chain of command at the shipping service as well as to top executives at Ketchum. It also sparked an e-mail from a FedEx executive that questioned whether the millions of dollars the company was paying Andrews' agency was money well spent.

Ketchum kept the FedEx account and Andrews didn't lose his job, but the incident epitomizes the vulnerability that all organizations face these days to the words and actions of individual employees.

Prior to the arrival of social media, few businesses needed a detailed policy laying out all aspects of public disclosure. They hired skilled media relations, investor relations, and public affairs people to do that. But now that social media makes it easy for anyone to make public disclosures, the rules have changed. Not long ago, the marketing department's job was to media-train a few executives. Today, the challenge is to media-train the entire company.

Social media policies have been around since the early days of blogging, and their content and tone vary widely depending on the company's attitude about online conversations, the regulatory and legal environment, and the characteristics of the employee population. They range from just a few hundred words to many thousands. The best policies are more than just rules; they guide employees on how to use social channels to the greatest benefit for the organization.

There are some excellent online resources on this topic. Chris Boudreaux has assembled more than 130 organizational social media policies at socialmediagovernance.com. There's a somewhat smaller database of policies at ComplianceBuilding.com[1] and on the Altimeter Group wiki.[2] Eric Schwartzman, co-author of this book, has published his social media policy template at socialmediapolicytemplate.com. These documents offer valuable guidance on what other companies are doing, but we recommend against simply copying and pasting your own company name into somebody else's document. An effective policy equips everyone in the enterprise with practical guidelines so that they can serve as your brand ambassadors.

Why Not Use Existing Policies?

That's a fair question. You probably have standards of employee behavior in place, and it might be easier to just beef them up to cover social media. The problem with that approach is that the guts of a social media policy—the purpose, definitions, objectives, principles, and the guidelines themselves—are mostly unique to the medium. You'll need to review your existing policies in the course of creating new ones. Start with your company's code of conduct policy, information technology policies, and any ethics or compliance policies and make sure any references to public disclosures, company information, and information security are up to date.

Here are a few things to look for:

- In the pre-Internet days, public disclosures were mainly limited to press releases, public filings, statements to the news media, and marketing brochures. Today, a Facebook status update may qualify. If your code of conduct discusses public disclosure, make sure the definition is current for all possible venues for such disclosure.
- If your code of conduct restricts employees from using company property for personal gain, consider how that might apply to a scenario in which an employee amassed a Twitter following as an outgrowth of his work on behalf of the company. Technically, that person would be in violation of company policy, even though his actions support your larger corporate objectives. Consider amending the existing policy to restrict employees from using company property "solely" or "exclusively" for personal gain.
- Make sure your information security policy distinguishes between confidential and public company information. A good rule is to say that if you can link to it, you can share it.
- Extend whatever responsibilities employees have to protect company information to cover external services. For example, posting a confidential document to Google Docs may be an unacceptable breach of security, even if the document is technically private, because the responsibility for security would be, in effect, transferred to Google.
- If your policy restricts employees from using company information systems to make solicitations, revise that to specify "inappropriate solicitations," since a good use of social media is to solicit information.

- Consider extending user ID and password control parameters with language such as "user names and passwords used to establish a social networking account on behalf of the company, and the direct URL to all company-branded social media accounts, must be registered with information security management." That way, an employee can't leave on bad terms and take control over the company's Facebook presence. This actually happened to one of Paul's clients. The manager of a local franchise quit in a nasty dispute with management and took with him the logon credentials to the franchise's Facebook page.
- Guidance on effective password management probably belongs in the security controls policy rather than the social media policy.
- Check out your company policy on e-mail use as well. It's not uncommon to find a clause restricting employees from including any personal information in their signature block, another counterproductive requirement, since the people we exchange e-mails with are often different from our social networking contacts, and links in a signature block to Facebook, LinkedIn, and Twitter pages can be a great way to cement relationships in the social sphere.

Corporate Policy Making 101

In large organizations, developing corporate policy is not unlike the legislative process. You need to assemble a coalition of influential stakeholders to support your initiative. Smart policy makers aim to appease a broad coalition of stakeholders. They clear the major hurdles first, even if that means leaving some stones unturned initially. They accept that perfect is the enemy of good and work to establish frameworks that can be improved over time.

In the case of social media policy, assembling stakeholders is probably the most challenging part of the process because of the generation gap. Forrester Research estimates that 30 percent of Americans older than age 55 don't use social media in any capacity. It's likely that many of the stakeholders you'll need in your coalition won't even understand why these tools are important.

Also, different stakeholders have different agendas. Here are some of the risks and opportunities that you may encounter.

Department	Risk	Opportunity
Human Resources	Violation of existing policies by employees Policing policy	Build goodwill with workforce Aid in recruiting
Information Technology	Information security and data loss	Reduce support requests from use of cloud services
Legal	Liability for unclear social media guidelines	None
Marketing	Aggravation of disparities between brand message and market perception	Reduce costs and increase efficiencies by enabling marketplace to self-educate
Customer Service	Productivity loss Complexity of enhancing existing CRM software Customer privacy violations	Increase efficiency through enhanced one-to-many communications
Public Relations/ Public Affairs	Employees' going "off message"	Communicate with wider audience Build stronger relationships with key communities
Compliance Officer	Lack of control over third-party channels Noncompliant behavior Enforcement of controls and corrections	Increase channels of communication Get "credit" from regulators for being proactive
Investor Relations	Violation of SEC Regulation Fair Disclosure Responsibility to update and nonselectively engage	Increase channels to investors and analysts
Executive Management	Upsetting the status quo	Thwart obsolescence and building a culture that embraces change

When you're deciding whom to approach in a given department, look for the most influential person who's going to require the least education. But you also want a single point of contact who has the ability to relay the rationale for developing the policy.

You can figure out who's up to speed on social media by asking people or by searching for names on relevant social sites. Request a meeting, brief the person on your initiative, and ask what that person would like to see a social media policy cover. Write down concerns to ensure that you can address them in the policy, and ask the person if he or she would be willing to serve as the department's point person. Explain that the person will be asked to review drafts as they are circulated and provide any feedback or recommendations along the way to make sure the intended policy meets the department's aims.

Try to find stakeholders who are unlikely to transfer to another department or leave the company. You don't want to have to start over again with a new stakeholder who may be hostile or disinterested. Make sure stakeholders are actively involved in the review and approval process so they take ownership of the result.

Sequencing the Chain of Events

Nab the most influential stakeholders first to make it easier to get others on board. Also, pay attention to the order in which you circulate your policy draft for review. Give first copies to those who are the most influential and educated about social media. As you progress through your request for comments review sequence, make it known who's seen it already; that's an implied endorsement to those further down the review chain.

Inadvertent sequencing derailed the initiative at a very large, public, regulated company where Eric was engaged to help create a social media policy. Rather than being circulated to the stakeholders as had been agreed, the initial draft for review somehow was sent to an attorney in the company's legal department who was not a stakeholder. As a result, the policy was essentially gutted of any useful guidance and replaced by three pages of legalese. The revised initiative didn't provide meaningful guidance to employees and was difficult for lay people to understand.

This raises an important point. To be useful, a social media policy must also be accessible. Let's talk for a moment about language.

Threat of "Bureaucratese"

In their zeal to limit corporate liability and obfuscate unintended consequences, legal advisers tend to pile on jargon that ultimately strips contracts of the meaning they are intended to convey. This undermines the whole effort, because the social media policy is as much a statement of principle as a set of rules. In a late 2009 analysis of 46 social media policies (Analysis of Social Media Policies: Lessons and Best Practices), SocialMediaGovernance.com creator Chris Boudreaux noted that "only one-third of sampled organizations portray social media as a positive opportunity for employees and their organization." In other words, most companies are playing defense. The message to employees is that social media can only get them into trouble. What a missed opportunity!

Contrast this with IBM's policy, which is often cited as one of the best. In the introduction, it states, "It is very much in IBM's interest—and, we believe, in each IBMer's own—to be aware of and participate in this sphere of information, interaction and idea exchange." In other words, using these tools is good for your career and for the corporation.

The language you use in your social media policy affects your corporate reputation. An easy to understand, reasonable policy posted online is a public disclosure of your company's regard for its employees. Social media is now an integral part of our social fabric. Recognizing this and offering proactive guidance that's easy for everyone to understand becomes a public relations activity as well, generating goodwill among existing employees, demonstrating fairness to job seekers, and giving you a potential edge over your competitors.

Clarity is about language, but it's also about anticipating difficult situations and offering guidance about how to proceed. In this respect, a lot of policies still come up lacking, according to Boudreaux. He notes, in particular, that few policies offer guidelines for the use of specific social networks and almost none cover use of company trademarks. "Support your employees and let them know where your boundaries lie," he writes. "Don't leave them guessing."

But whether you opt for a broader policy and a separate set of guidelines, one official policy that works for all parties, or a general policy for all employees and supplemental policies for specific business units, there is a core set of issues that you need to address. In the Appendix, we offer item-by-item advice on what topics to include in a social media policy.

Part Two

Tools and Tactics

CHAPTER SIX

Learning by Listening

Listening to conversations is how you find the low-hanging fruit in social marketing. The basics are easy to do, the results are immediate, the risk is low, and the learning is often compelling. There is a lot more to effective listening than just signing up for Google Alerts, however. In this chapter we describe some of the powerful tactics you can use to tune in to conversations at a deep level.

Business-to-business (B2B) marketers have it easier than their business-to-consumer (B2C) colleagues in the area of listening. In most cases, the customer base is smaller, there's less competition for top search rankings, and there are fewer conversations to monitor. There's also less anonymity in B2B social networks, which means conversations are more relevant, more meaningful, and of higher quality. You are more likely to trust information from sources you can identify. "Your professional identity and your public identity are the same thing," says LinkedIn director of global enterprise operations Brian Frank, "so you know who you're talking to."

Listening to the Crowd

Online conversation monitoring can be labor-intensive, and it has been frustratingly resistant to automation. There are dozens of paid services that listen to blogs, discussion boards, and Twitter streams to derive patterns or sentiment. Among them are Nielsen BuzzMetrics, Radian6, RelevantNoise, SAS, Scout Labs and Visible Technologies. These services range in price from a few hundred dollars per month to more than $10,000 per month, and all have one thing in common: they're imperfect.

Human speech patterns are devilishly hard for machines to understand, particularly when dialect, slang, and sarcasm are involved. A baby boomer who calls a TV ad "sick" is probably repulsed by it. A millennial who says the same thing is paying a compliment.

"We are a decade away from reliable, computer-based sentiment analysis," says Converseon chief executive officer (CEO) Rob Key, whose proprietary conversation mining platform uses seven different filters, one of them human, to monitor social media. "If you hear claims from analytics companies that their listening platforms are achieving 90% accuracy based entirely on machine approaches, be very careful. Where we're going to be three to five years from will be extraordinary. But we're not there yet."

There are many ways to find opportunity in conversations. "If you notice that a large number of people are unhappy with your competition's product or services, you may want to consider tapping into that concern when talking about the benefits of your product," writes Rick Sloboda, a blogger and senior copywriter at Webcopyplus in Vancouver, British Columbia.

Niche B2B companies can usually afford to monitor all the conversations in their segment, but for high-volume markets like office supplies or computers, there are probably too many discussions to track individually. In those cases, the best approach is to listen for trends.

The Deepwater Horizon Unified Command was "reading literally hundreds of posts and comments daily on our Facebook page," during the 2010 BP oil spill, says Navy Lieutenant Commander Jim Hoeft. "We didn't have the resources to respond to everyone. But when we saw a question trending, we allocated staff to respond."

One of the difficulties of monitoring conversations is that they're so dispersed. Google does a fairly good job of searching the static web, but as more discussions happen in near-real time on platforms like Twitter and Facebook, other tools are needed. A good listening platform is more analogous to a dashboard than to a stethoscope.

Listening to Keywords

Listening to customers online involves monitoring a portfolio of searches and analyzing the results. Understanding keywords is a necessary first step, as we discussed in Chapter 2. Monitoring tools can be used to track and follow multiple searches simultaneously over a wide range of platforms.

Keyword searches don't deal well with imprecision. Results are only as accurate as the keywords sued. Queries that surface off-topic results need to be revised and re-run until they find what's needed. The key to effective social media monitoring is to construct accurate complex queries at the outset. In Chapter 7, we explain the concept of constructing complex keyword queries. But for now, let's start by examining how to use those queries to set up a free social media monitoring dashboard in Google Reader.

Building a Social Media Monitoring Dashboard

Google Reader is an RSS reader, which is kind of like TiVo for the web. RSS (real simple syndication) is a protocol that enables a user to receive information without actively requesting it. Once you subscribe to an RSS feed, new content from that source appears automatically in your reader, usually within minutes. The publisher of that feed has a persistent connection to you until you unsubscribe. The value of an RSS reader is that instead having to search for relevant information, you save your complex queries in the reader and let the relevant information come to you.

Go to www.google.com/reader and use your Gmail address (create an account if you don't have one) and password to sign up for a Google Reader account. The first time you sign in to Google Reader, your account will look like the screen in Figure 6.1.

Figure 6.1 Monitoring Social Media with Google Reader.

The "Add a subscription button" is where you can add RSS feeds. Some people use this box to search for RSS feeds, but we're going to show you how to build custom feeds based on complex queries to monitor news, blogs, Twitter, Wikipedia, and Craigslist. Unfortunately, at the time of this writing there is no easy way to pull in a custom RSS feed to monitor discussions in Facebook or LinkedIn. Even on the paid social media monitoring platforms, Facebook is a major blind spot because of its registration requirement and because the social network wants to keep you where they can serve advertising.

But there's still a lot that can be monitored with Google Reader. For example, companies used to hire clipping services to monitor the news for relevant articles. But with Google Reader, you can do that yourself for free.

Go to www.news.google.com (see Figure 6.2) and enter a complex query into the search box. Click the "search" button and review the resulting links. If the results are relevant, scroll to the bottom of the page and click the RSS link. Most web sites that offer RSS feeds identify them with an orange badge like the one in Figure 6.2. To convert your Google News search results to RSS, click the orange badge or the RSS link.

If you are using a current web browser, the formatting of the page will change as it does in Figure 6.3. The Google News search has been converted to RSS. Select and copy the URL of that web page. In many cases, the process of loading a feed into Google Reader involves clicking just one button.

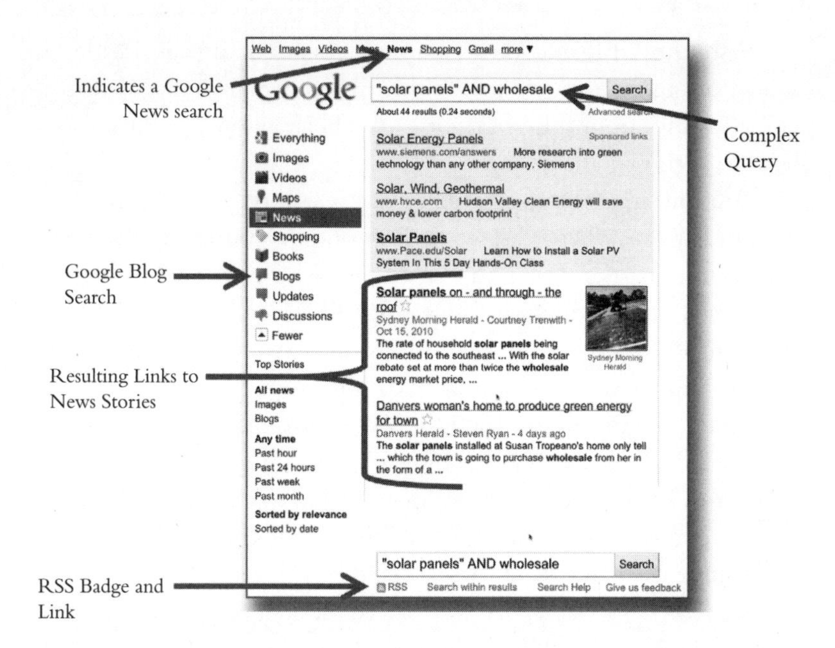

Figure 6.2 Converting a Google News Search.

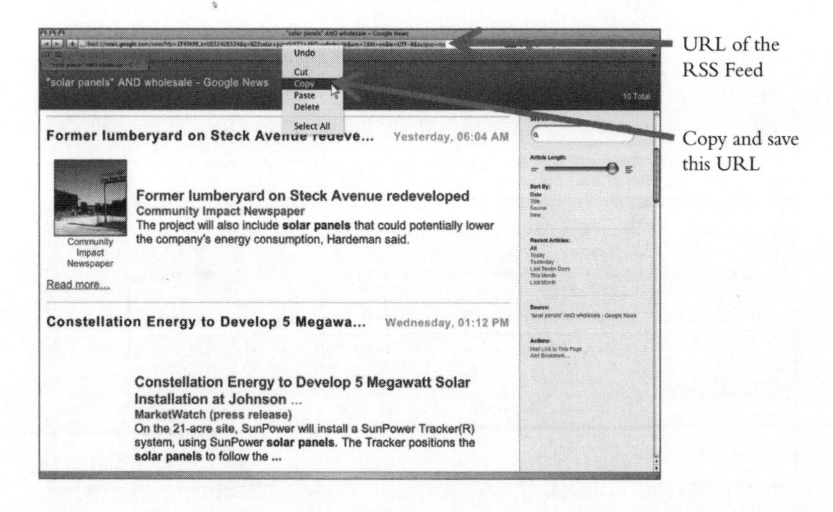

Figure 6.3 Subscribing to Google News as RSS.

Paste the URL into the "Add a subscription" box in Reader as shown in Figure 6.1 and click "Add." All new stories that appear in Google News from this point forward will show up in your Google Reader, as shown in Figure 6.4.

You can subscribe to a Google Blog search (Figure 6.2) the same way. In fact, anywhere you see an RSS option, you can subscribe to content on that page. Mozilla's Firefox browser (version 3 or higher) makes this easy by displaying an orange RSS icon in the address bar when an RSS-enabled site is in the browser window. Keep adding relevant sources to build your basic dashboard.

You may also want to monitor activity around your industry on Wikipedia, which is one of the most visited web sites on the Internet and is an excellent way to gauge popular sentiment. There's usually a lively debate taking place on Wikipedia's back discussion channel concerning the contents of each article.

Subjects of a Wikipedia entry are discouraged from editing the content because of conflict of interest. Nevertheless, you are allowed to flag false information and suggest it be changed, as long as you can attribute the information to a neutral, third-party source. Your corporate web site is not considered a neutral source, but a news article or an academic research report usually is.

Figure 6.4 Subscribing to RSS Feeds in Google Reader.

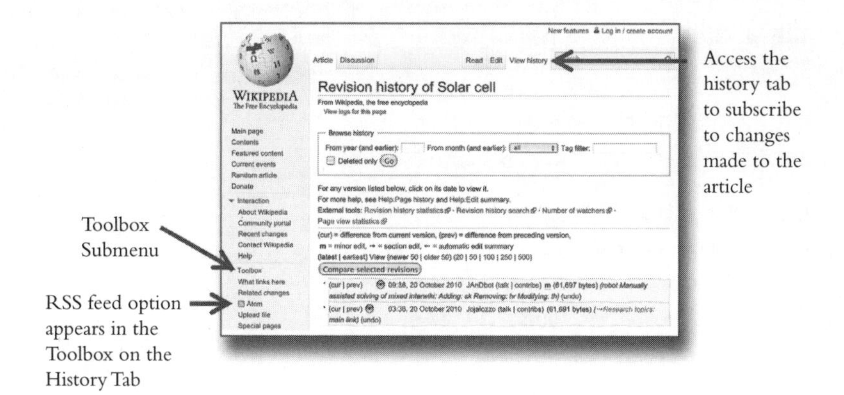

Figure 6.5 Subscribing to the Edits of a Wikipedia Article.

To subscribe to edits being made to an article in Wikipedia (Figure 6.5), select the "View history" tab, open the "Toolbox" submenu and click the orange RSS badge or the "Atom" link next to it to convert the revision history to RSS, copy the URL and add it as a subscription to Google Reader (Figure 6.1). An Atom feed is just another RSS format. It works fine in Google Reader.

If your business has aftermarket sales, like solar panels, forklifts, vending machines, or restaurant equipment, it may be useful to stay on top of what those items are fetching on the market so that you can keep your pricing competitive. Craigslist (Figure 6.6), which is one of the 20 most visited web sites according to Compete.com, offers an RSS option for subscribing to its classifieds listings. Again, click on the RSS badge, copy and paste the URL of the RSS page into the "Add a subscription" box in Google Reader.

You can use RSS to monitor Twitter as well, whether or not you have a Twitter account. Go to search.twitter.com (see Figure 6.7), enter a query, click the "Feed for this query" link next to the orange RSS badge, and copy the URL of the resulting web page. Use "Add a subscription" on Google Reader and all Tweets that match your query will be stored for you.

Another great feature of Twitter Search can be found under the "Advanced Search" link to the right of the "Search" button. Limiting keyword searches by geography can be a great way for regionally

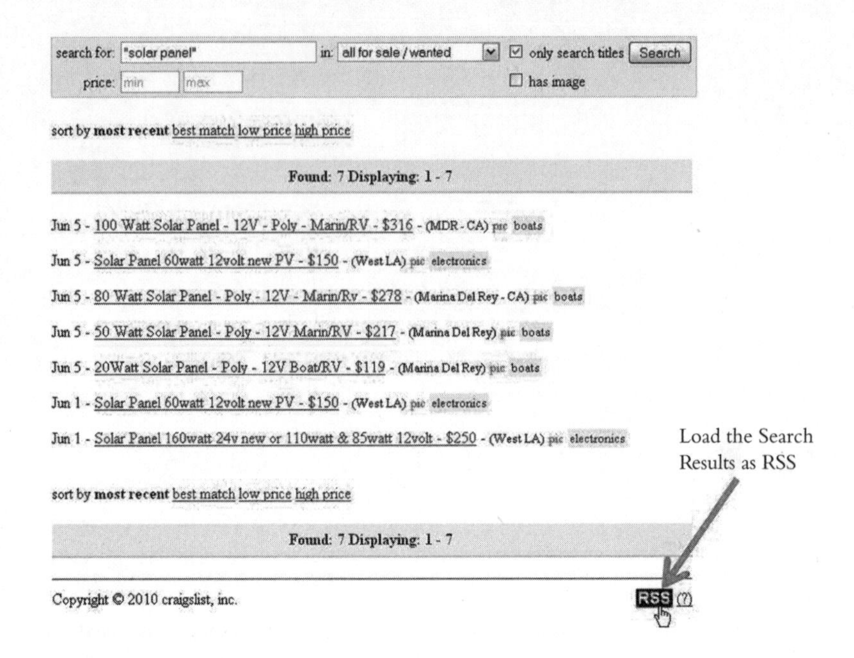

Figure 6.6 Subscribing to a Craigslist Query.

Figure 6.7 Subscribing to Twitter via RSS.

focused businesses to listen to customers in their area. For example, a Twitter Search (see Figure 6.8) for "solar panels" within a 100-mile radius of Chicago could be a good query for a Midwestern distributor of solar panels.

Figure 6.8 Twitter Keyword Search.

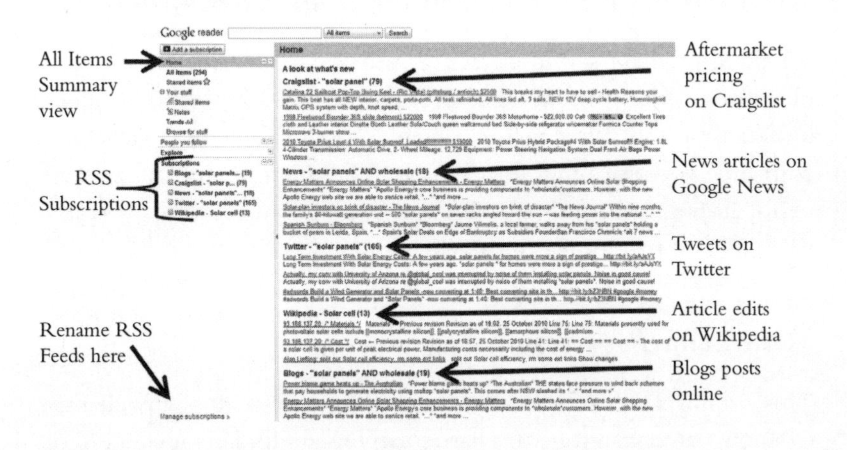

Figure 6.9 Subscribing to RSS Feeds in Google Reader.

There is no limit to the number of RSS feeds you can monitor in Google Reader. Figure 6.9 shows an account monitoring five feeds, each from a different source. We're monitoring information about solar panels in Craigslist, Google News, Twitter, Wikipedia, and Google Blog search. In this example, we've renamed the RSS Subscription using the "Manage subscriptions" link at the bottom of the left-hand column. You can also group subscriptions into folders.

Here are some other services you can bookmark and check on a regular basis:

Samepoint.biz.com

This is a social media search engine. It crawls blogs, Twitter, social networks, Q&A sites, review sites, podcasts, and document and photo-sharing sites, among others. Although not as comprehensive as Google, it saves you from having to set up searches on more domain-specific listening posts. Save queries as RSS feeds and the quality improves over time.

XinuReturns.com, Compete.com, and Alexa.com

All three of these services track a web site's performance in terms of inbound links, the number of pages indexed by search engines, bookmarks, and other factors. They're useful for telling how well your blog is performing, for example. Use them in tandem, because performance in inconsistent. WebsiteGrader.com scores your search visibility and recommends improvements.

WatchThatPage.com

This is a novel service that alerts subscribers by e-mail of any changes to a designated web page. It's particularly useful for keeping an eye on your competition.

BoardTracker.com

This search engine specializes in message boards and discussion groups, which were the earliest forms of social media and which are still the most active in some industries. Google also searches message board posts, but BoardTracker and competitor Omgili.com provide more focused results.

TweetDeck.com

Originally conceived as a reader for Twitter messages, this desktop application is now a functional tool for monitoring Facebook and LinkedIn traffic as well as saved Twitter searches. It's easy to create new columns that suck in all new mentions of keywords you specify or just track trending topics.

HootSuite.com

This is a social media client, like TweetDeck, but it runs in a web browser. Its advantages are the ability to schedule both tweets and status updates and the power to communicate from multiple Twitter and Facebook accounts from one page. HootSuite and CoTweet also have management features oriented toward corporate users.

CoTweet.com

Twitter suite that allows a team to collaborate on the management of a branded, corporate Twitter account. CoTweet is a direct competitor to HootSuite.

Trackur.com

This buzz monitoring tool claims to mine more than 100 million sources for keyword mentions and assign sentiment analysis to the results. The search is impressive, although the sentiment analysis isn't. Still, the basic free account is a pretty good deal.

You can measure page views or web traffic to a blog, or any web site for that matter, at Compete.com or Quantcast.com. These sites will also allow you to compare the traffic on different sites to each other.

Figure 6.10 Compete Screenshot.

In Figure 6.10, we copied the URLs of three different blogs about solar energy that we discovered through Google Reader and pasted them into the fields at Compete.com. The blogs at solarpanelspower .net and globalsolartechnology.com both draw significantly more traffic than the one at greenlivingexplained.com.

You might ask why we don't just recommend using Google Alerts for this process? Google Alerts is a popular service that sends you e-mail or updates your RSS feed whenever the keywords you enter match new entries in the Google search index. Nearly every marketer now uses Google Alerts, but Google Reader's dashboard-like interface provides a number of advantages over e-mail delivery.

For one thing, Google Alerts results are limted to the body of an e-mail and can't easily be searched unless you save every e-mail. In contrast, Google Reader lets you maintain an archive of links indefinitely. You can search the links you've collected over time without hunting through e-mail messages. Push technology like e-mail is also distracting. In contrast, a dashboard lets you check activity when it's convenient for you.

Google Alerts is great for information you need to know immediately. We recommend you use it to monitor keywords that might indicate a problem with your products, the name of an unannounced product or a dissatisfied customer. On a day-to-day basis, though, dashboards are more flexible.

Measure Marketing Effectiveness

Most web hosts offer some sort of web site statistics. If your web host doesn't offer any measurement options, or if your site is hosted internally on a company server, Google Analytics can provide insight on whether your web site traffic justifies the investment in your online marketing efforts. Once you have a way to measure how people get to and consume the content of your web site, you can use that information to see if your efforts are delivering worthwhile results. We can't anticipate all the ways to evaluate your web stats, but we can suggest some baseline evaluation metrics.

Keyword Validation

Review the keywords people search to find your web site. For most sites, search is the largest source of traffic. The other two traffic sources are referring sites, which are links posted by other site owners, and direct visits from visitors typing your URL into a browser or clicking a link in an e-mail. When you analyze the keywords people search to get to your site, you're testing your own assumptions about how people describe you. If the words they're using aren't the ones you'd expect, you'd better revisit your search optimization strategy.

Eric uses the web stats provided by his web host and Google Analytics (see Figure 6.11) to measure the effectiveness of his online marketing efforts. Google Analytics, which can be easily installed by publishing a unique tracking code on your web site, selecting "Traffic Sources" and then "Keywords," reveals a list of search terms people are using to find him. If the top 10 searches include keywords that match up with the products or services he sells, he knows his web site is doing its job because people with a need for his services are finding it through search.

You can drill down deeper into the effectiveness of your keywords by looking at the "Bounce Rate" (see Figure 6.11), which is

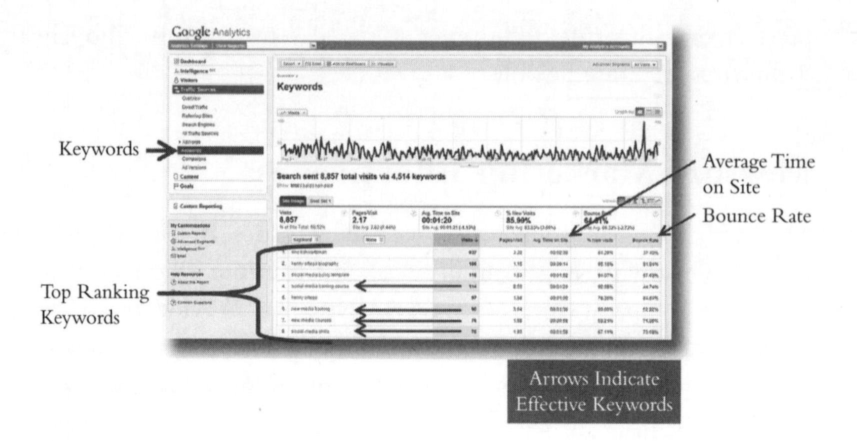

Figure 6.11 Keyword Effectiveness in Google Analytics.

the percentage of visitors that viewed only one page on your web site. If a keyword has a high bounce rate, that means most visitors browsed no deeper than the first page they saw. A high bounce rate may not necessarily be negative, though.

Blog visits often originate from search engines, and visitors usually only read the post that brings them to the site. If you see a high bounce rate, look at the "Avg. Time on Site" to see how long people stayed on the single page they visited. If the blog drives traffic to a landing page designed to convert site visits into measurable transactions, like e-commerce sales or leads, then the bounce rate and average time on site mean very little. That's because your landing page is generating results.

But if the page is intended to begin an engagement or education process, then a high bounce rate could be a sign that visitors aren't finding what they came there for. This means there's a mismatch between the keywords that are bringing you search traffic and the expectations of the people searching that keyword.

If your site ranks high for a complex keyword query like "patent attorney" AND Michigan, but the bounce rate is 90 percent or more and the average time on the site is 10 seconds or less, it's safe to assume your web site is not providing searchers with the information they seek. You need to reassess the effectiveness of the aesthetic design, layout, and content on your web site because people who are actively looking for your services aren't responding favorably to what they're finding.

To lower your bounce rate and increase the time visitors spend on your site, create entry pages optimized for specific search terms, and make sure the Web copy on those pages delivers on the expectations of the searcher. People will stay longer and dig deep if their search for a patent attorney in Michigan leads them to an entry page with the specific information they seek, rather than a long, bulleted web page listing all the legal specialties your firm offers throughout the north-central United States.

Top Content

The next measurement to pay attention to when reviewing web statistics is *most visited Web pages*. Eric wants people to visit his training calendar of upcoming workshops and his Social Media Boot Camp sign-up page. Figure 6.12 shows the most visited pages at ericschwartzman.com, using a free web analysis package called AWStats. The arrows indicate which of the most visited pages on Eric's site are designed to drive business. The two highest-ranking pages are his home page and his site's RSS feed. And although he'd certainly like more traffic overall, he knows that since the pages on his site that are designed to convert visits to transactions are ranking third and fourth in overall traffic, his visitors are viewing the pages he wants them to see.

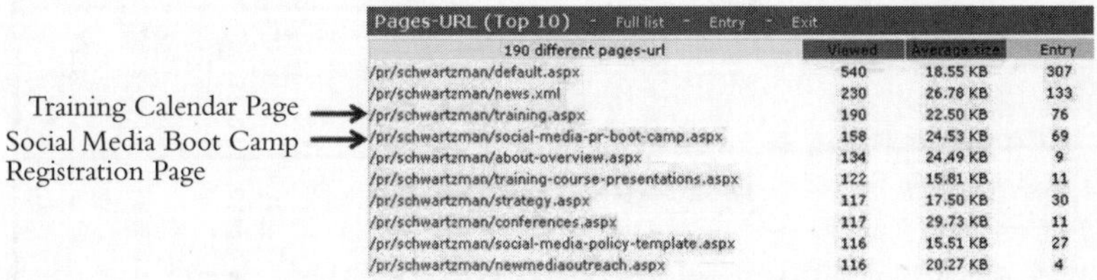

Pages-URL (Top 10) - Full list - Entry - Exit

190 different pages-url	Viewed	Average size	Entry
/pr/schwartzman/default.aspx	540	18.55 KB	307
/pr/schwartzman/news.xml	230	26.78 KB	133
Training Calendar Page → /pr/schwartzman/training.aspx	190	22.50 KB	76
Social Media Boot Camp Registration Page → /pr/schwartzman/social-media-pr-boot-camp.aspx	158	24.53 KB	69
/pr/schwartzman/about-overview.aspx	134	24.49 KB	9
/pr/schwartzman/training-course-presentations.aspx	122	15.81 KB	11
/pr/schwartzman/strategy.aspx	117	17.50 KB	30
/pr/schwartzman/conferences.aspx	117	29.73 KB	11
/pr/schwartzman/social-media-policy-template.aspx	116	15.51 KB	27
/pr/schwartzman/newmediaoutreach.aspx	116	20.27 KB	4

Figure 6.12 Most Visited Web Pages in AWStats.

Referring Sites

The last set of metrics we'll cover are referring sites. These are sites that transit a visitor to you via an inbound link. Yahoo! Site Explorer shows you all your inbound links, but the referring-site analytics show the visits that result from those links. Inbound links are valuable to your search rank because the more inbound links you have, the higher you tend to rank in Google. But inbound links that people actually click on are more valuable if they result in direct traffic.

Figure 6.13 is a screenshot from Google Analytics showing which referring sites are sending traffic to ericschwartzman.com. The graph indicates that of all the social marketing efforts Eric conducts, his podcast delivers the most qualified visits, because visitors coming from his podcast site spend more time and visit more pages than those originating from Twitter, even though Twitter refers more traffic. LinkedIn is the next most effective source of referrals, and Facebook comes in fourth.

Analyzing your keywords, most visited pages, and referring sites by bounce rate and average time spent brings your listening efforts full circle because it tells you whether or not your social media marketing efforts are working. The more you listen, the more you learn. But while you may be listening for marketing opportunities, you may wind up hearing things that could help your company in other ways as well.

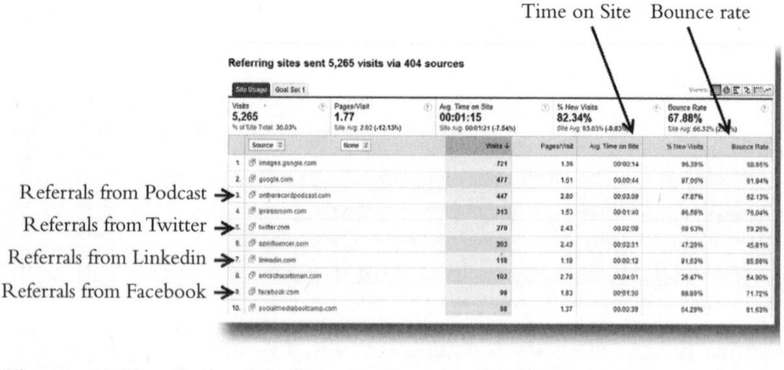

Time on Site
Bounce rate
Referrals from Podcast
Referrals from Twitter
Referrals from Linkedin
Referrals from Facebook

Figure 6.13 Referring Sites in Google Analytics.

Internal Feedback Loops

In this chapter, we've mainly talked about listening as a means to enhance your marketing programs, but the information you discover could help you in the areas of client services, product development, human resources, community relations, and elsewhere. You need a way to convey that intelligence. Corporate departments are often independent fiefdoms competing against one another for resources. It hasn't traditionally been marketing's job to share feedback with other departments, but that process needs to be put in place to truly benefit from the value of listening. Don't pass on information just because it isn't relevant to your marketing efforts. Make it a point to share comments that can help your developers, product managers, executives, and others who need to listen to their markets. This can be sensitive at first because people don't always welcome feedback, but once they hear feedback from the market, it can be a powerful motivator. It just may be the wake-up call that some of your skeptical executives need.

"You need to think big," says Converson's Key. "You need to infuse the value of social media across the enterprise for sustainable differentiation." If everyone is listening and responding when necessary, it makes your company faster and more responsive. That's the kind of competitive advantage you can't buy at any price.

RESPONDING TO WHAT YOU HEAR

One of the first things that will become apparent when you begin using a social media dashboard is that there are bloggers out there talking about you and/or your market. This is particularly true in the B2B sphere, where bloggers gravitate to the long-form format that enables them to discuss complex technical issues.

Blogging has evolved into the favored social media format for professional audiences. Although the medium's popularity among teens and young adults has declined by nearly half over the past three years, the population of over-30 bloggers has actually grown by more than 50 percent, according to a 2010 Pew Research Center report.[1] For many B2B publications, guest

(continued)

(*continued*)

bloggers are now the largest source of original content. ScienceBlogs.com is an invitation-only aggregator that brings together some of the most provocative scientific bloggers. Directories like Alltop.com and BlogCatalog.com syndicate blog feeds in hundreds of categories. And then there are the millions of independent bloggers who just talk because they care.

As trade media continues its precipitous decline and the importance of domain experts grows, marketers are increasingly courting these influencers. Software giant SAP has one of the best social marketing programs we've seen. It engages with influential bloggers regularly and maintains an open-door policy, with the goal of providing immediate response to any questions they ask. The company keeps profiles of key bloggers and matches them with appropriate executives in frequent briefings and meetings. It also gives them special treatment and special programming at the company's two big annual customer conferences. "We're engaging in conversations we never would have had before," said global communications vice president Mike Prosceno in an interview with ZDNet blogger Michael Krigsman.[2] "If people are going to cover SAP, why not let them hear from us what we're doing and why we're doing it?"

Chipmaker Intel is another company that has bought into the influence of B2B blogs. In 2008, it hand-picked 15 popular bloggers to get a year of behind-the-scenes perspective on activity inside the company in exchange for educating Intel communicators on how to connect through online channels. The bloggers got exposure, and Intel enjoyed bonus publicity through new channels like the enormously popular Rocketboom video blog.

Many communications professionals have a love-hate relationship with the whole idea of blogger relations programs. On one hand, they acknowledge that these new channels are important, but they are also overwhelmed by the sheer volume of relationships they need to maintain. We don't believe blogger relations programs are essential for every company, but we do recommend that you know the major influencers on your market. If volume is a problem, triage and focus on the most important sources.

Be careful about assuming that any service that claims to track blogs is completely reliable. There is no standard definition of a blog, so all kinds of content can get mixed in with search results.

The trick is to separate the wheat from chaff. In reality, few bloggers have much influence. One of the easiest ways to see whether a blogger deserves your attention is to check his or her activity level. Bloggers who post new entries once a month or less probably don't have a very large following.

Use some of the tactics mentioned earlier in this chapter to assess influence based on metrics such as inbound links, comments, and traffic estimates. You can also just search on the person's name to see if it shows up in mainstream media. Bloggers are becoming a favorite source of expertise for reporters.

You also need to verify that the blogger's topic is relevant to your business. While working on a project for a B2B client in the pharmaceutical industry, Paul was surprised to find that some of the most popular blogs by chemical engineering PhDs focused on topics like politics and cooking. On the surface, these people looked like important market influencers, but a little research established that their blogging interests lay elsewhere. Also consider the total of a blogger's online activity. The most prolific scribes are often also active in Facebook, Twitter, and special interest networks.

Finally, look at attitude. A blogger who is persistently sarcastic or negative may be trouble-in-waiting. Avoid people with an agenda.

When commenting on blogs, it's okay to include a link back to your web site but don't post links indiscriminately. Comment spam is a real problem for bloggers, and unless the host sees you adding value, you could actually make an enemy. Take the time to read the blog post and make an effort to contribute something useful.

Review previous blog posts and comments to see if the blogger is worth engaging in the first place. Someone who is unwilling to accept alternative points of view is probably more trouble than he or she is worth.

These are the axe grinders. Unless you want to become a missionary, you're not going to convert them easily into believers. Post respectful disagreements, but don't expect to have the last word. Sometimes the best you can do is register your opinion.

On the other hand, if you review the blogger's previous posts and comments and find the person to be tolerant, this is a better candidate for engagement. In his book *Twitterville,* Shel Israel offers guidelines from Richard Binhammer, a senior manager at Dell who leads the company's blogger relations effort. "Don't waste your time trying to convert atheists," Binhammer says. "Work on the agnostics in the room—doubters who might be turned into believers through conversation."

When executed with discipline, blogger relations programs can pay handsome results. For example, when ElectraTherm was preparing for the launch of the ElectraTherm Green Machine in 2008, it decided early that influential blogs would be part of its strategy. The company had only minimal awareness in mainstream media, and the launch of the Green Machine—a device that makes low-cost electricity from residual industrial waste—was a watershed event.

ElectraTherm had set up a working Green Machine at Southern Methodist University in Dallas to show off the technology. It was betting

(*continued*)

(*continued*)

that knowledgeable energy bloggers would validate the technology and create buzz.

The goal was to achieve 15 online media hits with a total audience of at least 1 million. The program used podcasts and webcasts to reach its media targets based on evidence that multimedia tools get much higher attention from journalists.

The company's public relations agency, PilmerPR, assembled a list of influential energy bloggers and studied their work. They contacted the writers individually to offer content for them to post, resulting in coverage in more than 20 blogs. "With each blogger with which we developed a relationship, we saw many other blogs linking to that post. Once the news was carried by a few of the major blogs, we had crossed the hurdle and saw a lot of resulting blog coverage," the company wrote in a submission to the Society for New Communications Research's Excellence in New Communications awards.

As word-of-mouth awareness spread, other media outlets took notice. The announcement was featured in the hugely popular Engadget and Gizmodo technology blogs as well as on the popular TreeHugger. All told, the launch reached an estimated 37 million people, far exceeding the company's objectives.

CHAPTER SEVEN

Understanding Search

On the Internet, people learn by searching. Through trial and error, they hone in on relevant content. You can learn from this activity and use it to increase your company's visibility and lead generation, but first you need a working knowledge of the somewhat esoteric discipline of keyword analysis.

Let's use an example: A Google search for "disposable surgical tools" returns roughly 64,000 links, while a search for "single use surgical tools" returns just 3. Obviously, the former search phrase is better, because it returns a much larger pool of suppliers for the customer to choose from.

The same logic applies to social media. A search for "disposable surgical tools" on YourOpenBook.org (a Facebook search engine) returns zero results, showing that no public conversation about "disposable surgical tools" exists on the world's most popular social network. On the other hand, a Google blog search reveals an active community of bloggers discussing topics related to "disposable surgical tools," showing blogs are a much livelier channel for marketers of these products.

Keywords research is the Holy Grail of online marketing. Once you learn what words and phrases your customers use and where they use them, you can seek out and engage the people you want to reach. In this chapter, we walk you through the process of listening with keywords and using them to optimize your web site and social media interactions for search.

Your overarching goal is to come up with a list of the popular words or phrases that your customers use to find and discuss your business. These may not be the same words *you* would use. Businesses tend to speak in terms of solutions while customers speak in terms of problems. The onus is on marketers to identify the search behaviors that lead people to a web site.

Your keywords must be accurate, but accuracy doesn't always yield the best results. For example, if you're blogging about "solar cells" but your customers are searching for "solar power," you're speaking two different languages. There are dozens of data points to consider, and just as many online tools to apply. We can't cover them all, but we will provide an overview of how to create an effective business-to-business (B2B) keyword strategy.

Keyword Research

We start with the process of finding the keywords your customers are searching. If you didn't know that businesses looking for "solar cells" were actually searching for "solar panels," how would you figure that out? Google offers basic tools for expanding your awareness of relevant keywords.

Start with the Google Related Searches (see Figure 7.1). At the time of this writing, Related Searches are found at the bottom of the first page of search results. They provide an even larger stable of keyword variations to consider. You should also look at how Google Instant, which displays popular search results as each letter is typed, selects top choices. This is another indication of your keyword competition.

Your keyword strategy should be consistent with your marketing strategy. If you're selling credit card processing terminals primarily on price, for example, adding keyword modifiers like "cheap" or "discount" will help frugal searchers find you. If you're a premium

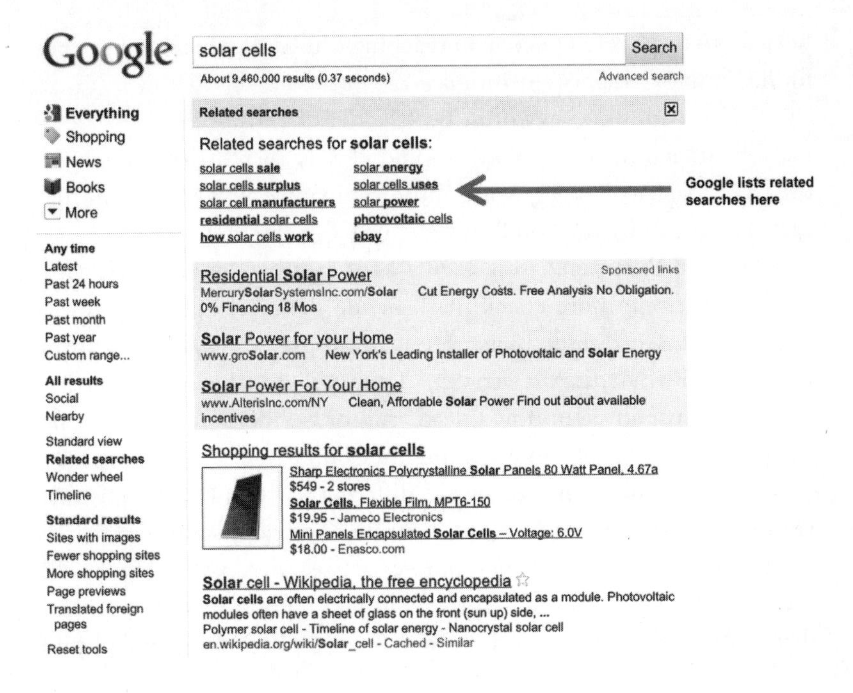

Figure 7.1 Google Related Searches.

provider, on the other hand, you might focus on early-stage, buying-cycle keywords like "how to process credit card transactions."

Trade terms and jargon are actually useful in this process because they can be used to reach a more qualified audience. Blogger Jim Cahill of Emerson Process Experts attributes much of his excellent search visibility to listening to his engineers. "The language they use to solve problems is rich in the keywords of their field," he says. "They're talking with customers all the time, and they speak the language of the customer."

Keyword research is a process. Electronics assembly materials company Indium Corporation uses blogs to search optimize its site for electrical engineers. "It was hard getting it down to 85 keywords. But we didn't want to have hundreds. We wanted to start relatively small and grow from there. We brainstormed in numerous sessions what keywords were effective in reaching our goal, which was getting found," said Rick Short at Indium.

When choosing keywords, be selective. B2B searchers are looking for efficiency, so keywords should closely match the content on the page. Never plant keywords indiscriminately next to content that isn't relevant to them. You'll shoot yourself in the foot.

"Typical B2B purchasing agents want to get in and out, allowing them to put one more check mark beside their ever-growing to-do list," wrote Gord Hotchkiss, president of search marketing firm Enquiro, in a MediaPost article. "They will not be in a forgiving mood if you send them down dead ends or tie them up in confusing navigation. This is all about making their job easier."

Once you have an idea of the different keyword variations that your customers are searching, you can use Google Insights for Search (Figure 7.2) to find out which phrases are searched most. Figure 7.2 shows that "solar power" is a much more popular search phrase than "solar cells." We can also see the seasonality and geography of

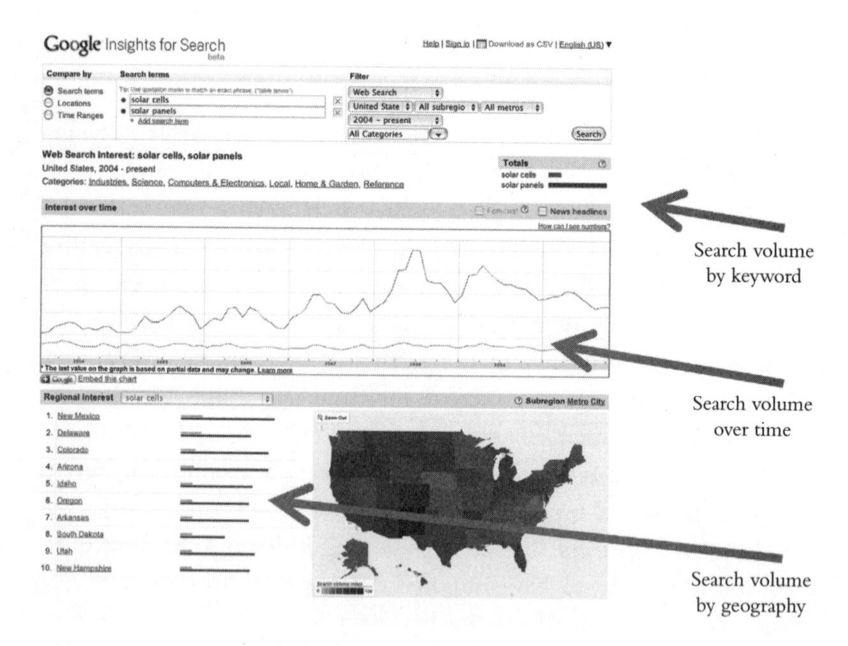

Figure 7.2 Google Insights for Search.

these search phrases. Searches for "solar power" peak in the summer months, probably because electricity rates are higher. That signals an increase in potential buyers and a greater opportunity for marketers to get found at that time of year.

Advanced Search

Use complex queries, which string together several different keywords in a single search, to ask a search engine a specific question. The Boolean operators AND and NOT establish the logical relationships between the keywords you're searching. Use quotation marks around a "multiple-word search" to narrow results to an exact phrase match. Without quotation marks, a search engine returns web pages that use all three words separately. So any page with "multiple" and "search" would show up in the results, whether they appeared in succession or not.

A search for "solar cells" AND "wholesale" would return any web page with the phrase "solar cells" as an exact phrase match and the word "wholesale" somewhere else on the page. On the other hand, a search for "wholesale solar cells" would return only web pages with that exact phrase. By the same logic, a complex query for "solar cells" NOT "solar system" would return web pages with the phrase "solar cells" and exclude web pages with the phrase "solar system."

Rules for Building Complex Queries

1. I'm interested in information on solar electricity but not the solar system.
   Search: *"solar electricity" NOT "solar system"*
2. I want to see which words people are using to search and discuss solar panels online.
   Search: *"solar panels" OR "solar electric" OR "solar electricity" OR "solar cells"*
3. I want information only about wholesale suppliers of solar panels.
   Search: *"solar panels" AND "wholesale NOT retail"*

Use geographic keywords to localize complex queries. A quick search in Google Insights reveals that demand for information about "solar panels" is highest in Colorado, Arizona, Michigan, Ohio, and Indiana. Equipped with this knowledge, try inserting geographic modifiers like "colorado" and "phoenix" to your search phrases to see if you can focus in on regional opportunities. B2B keyword modifiers like "RFP," "RFI," "wholesale," "manufacturer" or "price quote" with a term like "solar cells" are more likely to surface busines-to-business opportunities.

Not all keywords can be tracked for volume. When you drill down on low-volume keywords, Google Insights may display a "Not enough search volume to show graphs" message. In that case, try a tool like Trellian or Wordtracker, both of which offer free versions. In Figure 7.3, Trellian reveals higher-volume search phrases than "solar panels arizona." The numbers in the left column are proportionate to

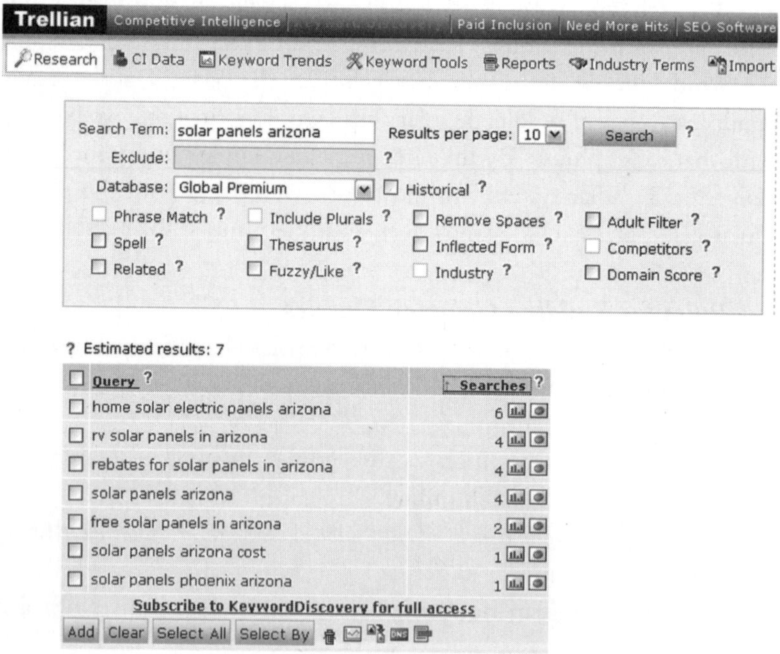

Figure 7.3 Trellian.

the other phrases in the chart. They indicate the ratio of searches to the other queries listed.

The discovery in Figure 7.3 that "home solar electric panels arizona" and "RV solar panels in arizona" are higher-volume terms than "solar panels arizona" indicates that this keyword cluster is aligned with consumer demand in that region. On the other hand, a Trellian search for "power cells" (Figure 7.4) reveals B2B-oriented keyword variations like "wholesale solar cells" and "solar cells surplus."

For B2B marketers, absolute search volume is less important than relevant search volume. Google Insights showed us that although "solar panels" got more searches than "solar cells," those searches do not appear to be coming from business customers. When we compared the related searches from Trellian for "solar panels arizona" to those

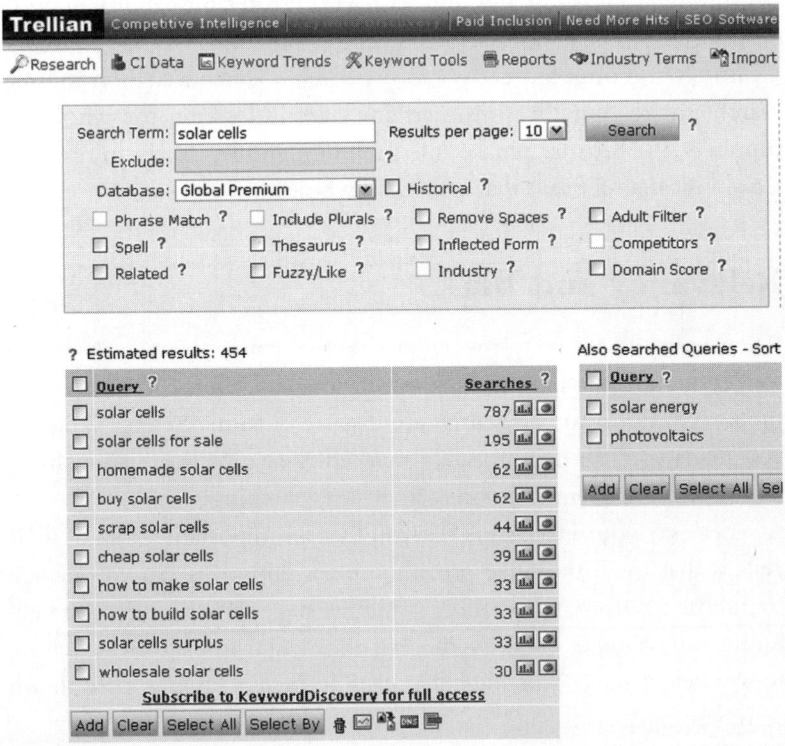

Trellian | Competitive Intelligence | Paid Inclusion | Need More Hits | SEO Software

Research | CI Data | Keyword Trends | Keyword Tools | Reports | Industry Terms | Import

Search Term: solar cells | Results per page: 10 | Search

Exclude:

Database: Global Premium | Historical

Phrase Match | Include Plurals | Remove Spaces | Adult Filter

Spell | Thesaurus | Inflected Form | Competitors

Related | Fuzzy/Like | Industry | Domain Score

? Estimated results: 454

Query	Searches
solar cells	787
solar cells for sale	195
homemade solar cells	62
buy solar cells	62
scrap solar cells	44
cheap solar cells	39
how to make solar cells	33
how to build solar cells	33
solar cells surplus	33
wholesale solar cells	30

Subscribe to KeywordDiscovery for full access

Add | Clear | Select All | Select By

Also Searched Queries - Sort

Query
solar energy
photovoltaics

Add | Clear | Select All | Sel

Figure 7.4 Keyword Variations Indicate B2B Demand.

from "solar cells," we saw that the latter keyword was surrounded by searches more likely to have been made by business customers.

Keyword strategy is important, but don't be so rigid in your approach that you intentionally avoid using sensible language just because it doesn't rank high. "Twenty percent of searches done in Google every day have never been done before, so create relevant content about your business, even if people aren't looking for it yet," writes Kipp Bodnar on the HubSpot blog.

Volume vs. Relevance

It's important for B2B marketers to understand the value of performing against low-volume search terms. "In B2B SEO [search engine optimization], keyword relevance is more important than popularity, because relevant terms and phrases have a greater probability of conversion," says Lee Odden, chief executive officer (CEO) of TopRank Online Marketing. Similarly, "solar panels" may be a higher-volume search phrase, but for customers in Arizona looking for wholesale suppliers, the broader phrase is less relevant and less likely to result in a site visit than a result that specifies "wholesale."

Relevancy and Bias

Relevant keywords are terms and phrases that your customers use when they're looking for the products or services you offer. But sometimes, the keywords customers search are distasteful to marketers. What do you do if you're uncomfortable marketing against the high-volume keywords your prospective customers are searching?

Let's say your customers tell you that an important value of solar cells is that they minimize greenhouse gas emissions. So you decide to publish a corporate social responsibility page with resources to help business customers quantify the environmental impact of switching to solar electricity. You want that page to be as visible as possible on search engines.

You search "greenhouse gases" in Google Related Searches (Figure 7.1) and find the phrase "global warming" is related to that search. You go to Google Insights for Search (Figure 7.2) and learn that "global warming" actually gets searched more than 10 times as often as "greenhouse gases." You decide to optimize your new web page for the phrase "global warming" by using it in the headline, subheadline, and lead and closing paragraphs of the web copy.

You send the new page to management and legal for approval, and they change the phrase "global warming" to the less politically charged "climate change." You argue that any company that cannot embrace the popular lexicon is in denial because its image is misaligned with its perception. But that doesn't cancel out management's concerns, because the company may be concerned about alienating some its customers. Google Insights provides no demographic breakdowns for its search volume reports. While "global warming" may be the most searched phrase, in the United States it has become a bitter wedge issue between partisans. "Climate change" is more politically correct.

B2B keyword strategy is about embracing relevant, popular language, but it's difficult to convince management to embrace keywords that alienate potential customers or conflict with brand aspirations. "If they see themselves as the low-cost leader, it's going to be tough to get them to search optimize for a keyword like 'cheap,'" said Greg Jarboe, the father of the search engine optimized press release, who learned this experience firsthand through his work with Southwest Airlines.

"One way to search optimize for alternative messaging that's inconsistent with a company's brand messaging is through a company blog that's intentionally written in a more informal tone, so as not to compete with the more formal messaging on the corporate website," says Odden. "And in the blog, you might create a post that's an argument for embracing 'climate change' over 'global warming,' which would require the use of both terms."

Mechanics of Search Engine Optimization

Now that we've established that SEO is closely aligned with keyword strategy, let's break down the fundamentals of how to use keywords to optimize your web content and online conversations for search.

SEO is not about coming up first when people search the name of your company, CEO, or trade name. Google gives you that one for free. The idea is to rank highly when people search for terms related to a business problem or need your company solves. Showing up on the first page of search results is the objective, because few searchers go beyond there.

SEO has become a profession is its own right. Blogs like Search Engine Land and Search Engine Journal are just two of the many online outlets covering the business, while traveling conferences like Search Engine Strategies and Search Marketing Expo are now worldwide events where specialists debate the intricacies of advanced topics like local search, mobile search, and landing page design.

If you want to specialize in SEO, these resources are top notch. We won't go into all the technical details, but we will give an overview of the process to aid in your understanding of how Google ranks web pages and what that means for you as a B2B marketer. To do that, we have to geek out just a little. If you can grasp these basic concepts, you'll be a more strategic online marketer.

An *inbound link* is a hyperlink that transits from an external web domain to your own. If Wikipedia is linking to your web site, that's considered an inbound link, because it transits from Wikipedia.org to yourwebsite.com. Inbound links are critical to understanding search engines.

One of the ways Google beat Yahoo! at the search game was by using social intelligence to establish relevancy. Yahoo! returned search results based on keyword density. The early search leader scanned the web and counted the number of times a phrase appeared on the page as a measure of relevancy. The web page that had the most mentions of "solar cells" ranked highest for that term. But this approach was rife with problems.

Marketers began stuffing their web pages with irrelevant keywords. They'd repeat the phrase "solar cells" over and over in white text on a white background just to elevate their search rank. The pages that ranked highest as a result weren't the most useful, just the most repetitive.

Google swooped in with a novel approach. Rather than use keyword density as a measure of relevancy, it consulted the wisdom of the crowd through inbound links. By treating inbound links as recommendations, Google minimized the impact of keyword spammers. Marketers could keyword-stuff their pages to their hearts' content, but if external domains weren't linking back to their web site, Google would pay little attention.

The Google algorithm is the Coca-Cola formula of the modern age. No one outside of Google knows exactly how it works, but the notion of the inbound link as a metric of relevance is now widely accepted. Getting others to publish hyperlinks from their web site back to yours is central to effective SEO. This approach is less susceptible to gaming, because it's tougher to control other web sites than your own. Inbound links are the currency of SEO.

"People are asking us to link to them all the time," says Nick Fishman, CMO of EmployeeScreen.com "We decide who to link to on the basis of relevance and expertise. Our reputation is all we have. We don't endorse just anybody that wants a link from our site."

There are different strategies for luring links. Some approaches exhibit a blatant disregard for ethics. These are known as "black hat" SEO and involve practices like launching a blog on a free service such as Blogger and writing keyword- and hyperlink-stuffed pages that link to a target web site. If you go this route, be forewarned that it may work against you. Google is very sophisticated at finding black hat sites and disqualifies them from consideration in search rankings.

White hat SEO, on the other hand, involves regularly publishing information that's genuinely useful to customers, using relevant keywords, and publicizing content in a way that makes it easy for people to find and to link to it. "Quality content will always be found," says Mike Moran, co-author of *Search Engine Marketing, Inc.*

Competitive analysis is about understanding who is currently ranking well for the phrases you desire and determining whether they're vulnerable based on the quality of their inbound links. Not all of the top-ranking sites you encounter will be real-world competitors. In the B2B space, a lot of academic and governmental institutions also compete for customers' attention.

Once you've discovered relevant keywords, check which sites rank highly for those terms. Search the phrase that matters to you and visit the top-ranking sites. Read their content and see how their site is organized. Ask yourself if you can do better. If so, you've just discovered a good keyword opportunity. If not, add modifiers to your search until you find an area of opportunity.

Remember, the sites that rank highest are the ones with the best inbound links. Use Yahoo! Site Explorer (Figure 7.5) to see who's linking to whom. Cut and paste any URL into the "Explore URL" field and check the inbound links to that URL. To see all inbound links to any web domain, just click on the "Inlinks" button, set the "Show Inlinks" drop-down menu to "Except from this Domain" option, and set the "To" drop-menu to "Entire Site" option. There are 5,163 links to all the pages at SiliconSolar.com. Unless you can lure better links, it's highly unlikely you'll outrank that site for that phrase.

Not all inbound links are equal. An inbound link from a site with a large number of high-quality links is more valuable than one from a site with just a few, or one with links from black-hat link farms.

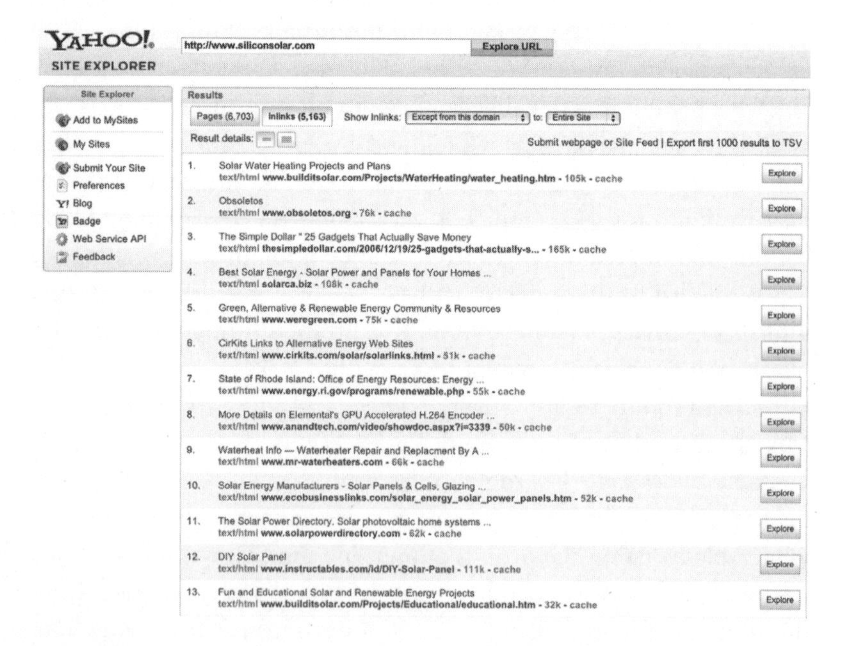

Figure 7.5 Use Yahoo Site Explorer to see inbound links from external domains to any web site or web page. Remember, if you find inbounds from high traffic sites such as .govs, .mils, or .edus, it may be tough to rank for the keywords the site your analyzing ranks high for, unless you can lure more or better inbound links.

A link from Wikipedia, for example, is much more valuable than one from most other web sites because Wikipedia itself has so many inbound links.

In Figure 7.6, the larger circles are sites that have more "link juice" because they've got the most or the best inbound links. Site B ranks highest because it has the most inbound links. Site C ranks second highest because it's the only site with a link from B, which has the most links. The arrows indicate the inbound links and the numbers are the percentage likelihood you'll visit that circle.

Not all domains are equal. A link from a .gov, .mil, or .edu domain is particularly prized since owners of those domains must be qualified by a government or academic bureaucracy, which have tighter restrictions on outbound links. A site with a lot of inbound links from .gov or .edu domains is exceedingly difficult to topple.

For inbound links to have search rank value, they need to be attached to *anchor text,* which is the blue link text. Publishing the URL SiliconSolar.com on a web site doesn't give Google much to go on. However, using the term "solar cells" as anchor text for a hyperlink to

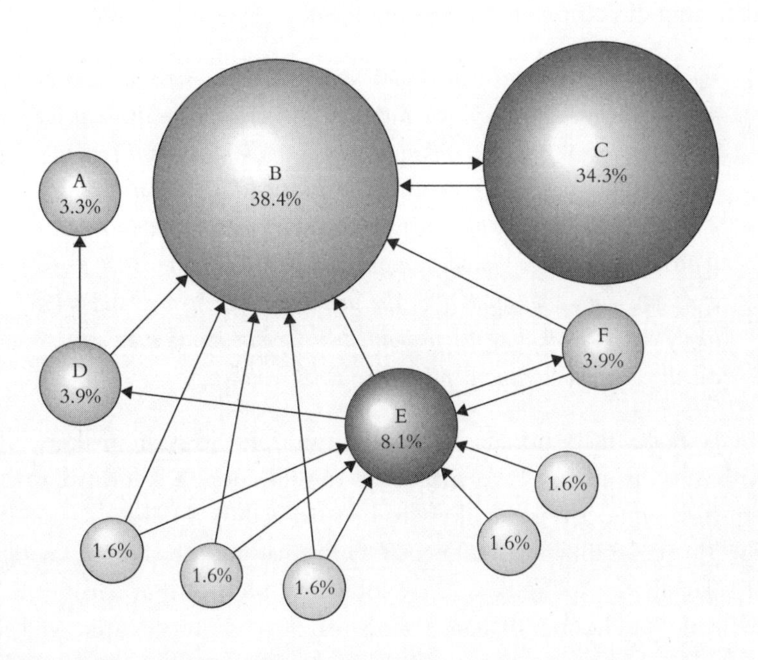

Figure 7.6 Google Page Rank Diagram.

that URL is very meaningful. Google looks for other sites that use that same anchor text. If it keeps finding the phrase "solar cells" pointing to siliconsolar.com, the search engine assumes that URL is relevant to that search query and ranks the site accordingly.

The best way to rank high in Google for a particular keyword is simply to have the best, most accessible content online about that search phrase. You can't game search these days. If you have the best information on your web site, you'll rank high because people will link to it.

Don't be too aggressive in the use of keywords in your web copy. Cramming all the keywords you can onto every page won't help and may actually hurt you. Readability is more important than repetition. Quality content is what gets results.

Lee Odden suggests making a list of all your keywords and mapping them to the various sections of your web site. Then he varies the usage of those terms evenly across those pages. That way he can use all his strategic keywords, but without cramming them into a single page.

In a guest post on the Search Engine Land blog, Proteus SEO managing director Galen DeYoung wrote:

> *Customers "may start with search terms related to their problem or need (e.g., speech privacy). Or they may use search terms that involve the name of a potential solution (noise masking systems). They may start broadly (office acoustics) or narrowly (healthcare acoustic design), or they may be looking for the solution provider (noise consultants) or the industry (acoustical consulting). The key to B2B SEO is a complete understanding of the prospects, their issues, and their likely actions as they search for solutions. Good optimization considers all potential starting points of the B2B searcher."*

Because B2B purchases involve multiple decision makers, all with varying needs, B2B marketers should adopt a keyword strategy that includes phrases likely to be searched by different job titles. For the chief financial officer (CFO), that may be "cost savings of solar energy." Engineers may look for "high-output solar cells," and the purchasing manager may search "wholesale solar cells."

Unlike the impulse-driven world of consumer marketing, B2B buyers need consensus to make smart decisions.

"The goal of most B2B searchers is research," writes De Young. "Your job is to increase the number and quality of those encounters by offering opportunities for them to engage with you. SEO helps not only create the first encounter, but, ideally, it also creates multiple subsequent encounters throughout the buying cycle." If you've ever searched different keywords and continued to see the same company rank high in the results, that's a company that's getting it right.

Once you know the keywords in mind, you can apply that knowledge to your content strategy. For example, keywords could become the editorial calendar for a corporate blog. You might publish a blog post about solar energy savings, create a technical bulletin about high-output solar cells, and even tweak the language on your pricing page to incorporate the term "wholesale energy cells."

It's also important to make your pages visible. Search engines aren't necessarily going to find every page in your site. The deeper a page is buried in the navigation hierarchy, the less visible it is. Search engines start at the root domain and attempt to index every page that is linked to from another page. But not all pages are linked. For example, a landing page that is put in place for an e-mail promotion may not be incorporated into the site's navigation scheme. There's a high likelihood that such pages will escape search crawlers. Using a site map to index every page increases the chances that such pages will be found. This is important because search marketing firm HubSpot has documented a strongly positive correlation between the number of indexed pages and median leads.[1] "For every 50 to 100 pages of indexed pages in Google, leads achieved double digit growth," HubSpot reported. "Lead growth experiences significant acceleration for customers with more than several hundred indexed pages."

Social Media Optimization

You can also use keywords to find customers on social networks, but you need to first validate those keywords in social media to see if the phrases people search for on Google are the same ones they use on

Facebook. That can be tricky, because social network search engines don't necessarily work the same way that Google does, and much of the content may be shielded from public view. Social network search is growing in importance, though. In March 2010, Facebook passed Google in all monthly visits for the first time, although Google still leads by far in the number of unique visitors. "The search that happens behind the login on social networks is becoming increasingly important," says Odden. "Companies need to consider optimizing their content within social networks as well."

In fact, a new kind of search is emerging based on ask-and-answer principles, according to Andrew McAfee, principal research scientist at the MIT Sloan School and author of *Enterprise 2.0.* Twitter users understand this well. If you're looking for a steakhouse in Chicago, you can search the web for restaurant reviews, or you can ask your followers. It you're being followed by people you know and trust, they may yield better information faster.

This introduces another whole level of complexity. Search optimizing the corporate web site is one thing, but Facebook, Twitter, and LinkedIn are creating a new kind of search metaphor that will require a different—and still mostly unexplored—kind of optimization.

People are already learning to leverage this technique. LinkedIn members are optimizing their public profiles on the assumption that hiring managers will increasingly find them by search and Facebook marketers are experimenting with www.youropenbook.org which searches public Facebook status updates. "In the future, there will be no job boards. There will be a global marketplace of talent online, and employers will search it for new hires," says Frank. The United States Marine Corps Recruiting Command might search "just graduated high school" on www.youropenbook.org to find prospective recruits. Another way to optimize a LinkedIn profile is by joining and participating in trade groups. In Chapter 13, we describe how status is the currency of professional networks.

CHAPTER EIGHT

Choosing Platforms

Although we asserted earlier in this book that platform selection is one of the last factors you should consider in developing social marketing programs, making the right choice is critically important. This chapter examines the major options and provides guidance for their use.

Platforms that perform best in business-to-consumer (B2C) environments are not necessarily the ones favored by business-to-business (B2B) marketers. In addition, we believe that companies should make it a goal to drive visitors to their own web sites, where they can engage in richer conversations, showcase their products and content, and own a record of interactions. These days, though, most conversations start in public spaces.

In the next three chapters, we'll talk first about public web 2.0 options such as blogs and Facebook. Then we'll offer guidance on choosing a platform on which to host your branded, destination web site. Finally, we'll show you how innovative B2B companies are using these platforms in concert with each other to achieve results.

The Big Four and More

Four years after MySpace became a cultural phenomenon, we can finally count the number of social networking pure plays winners on one hand: Facebook, Twitter, YouTube, and LinkedIn. Not only do they dominate the landscape of online interactivity today, but they are likely to do so for the next several years. Each of these platforms is being used successfully in B2B marketing, but not all of them have equal value. Whether or not you choose to play, you should understand where they're strong and how other B2B marketers are using them.

Social networks may be hot, but mature platforms like blogs and podcasts still have an important role, particularly for B2B companies. Let's look at the pros and cons of each option.

Blogs

Blogs have been around for more than a decade and have already gone through the hype and disillusionment phase that characterizes any hot consumer phenomena. By some estimates, more than 200 million blogs still lurk on the Internet, but our experience is that only about 20 percent are tended regularly. That's still good for a 1.4 million new blog entries every day, according to comScore. A large percentage of these are in B2B markets.

Blogs are the Swiss Army knife of social media. Simple to create and easy to update, they deftly accommodate multiple media types such as audio, video, and widgets, and they have excellent search engine performance. As truly *social* media they fall short because discussions are limited to a simple post-and-respond metaphor. Think of them as the online equivalent of a business presentation. The blogger is the speaker and the person who controls the microphone. The audience mostly listens and has a chance to challenge and respond at the end.

B2B marketers cited blogs as the most effective social platform in research conducted by *BtoB* magazine and the Association of National Advertisers (ANA) in early 2010. The principal advantage of blogs for B2B purposes is their depth. Entries can be of any length, and graphics and multimedia can be incorporated to illustrate a point. In the technical realm in which many B2B professionals dwell, blogs are the best way to explain complex concepts and engage in audience discussions of equal depth. It's not surprising that technology companies have swarmed to blogging platforms as a way to connect developers with information-hungry constituents.

Their search engine performance shouldn't be underestimated. Search engines are hardwired to favor web sites that they, in their algorithmic wisdom, considered to be useful. For example, type "buy a PC" into Google and note that the search results are much heavier on blog content than marketing come-ons. That's because Google's finely tuned engine favors how-to advice over salesmanship.

Facebook

The success of Facebook is legendary. With more than 500 million members in just 3 years as a mainstream social platform, it is the fastest-growing consumer phenomenon in history. The key word here, though, is "consumer." Facebook's freewheeling informality make it a marginal platform for many B2B companies, but given the social network's ubiquity, this could very easily change. Even today, B2B marketers can find pockets of value.

Facebook is the ultimate word-of-mouth marketing vehicle. All marketing on Facebook is permission-based. The administrator of a Facebook page (previously called a fan page) may communicate only with members who register their interest. Members vote for the companies and causes they like by registering their approval with a "Like" button and sharing their activities and preferences with others. Members' activities, such as joining a page, are automatically shared with their social network through a constantly updated news feed. In addition, members can recommend that others join groups or fan pages that they like. There is no such thing as unsolicited contact because members may receive messages only from organizations they choose to endorse.

One feature that is unique to Facebook is its applications. These small programs usually involve games or self-assessment tests, and some have achieved huge numbers in the consumer realm. However, B2B applications on Facebook are relatively rare. One of the few we found was "A Mini with HP Supplies," which challenges fans to submit photos dramatizing the life of an office manager in exchange for a chance to win a Mini Cooper automobile. The contest page drew more than 15,000 members. Facebook makes most of its money on targeted advertising, but it is beginning to charge businesses for promotions like contests.

B2B companies have found Facebook to be an effective vehicle for recruiting. Ernst & Young, Deloitte, and Sodexo are among the firms that have had success there. In a novel twist, copper producer TVI has also adopted Facebook as a way to communicate with investors.

LinkedIn

If Facebook is a T-shirt, then LinkedIn is a button-down and blazer. The 9-to-5 counterpart to Facebook's perpetual house party is built on résumés, professional networking, and a vast collection of no-nonsense topical discussions. The *BtoB* magazine/ANA research found that 81 percent of B2B marketers said they use LinkedIn, compared with just 25 percent of B2C marketers.

LinkedIn's most distinctive feature is Connections, a six-degrees-of-separation metaphor that maps members to each other via their common contacts. Although members may message only their primary connections directly, they can request introductions and forward messages via intermediary connections. You can also upgrade to a premium account, which allows you to send three Linkedin InMails directly to connections outside of your network. At a cost of $7.50 per InMail, they are rarely misused and have a 40 percent response rate, according to Brian Frank, Director of Global Enterprise Operations at Linkedin.

LinkedIn is strictly business, and that's what makes it such an attractive option for B2B marketers. There are groups for almost any professional discipline you can imagine, and discussions are focused and active. It's easy to start groups, and you can also drop in on relevant discussions to find out what's on the minds of business customers. "Our LinkedIn groups are all under 200 people and they're all customers of ours," says CME Group's Allan Schoenberg. "You can ask anything and get a reaction."

LinkedIn is also a lead generation machine. Its novel approach to company profiles presents a view of businesses from the bottom up, enabling members to identify mutual contacts of employees they might be trying to reach. Its Answers feature is a great way for members to showcase their expertise by helping others solve problems in full view of others. Not surprisingly, LinkedIn is particularly popular with consultants and small business owners who have extensive domain knowledge. But it's also a good way for businesses to augment campaigns by forming regional and/or topical groups within their areas of focus. The site is a popular way to promote events and has even sparked a class of unofficial, regional networking events where LinkedIn members meet and mingle.

YouTube

The world's number one video-sharing site—and number two search engine—has clocked some astounding growth in its 4 years in the public eye. YouTube reportedly logs more than 20 hours of video uploads every *minute* and in 2009 passed the 1 billion daily download mark. YouTube is a rudimentary social network, but its strength is as a video library with the capability to let members easily share content and embed videos in their own web sites.

A particularly valuable feature to businesses is member commentary, which can quickly provide an informal poll of a video's appeal. Many businesses find that YouTube is a cheap way to get bonus exposure for promotional, training, and demo videos that are no longer needed in active campaigns. It's also a good way to test concepts for new promotional campaigns, share customer testimonials, or just show employees doing their jobs. A counter keeps track of the total number of video views both on the site and through viewers of the video embedded elsewhere. But it should be noted that the counter registers each time a new viewer starts rather than finishes a video, and YouTube's autoplay functionality exaggerates that number. In fact, the "views" counter would be more accurately described as a "play starts" counter.

Consider YouTube as a possible home base for all of your public video assets. Once stored in a branded channel that you own, they can be easily streamed through any web site that supports embedding. The principle downside of YouTube is its 10-minute length limit. Business-focused services like Viddler, Vimeo, and Blip.tv offer more latitude with a premium account for a modest fee.

Twitter

The social networking growth story of 2009 was a topic of constant controversy. Twitter eclipsed the 100-million-member mark in early 2010, but research has indicated that the percentage of active users is quite small. SocialMediaToday.com estimated in early 2010 that although 87 percent of Americans had heard of Twitter, only 7 percent actually used it.

For B2B marketers, however, Twitter is a must-have. As of the end of 2009, more than one third of the Fortune 500 and nearly half of the top 100 companies had a Twitter account, according to research published by the Society for New Communications Research. By comparison, just 22 percent of the Fortune 500 had a public-facing blog, despite the fact that blogging has been mainstream for five years. The *BtoB*/ANA research found that Twitter was used by 70 percent of B2B marketers, compared with 46 percent of B2C marketers.

Entire books have been written about Twitter, and it's difficult to summarize all of its applications in a few paragraphs. Its 140-character limit, which is often perceived as a limitation, is actually a virtue, because it's easier to come up with 140 characters than a blog post. People post messages to Twitter that they would never publish to a blog. Although that creates a certain amount of meaningless chatter, tweets can be filtered and grouped in a way that yields meaningful trends. Insights gained from Twitter are likely to have greater immediacy and emotion than those that appear in long-form media because the service encourages spontaneity and impulsivity. Twitter is also so fast and used so candidly that trends can become evident there more quickly than any other medium.

Twitter has one of the oldest demographics of any form of social media, and it is particularly popular with professionals in the technology, marketing, and communications fields. Nearly all major media outlets now have a presence there, which means that marketing campaigns that have a media outreach component should make Twitter a core tool. Twitter has also been shown to draw a highly brand-aware audience. A 2010 Edison Research study found that 42 percent of active Twitter users learn about products and services via Twitter and 49 percent follow brands or companies.[1] The percentage of "Twitter users talking about marketing and brands far exceeds the usage on the other social networks," according to Tom Webster, vice president of strategy and marketing at Edison.

Podcasts

Media hype elevated podcasts to prominence before they were ready. Once seen as a replacement for terrestrial radio, podcasts never lived up to their potential in consumer markets. What is often overlooked is their remarkable B2B success.

Podcasts are downloadable audio programs that play on a computer, an iPod, or other mobile device. They're reasonably easy to create using inexpensive recording devices or computers with open-source software. Although the term "podcast" technically refers to the delivery of an audio or video file via RSS, it has come to be used for downloadable audio or video as well. Recent market figures are hard to come by, but eMarketer estimated that the 2009 audience would more than double by 2013 (see Figure 8.1). The research firm has also estimated that regular podcast listeners are twice as likely as nonlisteners to have incomes exceeding $100,000. Video podcasts are a more

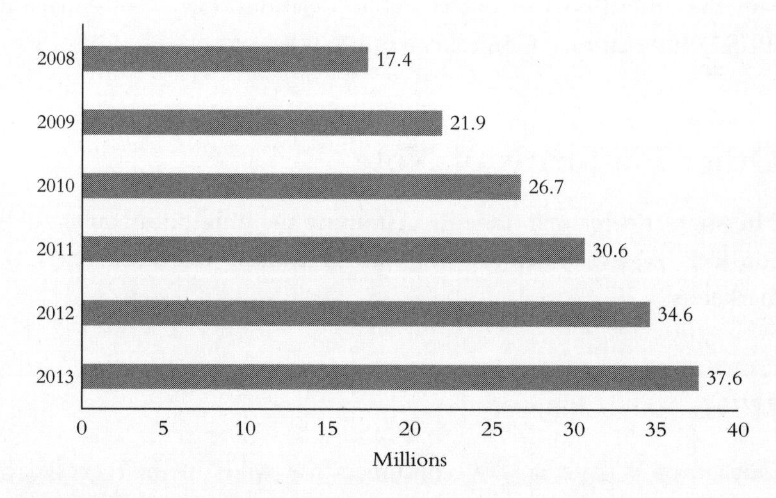

Figure 8.1 Estimated U.S. Podcast Audience.
Source: eMarketer.

recent evolution. In both cases, the process of loading the program into a mobile device for playback on the go is the same but podcasts can also be consumed via desktop using iTunes and Google Reader.

Podcasts are one of the hidden success stories of B2B marketing. The audio format is extremely time efficient; it allows busy professionals to consume information when they are occupied with routine tasks like commuting, exercising or mowing the lawn. They're an excellent way to capture presentations, speeches, and even meetings for playback to people who couldn't be there. When combined with PowerPoint in a package called a "slidecast," they can also be self-contained presentations.

Business-to-business technology companies like IBM, Cisco, and National Semiconductor have public libraries containing hundreds of podcasts. But it's not just technology firms. The management consulting firm McKinsey & Company has podcasts on topics such as finance, high-tech, and international business. Bosch Rexroth has a series on lean manufacturing. The Missouri Industry Beef Council has produced more than 200 podcast interviews with its members. There are dozens devoted to various aspects of marketing, including the excellent For Immediate Release: The Hobson and Holtz Report and, of course, Eric's award-winning On the Record . . . Online podcast, the official podcast of the Public Relations Society of America (PRSA) International Confernece since 2006.

Other Platforms of Note

The six platforms mentioned so far aren't the only ones you should consider. A few other services have particular relevance to B2B marketers.

Wikis

Outside of Wikipedia, few consumers use wikis in their everyday activities, but inside businesses, this simple collaboration platform is extraordinarily popular. A wiki is basically a big electronic whiteboard upon which anybody can post nearly any kind of content and also change and annotate content contributed by others. Wikis have almost no value as marketing vehicles, but they have one great advantage for businesses that are dipping their toes in the social marketing waters: they're a great tool to deploy inside the organization for collaboration. In fact, IBM's main internal wiki gets more than 1 million page views a day, according to social media communications manager Adam Christensen. Other big organizations like the Central Intelligence Agency and pharmaceutical giant Pfizer have spoken publicly about the significant value they've derived from internal wikis.

Wikis underlie popular customer communities at IBM, Hewlett-Packard, Intuit, T-Mobile, and the Dell TechCenter, which we profiled at the beginning of Chapter 1. They can be deployed internally to introduce social networking concepts to reluctant employees and then moved outside the firewall as a safe place to interact with customers. Peter Kim maintains a massive list of social media marketing examples, including several wiki-based customer communities at wiki.beingpeterkim.com/master-list.

SlideShare

Founded in late 2006, this presentation-sharing service operated quietly under the radar until 2009, when membership grew 400 percent and monthly page views topped 60 million. Co-founders Rashmi Sinha and Jonathan Boutelle had probably sat in enough new business meetings to understand that PowerPoint is the tool of choice for pitching business so they built a site that became the equivalent of YouTube for PowerPoint presentations. It has attracted a blue-chip member base, more than 60 percent of whom identify themselves as business professionals. Spend a few minutes browsing the presentations on SlideShare, and you'll quickly see that this site offers a laser-focused collection of B2B visual essays, many of which are designed to shore new business prospects.

SlideShare offers the same basic functionality as YouTube. Members can upload and download presentations, create channels, and comment on one another's work. The simple rating system is limited to a polite "favorite" metaphor to recognize exceptional value. Members can also follow one another, create groups, post status updates and embed presentations in another web site. SlideShare is one of only a handful of third-party applications supported by LinkedIn.

In 2009, the service added two features aimed at B2B marketers. Companies can now purchase branded spaces where they can consolidate their own presentations as well as those of others. Members can also pay to generate leads by capturing contact information from member downloads. SlideShare has the YouTube-like appeal of being a convenient source of bonus exposure for existing content as well as a place to showcase expertise.

Ning

This is probably the fastest and easiest way to get your feet wet with branded social networks. Ning was originally a free service, but in 2010 it abandoned that model in favor of monthly fees ranging from $2.95 to $49.95 per month. Still, the cost is trivial compared with the value of learning the tools and tactics of social networking. There are some surprisingly large communities operating on Ning, many with tens of thousands of members.

The chief value of Ning to marketers is that it provides many basic community features at an affordable price. These include personal profiles, forums, groups, photo- and video-sharing features, and blogs. For marketers who want to test communities inexpensively, it's a great choice. However, experienced users tell us that successful community operators almost invariably want to migrate to more functional platforms as their needs grow. Be sure you can move people and conversations under those circumstances.

Scribd

This 2007 startup is trying to do with PDF documents what SlideShare has done with PowerPoint: make reading a social experience. It's another way for B2B marketers to find new life for content that might otherwise be relegated to a dusty archive.

The core of the service is a reader technology that can handle anything published in the Microsoft Office format, as well as text and Adobe PDF documents. Scribd addresses a unique need in the market: most text content today is created in one of these formats, but posting such material on a web site while retaining format and images is beyond the skills of the average computer user.

Scribd's reader makes it possible to read documents on the screen as if they were on a printed page. The company has been a leader in championing the new HTML5 standard, which delivers reader-like capability on standard web pages. As with SlideShare and YouTube, the reader can be embedded on other web sites and documents can easily be shared via integration with Facebook, Twitter, RSS feeds, and other popular services. Members can even sign up to have their reading choices automatically shared with their networks of online friends.

Scribd is hugely popular with professional publishers, who take advantage of its e-commerce capabilities to deliver samples of their products and invitations to download or buy for a fee. What may interest B2B marketers more, however, is the service's value as a way to distribute manuals, white papers, technical publications, and regulatory filings for popular consumption. Companies can create branded channels, attract subscribers, and subscribe to others. It's just one more way to tap into an existing audience and potentially find leads.

It bears noting that at the time of this writing, viewing documents embedded in third-party web sites via Scribd was a hit or miss endeavor. As the company grows and secures resources, this should change, but currently we're seeing the "load" graphic spin indefinitely and service's widgets fail to load, so at this point, you may want to steer clear of using their embed codes.

Now that we've covered the major public platforms, we'll tell you why we think your own destination web site is the heart of B2B social marketing.

CHAPTER NINE

A Non-Techie's Guide to Choosing Platforms

In its 2010 Trust Barometer, the giant public relations firm Edelman asserted that because most people see all stakeholders as equally important and because people need to hear something multiple times to be convinced of its veracity, companies should "be everywhere, engaging everyone."

But the reality is that given the explosion of social media sites and the amount of time organizations have to invest in them, you need to focus your resources on those social media channels most likely to deliver a return. In B2B marketing, where purchasing decisions can be major commitments that require educating multiple stakeholders and building group consensus over the long term, picking channels with longevity is key.

The conundrum is how to maintain relationships with those customers using platforms that are here today and may be gone tomorrow. Interruptions compromise sales. If you wind up on an obsolete platform, you will face the task of moving your data elsewhere. That's a complex process, and it is particularly disruptive to B2B marketers, because sales cycles are longer and purchases are more heavily considered. If you lose access to your customer interaction history, it's difficult to keep prospects moving through the sales funnel.

In this chapter, we walk you step-by-step through the process of mitigating the risks associated with selecting a platform to host a destination web site.

Destination Web Site as Home Base

In social marketing, your corporate web site is your home field advantage. As a source of official company information, people trust what you say about yourself at your own domain more than they do on your Facebook company page. After all, anyone can launch a Facebook page, but only your organization can upload content to its own destination site. A December 2008 study by Forrester Research analyst Josh Bernoff reported that a scant 18 percent of U.S. Internet users say they trust social networking site profiles from a company or brand.[1] Half of industrial buyers have selected one supplier over another primarily based on the capabilities of that supplier's web site, according to the 2008 ThomasNet Buyer-Seller Disconnect Study by Outsell, Inc.

John Shea, new media director at the Federal Emergency Management Agency, endorses this principle. "If you're concerned that information came from a social network, look back here to the FEMA.gov website so you know it's authorized information," he says. "A lot of what you see out there are folks who pretend to have the right information, or think they have the right information, but there's nothing that says its official unless it can be verified on a .gov site." That doesn't mean you should avoid public networks, but back-end those conversations with content on your official site as well.

Think of your web site as the homeland, and your presence on social media services as embassies, suggests Steve Rubel, SVP, Director of Insights for Edelman Digital. You should build relationships via social media, but without neglecting the importance of driving people back to a place where you can have more influence over the conversation.

Use social networks at the top of the sales funnel. If your objective is to generate leads, seek out conversations happening in public spaces, give out free advice, and entice people to follow you home. The page they land on should both validate what was said on the social network and encourage them to take a desired action.

"If you're making money through e-commerce on your corporate site, why would you be so quick to send traffic away?" asks Jeremiah Owyang, partner at the Altimeter Group. "Most companies say it's because they want trust or word of mouth, but they haven't thought through what that actually means."

Control the Interface, Not the Conversation

Most of the worrying we hear from companies about social media engagement centers around the bad things people might say about their product or service online. But what's more important is where they say it. If it's on your own destination web site, you're in a better position to refute misinformation and convert conversations into transactions.

If you make your destination social so stakeholders can converse about the business in which you compete in your homeland, you generate editorial content against which you can promote your own products and services. Think of how you can leverage content and conversation on your own site to promote your company in context.

Content Management Systems

Before you start tweeting links back to your corporate site and inviting people over, clean up your house first. Start by choosing a content management system (CMS).

A CMS is a platform for managing web content. A blog is an example of a simple content management system. So is Twitter's 140-character tweet field. A CMS lets you create and format content to display on a web site.

A CMS can come in all shapes and sizes. What's important to know is that you don't have to reinvent the wheel. There is a vibrant industry of packaged CMS platform providers and chances are there's more than one that's right for you. But regardless of the CMS you select, two things you need for sure are data portability and interoperability.

Data Portability and Interoperability

Interoperable systems play nicely with others, so they're compatible with other types of software. Having data portability means you can easily back up your data or migrate your content and contacts to applications like customer relationship management (CRM) systems or another CMS in the future.

When you use popular social networking sites, you relinquish control of your customer data to the service provider. Social networks like Facebook have a vested interest in tying you to their platform, so most don't make it easy to move data elsewhere.

For example, if you use Facebook Events to invite your "friends" to a webinar, the attendee list is excruciatingly difficult to export. If you ran into someone who attended your webinar at a trade show a year later, you'd like to be able to pull up his customer card and see a history of your interactions. CRM software enables this, but if you rely exclusively on third-party web 2.0 services, the task is nearly impossible.

There's also no guarantee that a third-party social network will be around for the long term. In 2002, a social networking site called Friendster was all the rage. The next year, its dominance was usurped by MySpace, which was trumped by Facebook a few years later. Today, Facebook looks unstoppable, but so did IBM in its heyday. The fact, no one knows what's next. Make sure your customer data and interactions can be exported in an interoperable format.

We've seen numerous cases in which marketers were surprised to discover that their corporate site couldn't easily be integrated with their CRM or e-commerce service. Here's how to make sure that doesn't happen to you.

Getting Ready to Pick a Platform

One big reason companies fail at platform selection is because they delegate the task to an internal information technology (IT) department whose primary function is infrastructure, not interface. Marketers need to be closely involved in providing guidance on business needs. Writing out detailed business requirements based on case studies is a complicated process. It can be long and tedious, but believe us when we say it's absolutely critical. You need to think about what features you will need 2 to 3 years from now and write them into the needs definition from the start. Otherwise, your destination site will become a pair of handcuffs when you seek to expand it. You can't choose the right CMS if you don't know what you need it to do.

Start by interviewing representatives from different departments in your company to gather requirements and determine current and future use case scenarios. Work with a user interface designer to translate business requirements into functional specifications and web site wire frame drawings, which are line drawings showing specifically how the site's interface will work.

For example, you may not need the ability for customers to easily share the e-commerce transactions they make on your web site on Linkedin today, but you may want that functionality in the future. It's difficult to think ahead to all the possible options, but choose a platform that's interoperable enough to support the most likely scenarios. Look for a robust ecosystem of third-party plug-in providers.

Platform Options

When choosing platforms, you have four basic options:

1. Public web 2.0 services such as Blogger, Flickr, and YouTube
2. Licensed proprietary or open-source software such as Microsoft SharePoint or Joomla
3. Software as a service (SaaS) providers, which lease access to a proprietary platform that's hosted on the Internet
4. Homegrown applications

It's difficult to imagine a scenario in which the fourth option makes sense these days. The homegrown option is expensive and risky, and failure rates are high. We recommend against do-it-yourself solutions unless the features you require are so highly specialized that no viable commercial alternatives exist. Frankly, with the exception of the US Department of Defense, which is building its own CMS for security reasons, we haven't encountered that situation yet.

Public Web 2.0 Services. It's possible to build a destination web site on the back of public web 2.0 services like Google's Blogger, Yahoo!'s Flickr, YouTube, and Facebook. Blogger lets you point your domain name to your blog so your pages are parked at your domain. You can design a custom template based on your brand identity. The aesthetics of a YouTube channel can also be customized to a certain extent. You can even use public services to back-end your web site. For example, you can syndicate Flickr photos and YouTube videos on your own pages or use Facebook Connect to make it easy for visitors to register and collect Facebook Friends instead of customer profiles in a CRM database.

Public web 2.0 services are easy to use, require no client-server maintenance or software updates on your part, and can be deployed in minutes. You sign up for an account, publish content, and never have to worry about installing security patches, upgrading the CMS or managing a server.

However, you have no control over back-end functionality or navigational hierarchy. There's no version control, archiving, or workflow management. Data portability and interoperability are intentionally restrictive because the providers want to lock you in. It's difficult to market around your content because the site operator is already doing that for their advertisers, who underwrite the cost associated with maintaining your "free" account. These services also often have weak support for nonpaying users or no support at all. If you have a problem, you're on your own.

This happened to one of our clients: Her organization's 1,000-member Facebook page inexplicably disappeared because, she was told, it violated Facebook's terms of service. There was no further explanation from Facebook, and it was months before she was able to reach someone at the company who could resolve the problem.

Terms of service may absolve the public network from any liability for problems. Here's a passage from Blogger's contract: "You agree Google has no responsibility or liability for the deletion of, or the failure to store or transmit, any of the content and other communications maintained by the service. Google retains the right to create limits on use and storage at our sole discretion at any time with or without notice." In other words, Google has no liability for anything that happens to your Blogger data. (In fact, there are ways to back up and export Blogger data, but Google doesn't make that easy to figure out.) And if they want to impose other restrictions on usage in the future, they have reserved the legal right to do.

Licensed Software. The second option is to license software and host it either on your own servers or externally with a web hosting company, also known as a co-location provider. If you host a site yourself, you have to provide for the time and expense of installing security updates and software upgrades, arrange for backup and disaster recovery, and build the necessary infrastructure to support growth.

The license-and-install option requires extensive IT support, but once the site is up and running, you have considerable autonomy and flexibility. There are two categories of licensed software: proprietary and open source. In the case of proprietary solutions, you pay a licensing fee to use the software. In the case of open-source software, you pay no licensing fee but are responsible for customizing, deploying, and hosting. This sometimes carries considerable cost. Many vendors, such as Jive and SocialText, offer both on-premise and hosted (SaaS) options.

If you go the licensed software route, spend the money up front for a functional specification and produce wire frame diagrams to illustrate desired functionality. You will make a significant up-front investment, so be sure the platform will serve your purpose. Since the implementation costs are front-end loaded, you've got much more to lose if the platform underperforms, because you're not going to be able to use it until most of the work has been done.

Be precise about the functionality the vendor needs to deliver. For example, you might specify that the platform should support streaming webcasts with text chat and polling, automatic importing of attendee names into your CRM system, and synchronization with your e-mail marketing application. Schedule dedicated time to test the completed system and ensure that those features work and don't sign off on delivery until you've assured they function at the scale you need.

Provide complete specifications up front. The vendor is under no obligation to implement new features that weren't in the original contract. If you're depending on the new system to be working by a certain date to support a product launch or trade show, write that into the contract and be sure the vendor has a contingency in place in case it misses the deadline. Grand plans are derailed by details, so sweat the little stuff.

Software as a Service. SaaS services are accessed over the Internet, usually from a browser. The advantage of SaaS is that the service is less expensive up front and provides the latest features without the hassle of software installation and testing. The provider earns its keep by demonstrating value over time, because the cost and trouble of switching platforms is relatively low. Time to market is also faster, because the SaaS provider has the software and hardware in place and has usually deployed the platform successfully for other clients. Salesforce.com, CrownPeak, HubSpot, and iPressroom (which Eric founded and sold in 2009) are some of the hundreds of providers that deliver their products as services.

Another advantage of SaaS is technical support. Most SaaS vendors offer so-called service-level agreements (SLAs) that guarantee uptime, customer response times, and service quality. Read these agreements carefully, though. Many vendors don't guarantee SLAs beyond giving back a couple of months' worth of free service, and no vendor will compensate you for lost business. Specify the largest penalties for nonperformance that you can get.

The big downside of SaaS is that you've got to keep paying as long as you're on the platform. Also, some internal IT organizations prohibit the uses of hosted services outside the firewall. There is some risk involved because vendors may fail or be acquired. Perhaps most important, the data on a SaaS platform doesn't live on your site. If you go the SaaS route, be sure to obtain an ironclad guarantee that you can get your hands on that data whenever you need it.

Use this Q&A to help decide which platform is right for you.

1. **What measurable actions do I want prospects to take?**
   The answer to this question determines the feature set your platform needs to support. If you want to use a public social network to help customers educate and support themselves, consider a platform like Jive or WetPaint that lets participants easily add to a shared body of knowledge. If you want to enable people to collaborate, you'll need a platform that supports activity streams, like the newsfeed on Facebook or the tweet stream on Twitter. If you want to build landing pages that send leads to another system such as Salesforce.com, you'll need a CMS that's interoperable with your CRM package.
2. **What specific functionality do I need?**
   For example, if you plan to display banner and tower ads alongside your content, you need a platform with ad server functionality, including the ability to rotate ads dynamically. If you plan to create a lot of your own content, you'll need to be able to specify page titles and metadata for search engine optimization. If you want to send e-mail newsletters to an opt-in list, you'll need a system that supports e-mail marketing or that can be integrated with a third-party e-mail marketing system. Think of everything you might ever want to do with your service and specify it in the front-end definition. It's a lot more expensive to add features later than to demand them at the outset.
3. **Am I tech savvy enough to support myself?**
   If you are technically proficient enough to customize a site to your liking, go with an open-source CMS platform like Drupal, Joomla, or WordPress. There's no software license fee, and the open-source community protects you

against obsolescence. Major B2B marketers like Cisco and IBM use open-source platforms, so these systems are tested and proven.

If you have budget but no support, go with a SaaS provider and negotiate an SLA that gives you as much support as you think you'll need. If you've got no budget and no support, public web 2.0 platforms are your only option.

4. **Does the internal IT organization have the resources to support me?**
   If you've got the technical resources on staff but you're competing with other projects, you could hire an outside firm to get you up and running on licensed software, but it's going require a heftier up-front investment than using a SaaS provider. However, you also have more control over the final outcome. Support may be more challenging because added fees are involved and systems integrators are also pulled by obligations to other clients.
5. **Do I need regular offsite backups?**
   If you go the license-and-install or cloud-hosted route, make sure you maintain an offsite backup in safe locations where you can get to it. If you go with the SaaS approach, get assurances you can make a copy of the data whenever you need it.
6. **Do I need disaster recovery?**
   Disaster recovery allows you to maintain backups of your web site in remote data centers. If one site goes down, another site automatically takes over. SaaS providers have this feature built in. If you host the site yourself, you need to make your own arrangements. If you're hosted on a public web 2.0 platform, the decision is out of your hands. While major public platform providers generally have good infrastructure in place, none that we know of will guarantee against data damage or loss.
7. **How quickly do I need problems resolved?**
   When your web site is down, minutes can seem like hours, so think about how much downtime you can withstand. Systems integrators and co-location vendors usually provide

several classes of service, ranging from instantaneous to leisurely. The faster the response, the higher the price. This is one advantage of SaaS solutions. Those vendors can't afford downtime, so they invest considerable resources in reliability and redundancy.

8. **How compatible does the platform need to be with my company web site?**
   You don't need code-level compatibility. You can load templates that match the look and feel of your existing web site into a CMS, redirect from an existing domain, and achieve nearly seamless integration. But if you want the headlines from your blog posts to appear on your corporate home page or clicks from the blog to trigger forms from a commerce engine, you'll need a CMS that can integrate at that level.
9. **What's my budget?**
   Got cash but no resources? Go with SaaS providers and leave the heavy lifting and support to them. Got resources but no cash? Go with an open-source solution and save on the software licensing fee. Got plenty of Microsoft-certified engineers? Go with Microsoft SharePoint. Got no cash and no resources? Go with Web 2.0, but favor those free platforms that are interoperable and make it easy to migrate your data.

   If you do go the Web 2.0 route, point your account at a web domain you own. That way, you can more easily migrate and redirect the URLs to new ones later. You won't abandon your inbound links and inadvertently sacrifice your search rankings. When Eric moved his Spinfluencer blog from Blogger to WordPress, he didn't want to orphan several valuable inbound links from Wikipedia. By pointing his Blogger blog to the spinfluencer.com domain he owned, he was able to redirect all his Blogger permalink addresses to the new ones on the WordPress platform. SaaS providers try to be very flexible about embedding their services within your existing web site. However, such options don't exist with Facebook, LinkedIn, or most of the most popular public social networks.

The Future of the Destination Web Site

The question of who owns what pieces of a web site is becoming more challenging as options proliferate for embedding web 2.0 services. No matter what platform you use, you want one that easily supports the scripts and embeds that enable activity streams from elsewhere to show up on your web site.

You're no doubt familiar with embed codes through the many widgets that have sprouted up in recent years. These are commonly used to display books from Amazon, show off Flickr slideshows, or display the owner's most recent tweets. In the future, these widgets are going to get a lot more sophisticated and a lot better integrated with the sites that display them. A few examples:

- Facebook's Open Graph permits any site owner to integrate the Facebook "Like" button and to enable discussion between Facebook friends without requiring them to leave the site.
- Twitter's @Anywhere platform enables visitors to any web site to interact with a filtered tweet stream in real time. You could use this, for example, to show a live Twitter feed of comments about your industry or product and let visitors participate without leaving your site, or to gather followers on your destination web site.
- Google Wave was a collaboration engine that could be used to embed an activity stream on a destination web site. We thought it had a great deal of promise for B2B marketers. But unfortunately, Google shuttered the service before it had time to become widely adopted, which reinforces the importance of building a destination site on a platform you are not beholden on others to access.

Google open web advocate Chris Messina suggests that in the future activity streams might be used to keep project team members abreast of deadlines and the actions of their colleagues without requiring them to visit a special site. B2B marketers could embed activity streams on topical pages within their own web sites to make it easy for visitors to engage in relevant real-time discussion.

In other words, the web site itself is increasingly becoming an aggregation of services and activities that originate elsewhere. As technology makes it possible for our online scribblings to appear wherever we choose, web site owners will increasingly find themselves acting as curators of external services. For B2B companies, whose relationships with customers are often characterized by rich technical discussion, this ability to become a portal for all kinds of relevant information will unlock new marketing opportunities by allowing markets to self-educate through organic, online sharing and interaction.

Part Three

Going to Market

CHAPTER TEN

Social Platforms in Use

Here are several examples of how innovative business-to-business (B2B) companies are applying one or more of the platforms described earlier in this book.

Emerson Process Experts (Blog)

It took two years for Jim Cahill and Deb Franke to convince the management at Emerson Process Management that a blog was a good idea. Their reticence was understandable. It was 2005, and blogs were widely perceived to be the domain of teenage diarists and scandal-mongers. Why would anyone want to get mixed up with that? And why would they want to read about equipment that manages large industrial plants?

Cahill and Franke persevered. Some technology companies were creeping into the blogosphere at the time and clearly enjoying good results. By pointing to successes elsewhere, the two eventually overcame objections by arguing that, as communications people, they understood the pitfalls and how to manage them. A blog called Emerson Process Experts was born.

Four years and more than 500 blog entries later, Cahill is enjoying the new job title head of social media at Emerson Process

Management. Emerson Process Experts was named Best Corporate Blog by *BtoB* magazine in 2010, and Cahill is now leading the company's charge into Twitter and Facebook while institutionalizing best practices among all the Emerson Process Management divisions.

The blog has brought numerous business opportunities into Emerson, including an invitation to bid on a large new plant for a contract that could total hundreds of millions of dollars. "I have the e-mail from that company on my wall next to a sign that asks 'Is there any value in blogging?' " he laughs.

Even after four years, Emerson Process Experts remains an enigma in a heavy industry that has done little with social media. Topics like "Sensing Liquid Levels with Vibrating Fork Technology" may cause the average visitor's eyes to cross, but the elite engineers who run giant process control systems can't get enough of this kind of technical wisdom.

And for a blog this specialized, the traffic is pretty impressive. About 2,000 visitors stop by on an average business day, and 15 to 20 messages land in Cahill's inbox every week. Although most are routine, a few gems inquire about business opportunities. After replying with a thank-you message, Cahill forwards them on to the sales team.

One reason for the blog's success is the search engine magic it delivers. Search on "process control" or "process management" and depending on the day, Emerson ranks in the first or second page of search results. Rarely used terms like "compressor surge control" deliver Emerson on Google's first page. The secret is the lack of competition. As an established presence in a community with few other bloggers, Cahill is a big fish in a small pond. And as we know, Google loves blogs.

Cahill approaches his job with a reporter's eye. He isn't an engineer, but with more than 20 years at the company, he understands the lingo and is able to write in the customer's language. "When I pass people in the hall, I'll ask if they had any recent customer interactions that were interesting," he says. "I'll dig into those stories."

His advice to prospective B2B bloggers: "Be prepared to stick with it for a while; it takes a couple of years to build up your presence.

Listening is a key skill. Blogging isn't just pushing out information, it's responding to the interests of your market."

CME Group (Twitter)

The world's largest futures exchange is also one of the most popular entities on Twitter, with more than 750,000 followers. At the time of this writing, that put CME Group (formerly the Chicago Mercantile Exchange) ahead of well-known brands and celebrities like *The Today Show,* Dr. Phil, and Danny DeVito.

The exchange has been active in social media channels since the early days, having launched a Facebook account in 2007 and since adding Delicious, Digg, StumbleUpon, Twitter, and a corporate blog. Equally remarkable is that CME Group's market is highly regulated and has been under particular scrutiny since the 2008 mortgage bond crisis. Whereas most financial firms have preferred to stay out of the spotlight during the past couple of years, CME Group has talked in every channel it could find.

As is often the case with B2B companies, the online initiative was driven by the corporate communications department, and particularly by Allan Schoenberg, a career communications professional with a background in technology. "I was an early adopter of Twitter as I'm an early adopter of a lot of [social media] tools," Schoenberg says. "We got on Twitter when there were less than a half million people using it. In the early days, people could find us very easily." The Exchange's tweeters got to know a few people at Twitter, who added the Exchange to an elite list of people the company recommends its members follow. A partnership with StockTwits, the popular real-time investment discussion forum, helped, as did a broad-based effort by CME Group to promote its Twitter presence through press releases, speeches, and its web site.

Given the regulatory climate, the company has stepped carefully. Only designated employees are allowed to speak on behalf of the company, and they are thoroughly briefed in Securities and Exchange Commission (SEC) disclosure rules as well as the SEC's social media guidelines. Schoenberg's team also leveraged good relationships with the company's legal and information security teams to get buy-in at the front end.

About 80 percent of the tweeting content is about the marketplace and the economy, with the other 20 percent related to CME Group. Still, Schoenberg says, even the company-specific messages are intentionally nonpromotional. "One of the key drivers of our success is that [our Twitter feed] is about our audience and what they want," he says. "Now they know that if it's coming from us, it's a credible source." Company tweeters also make a conscious effort to respond to any messages that demand a reply.

Among the tactics the communications team has used is profiles of partners, traders, and other financial professionals who are active in the Twitter stream. As Schoenberg sees it, content equals visibility and Twitter is only one of many tools that are available.

Company management has seen the visibility CME Group is receiving and fully supports the social initiatives. So far, the communications group has run with the social media ball, but that's about to change. "One of the key goals for my team this year is to educate everybody within the company," Schoenberg says. CME's impressive visibility on Twitter has aroused interest from employees who are now asking to contribute to the company blog. By letting CME's skilled communicators introduce the rest of the company to Twitter, employees at all levels were able to learn how use this new channel for responsible, external communications by simply following the company's Twitter feed, and monitoring the interaction. With all the other social platforms the company has on deck, there will be plenty to keep them busy.

Infusionsoft (Video, Social Networks)

With prices starting at $199 per month, Infusionsoft has staked out premium-priced territory in the cost-competitive e-mail marketing business. Yet it has still managed to grow its user base nearly eightfold over the past two years. One reason is that the company bundles sophisticated enhanced services like print delivery and customer relationship management (CRM) into its product. Another is that it constantly innovates in its use of social marketing. Video is a key tool.

The e-mail marketing business enjoys high retention rates because the value of the service increases the more customers use it. That means the key objective is getting new customers in the door. Word of mouth is a critical marketing tool, particularly in the small business market that Infusionsoft serves. Customers frequently select vendors based on input from their friends.

Infusionsoft's library of more than 100 videos on their YouTube channel communicates the company's customer service commitment through quotes from dozens of employees. A premium account on Vimeo showcases in-depth product demonstrations and tutorials that don't conform to YouTube's 10-minute limit. Much of the library was assembled for an innovative promotion program called "Double Your Sales" that guarantees a refund if customers don't see an uptick in business.

Infusionsoft promotes its activities through a mosaic of social platforms, including a blog, groups on LinkedIn, and a Facebook page with more than 2,500 fans. It runs a public customer support portal and even a site where customers can submit and vote on ideas for new products.

Its Twitter account has attracted more than three times the following of much larger competitors. The secret? The company targets small business owners, follows as many of those people as possible and regularly comments on their tweets. "We reply to nearly every comment and engage with a lot of people," says Joseph Manna, Infusionsoft's community manager and social media evangelist.

One Twitter promotion asked, "If you had Infusionsoft free for a year, what would you do?" Several hundred respondents clicked through to a landing page to share their ideas. The promotion reeled in several new customers. "Some people who won are still talking about us on Twitter," Manna says.

The company has a knack for offbeat tactics that attract attention. In early 2010, Infusionsoft locked marketing vice president Tyler Garns in a room for a 12-hour live video webcast distributed by Ustream. Garns showed slides, chatted with guest speakers, and took questions from the audience via chat. The experience was exhausting for Garns, but the payoff came in the form of more than 1,100 viewers and several new customers.

Over the 2009 Thanksgiving holiday, Infusionsoft posted a Black Monday promotion on Facebook, offering bonus services to people who became new subscribers on the traditionally busiest online shopping day. The promotion was almost a spur-of-the-moment decision, having been conceived the day before Thanksgiving, says Manna, but speed is one of the beauties of social networks. "People signed up and all of them have been maintained," he says.

By enabling word-of-mouth marketing, Infusionsoft cut its sales cycle time by about 30 percent in one year. "Social media efforts were a main contributor to that change," Manna says.

Avaya (Twitter)

When Paul Dunay joined data networking firm Avaya Inc. as global managing director of services and social marketing in 2009, he quickly set to work building the company's social media capabilities. Already an award-winning blogger and author of *Facebook Marketing for Dummies,* Dunay was looking to apply the advice he had been giving others as a consultant to a real business case. He thought Avaya could use social tools to better convey its product differentiation message and to respond to what other people were saying.

One of Dunay's key objectives was to focus on conversations rather than audiences. By using social channels, Avaya could more quickly spot issues and opportunities. Twitter would be the key for listening to and resolving issues, as well as finding prospects.

Avaya established a corporate presence in four key social media realms: blogging, forums, Facebook, and Twitter. Dunay assembled a cross-functional, global, and virtual social media team comprised of seven people from communications, marketing, support, legal, and other business units. Since then, this virtual team has grown to number 125 people who monitor social channels as an adjunct to their regular jobs.

The group monitors between 1,000 and 3,000 mentions of the company each week using a combination of TweetDeck and conversation monitoring software Radian6. A team member who "hears" about an issue requiring action posts it on an internal microblogging application called Socialcast. The issue is assigned to an Avaya staffer who has the knowledge and authority to address it.

The tactic paid dividends almost immediately. In June 2009, a team member responded to a 57-character tweet that mentioned Avaya. "Time for a new phone system very soon," the tweet read. Moments after the tweet was posted, an Avaya team member spotted it and notified Dunay, who responded that Avaya was ready to help. Two weeks later, Avaya closed the $250,000 sale.

In late 2009, Dunay proposed a promotion of a 40 percent savings on technical services for new customers. Two hours after the tweet was posted, a government customer responded and the sale was closed early the next quarter. The initiative has also led to several smaller sales.

Today, Avaya operates more than 15 branded Twitter accounts, covering everything from corporate business to support, services, small business, and international accounts. The company also operates 42 Facebook groups, 5 Facebook pages, an external blog with 15 writers, and 12 LinkedIn groups. Inside the firewall, the company operates 14 blogs and numerous wikis.

The initiative has led to higher retention rates, customer satisfaction scores, and profitability, Dunay says. Avaya has also been twice recognized by J.D. Power and Associates for "Providing an Outstanding Customer Experience."

IEEE (LinkedIn)

You can't get much more B2B then the IEEE, which bills itself as "the world's largest professional association dedicated to advancing technological innovation." Formerly called the Institute of Electrical and Electronics Engineers, the group's roots are in engineering and its lifeblood is membership. IEEE spends much of its promotional money on online advertising, because that's where the engineers can be found. When marketers embarked on a pay-per-click campaign in early 2009, they elected to try a targeted promotion on LinkedIn and measured the effect on conversion rates.

LinkedIn was more expensive than Google, but the quality of leads promised to be higher. IEEE was betting that LinkedIn members would be more forthcoming about their identities on LinkedIn than users on other social networks. For this campaign, the target was engineers in technology companies and ads only appeared on pages viewed by members who met that profile.

"The more niche the audience, the better LinkedIn works," says Danielle Leitch, an executive vice president at Peter Nasca Associates, the marketing communications firm that coordinated the campaign.

Results more than justified the higher cost per lead. Two months into the campaign, the conversion rate for visitors from LinkedIn was three times that of other venues, and bounce rates were 10 percent lower. Bounce rates are an important factor in pay-per-click campaigns because advertisers pay for the click and not the conversion. Visitors who click through to the landing page and then leave are wasted money. Bottom line: "The quality of the lead was orders of magnitude better on LinkedIn," Leitch said.

Cree (Video, Contests)

You'd think an ad showing people slumped at their desks, sleeping in chairs, and drooling on the floor would never make it off the drawing board. But for the Cree LED Revolution, workplace lethargy has been just the ticket for getting its point across.

"The LED Lighting Revolution Tackles the Workplace" is a video that underlies an integrated social media campaign that promotes an entire industry. Combined with a blog, Facebook, and Twitter promotion, the program has "far exceeded our expectations," according to Michelle Murray, head of corporate communications at the Durham, North Carolina–based Cree.

Cree is a 23-year-old maker of LED chips that's making a bold move into a new market. The core products that make up more than 80 percent of its business light up the displays of cell phones and cameras. A couple of years ago, the company placed a bet that the same technology could also be used to light homes, offices, and even city streets, yielding huge cost savings. The Cree LED Revolution is all about evangelizing that concept.

The lighting market isn't exactly accustomed to revolution. The last major innovation in the technology was nearly 100 years ago, when fluorescents came on the market, and led, of course, to the more recent growth of compact flourescents. LEDs are starting to get hot (and we mean that figuratively; they actually generate very little heat) because they emit the same number of lumens as an incandescent bulb for less than a quarter of the power.

Cree's current mission is to raise awareness of LED technology's benefits so architects and contractors will start specifying it in residential, commercial, and public engineering contracts. But there's a catch. LEDs are significantly more expensive than convention light bulbs. In late 2009, the company embarked upon a major social media initiative anchored by online video, a photo contest, a blog, real-world stories, and a footprint in multiple social media venues. The idea is that a rising tide of LED adoption will lift all boats, with Cree getting more than its fair share of the business. "My number one marketing message now is that LED lighting is ready, and my number two message is that Cree makes the best LEDs," Murray says.

The dour tone of the "Tackles the Workplace" video, which was created by Shelton Group of Knoxville, Tennessee, was the subject of much debate within the company prior to its rollout last fall. After all, advertising is supposed to be happy. But Cree was trying to make a point: lousy lighting makes the workplace a dreary and sleep-inducing place, which drags down productivity. The video ends with a collage of bright LED alternatives.

"Tackles the Workplace" has one other thing going for it: it's funny. "We thought it would draw attention to the problem," Murray said. It's done that. The video garnered more than 5,000 views with a minimal push in its first six months. Overall, the CreeLEDRevolution.com site averaged a 25 percent increase in monthly unique visitors in the eight months after the video was released. Regularly updated blog content, new case studies, and YouTube videos all helped drive awareness. Cree LED Revolution was subsequently folded into the company's other marketing programs. At a recent trade show,

Cree devoted an entire wall of its booth to a demonstration area, where social media specialist Ginny Skalski showed off the site while a live Twitter stream scrolled by on a flat-screen monitor.

Skalski is the Revolution's eyes and ears in social media. A former newspaper reporter, she joined the company in late 2009 to manage its blog, Twitter, Facebook, and other online outposts. One of her first tasks was to organize a blogger outreach campaign. That drew attention from top lighting bloggers (yes, there are such people) like Jim on Light and conservation blogs like Energy Circle.

Cree's blog covers energy efficiency and the growing use of LED lighting. On Twitter, Skalski is @Cree, delivering a steady stream of updates about the same topics. "I'm a Twitter addict," she says. The Facebook group has more than 1,000 fans.

The web site makes liberal use of digital media. LED lovers can submit photos and videos of their successes. Cree groups these mini–case studies on a map in a manner that dramatizes the spread of the technology across industries and geographies.

Skalski also knows how to handle a video camera herself. At one point she placed one chocolate bunny under a 65W incandescent lamp and another under a 12W LED light, started the camera and filmed the results. Ninety minutes later, the incandescent bunny was a gooey pool while the other rabbit was barely sweating. Two months after that, the experiment had 20,000 views and a dozen embeds on YouTube. Cost after the capital outlay for the camera: about $12 for the chocolate.

The Cree LED Revolution includes another dimension that's uncommon in B2B scenarios: a photo contest. Visitors can submit snapshots of dismal lighting conditions in their home or office and have a chance to win free products. The gallery demonstrates why there's so much potential for LED in the workplace.

Skalski embraces the social media philosophy of one-to-one relationships, and her most memorable stories involve interactions with customers. For one photo contest winner who owns a guitar shop in Sacramento, Skalski arranged to have bonus light fixtures delivered if the man would write a jingle about LED lighting. He did. You can find the song on the site.

Cisco Systems (Simulation Game)

The excitement around virtual worlds has died down considerably since Second Life faded from the spotlight, but Cisco has remained a tireless advocate of simulations as a way to enhance human interaction. With myPlanNet, the company found a way to connect with the young IT professionals who comprise the next generation of network managers in a way that was educational and fun while also reinforcing Cisco's track record of 25 years of leadership in building the modern Internet.

Cisco myPlanNet is a simulation game that puts the player in the role of chief executive officer (CEO) of an Internet service provider. Over time, the player's business grows from a small dial-up provider into a multifaceted technology company spanning broadband, mobile, and collaboration services. The primary target audience is the "young professionals of tomorrow" who are interested in networking technology, as well as current Cisco customers and partners.

"The objective was to create learning opportunities by allowing players to bring services to life and discover Cisco's role in the evolution of the Internet," says Steve Liu, a Cisco marketing manager. "It's an interactive way for young professionals who are entertaining the idea of data networking to see how the Internet was built and what it's preparing them to do."

Conceived as an entry in an internal innovation contest and built on a $200,000 budget that is considered tiny for gaming software, myPlanNet surpassed its download goal within three months and logged more than 30,000 players within the first six months. The related Facebook page had attracted more than 70,000 fans by mid-2010, with players coming from at least 2,500 different companies and 130 countries. In fact, the largest population of players isn't from the United States; it's from Indonesia. Administrators stoked activity with contests, a "CEO quiz," and opportunities to win prizes.

The skunkworks Cisco team that built myPlanNet had to ration its promotion budget carefully, so members invested mainly in word-of-mouth marketing. The $30,000 launch budget was spent on demos, welcome ads, content syndication, and Facebook. A social network based on the Jive platform provides technical support and enables players to swap tips and talk trash to each other.

There are plenty of benefits to Cisco. By watching players' activities and comments, the company has learned about how they prefer to engage with technology and with each other. The program has also been a low-cost way to spread awareness about a company that many of the players may have thought dealt only with chief information officers (CIOs). Media coverage in the *Washington Post,* the *San Francisco Chronicle, NetworkWorld, Computerworld,* and elsewhere was a bonus.

Deloitte Development LLC (Facebook)

"In a highly commoditized business, perhaps our largest differentiator is our people," says William Barrett, global director of online strategy at Deloitte, the global accounting and consulting firm. With 169,000 employees worldwide, Deloitte needs to maintain a pipeline to attract new talent. Deloitte has been on Facebook for a while, but the details of presence had been mainly left up to individual country managers. As a result, by early 2010 its brand had become fragmented. Meanwhile, the Global Facebook Page was "a dormant and rudderless site," Barrett says.

Nevertheless, the 25,000 fans that the company had collected across its far-flung Facebook properties was an underutilized asset. An internal social media committee was formed with representatives from multiple countries. Its purpose was to develop a unified look and feel for all Deloitte-branded pages. The company also made the decision to invest resources to monitor content and address incoming comments. "The global page would function as a first-stop landing page for all those new to Deloitte on Facebook," Barrett says.

The page is now a beehive of activity. Its video library promotes career opportunities and celebrates the company's involvement with highly visible destinations like the World Economic Forum in Davos. One tab features the company's Twitter feed. A gateway page lets visitors easily click through to any one of 18 country-specific pages.

The company even set up a fantasy league for the 2010 World Cup soccer tournament.

Results were immediate and dramatic. Within six months, membership had nearly tripled and career inquiries were coming through the door. "We have also been able to enforce our branding guidelines, resulting in a more unified and consistent Facebook presence for our brand," Barrett says.

CHAPTER ELEVEN

Pick Your Spots: Planning Social Marketing Campaigns

Here's an all-too-common situation we encounter when going in for an initial client consult: the company has been experimenting with various social media platforms for a year or so; it has a blog, a Facebook fan page, a LinkedIn presence, and a couple of Twitter accounts. Marketers had big expectations, but their performance has been underwhelming; the blog gets about one treasured comment per month, Facebook fans topped out at around 90, and Twitter followers are in the low triple digits. The company is frustrated, the marketing director is on the hot seat, and top executives are questioning whether this whole social media thing is just a waste of time.

The time-waster isn't the media, but rather an undisciplined approach to using it. In these cases, the companies have been experimenting, which is a good thing. The barriers to entry for social tools are so low that you should be constantly testing new ideas. Follow up on the promising technologies and quickly discard the ones that don't have much value. However, there is no overarching strategy. The tool has become the goal rather than the means to a goal. Marketers have either bought into the hype because they've been told that social marketing is a panacea or because they're playing a game of Follow the Leader with their competitors.

Social marketing takes discipline to achieve results. Simply showing up and dabbling won't work. Case in point: In a *BtoB* magazine 2010 survey of 387 marketers about their use of Twitter, 54 percent reported posting tweets once a week or less. Among that group, 51 percent indicated they were satisfied with the return on investment (ROI) of Twitter. In contrast, respondents who posted at least once a day reported satisfaction rates 10 points higher. Similarly, respondents with more than 5,000 followers reported a 77 percent satisfaction rate, whereas those with fewer than 500 reported 51 percent satisfaction (see Figure 11.1).

The point is clear: Results come from only frequent and purposeful use of tools. You need a strategy.

"Strategy" is a loaded word in big companies. It implies hours of meetings, months of research, and thick reports that nobody reads. We don't wish that on you. We're talking about a strategy that supports a short-term goal like increasing leads 50 percent in 12 months. It means constant experimentation, revision, and the willingness to discard ideas that aren't working.

This new approach is well summed up in the title of the book *Do It Wrong Quickly* by veteran IBM technologist and marketer Mike Moran. "The way to eventually do it right is to admit that what

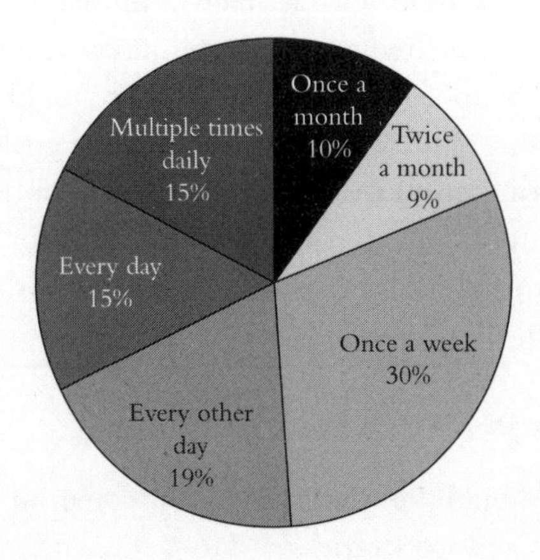

Figure 11.1 How Often Do You Post Tweets?
Source: BtoB magazine.

you are trying right now is probably wrong," he writes in the preface. "We need to accept the fact that our first try will stink on ice, and then we'll start making it better so that it stinks a little bit less each day." When your mistakes aren't expensive or embarrassing, then you won't worry so much about making them. The good news about social marketing is that mistakes are rarely expensive.

Strategy is sorely lacking in most social media programs we've seen. In most cases, clients come to us asking how they can get going on Facebook or Twitter. We tell them that's the wrong question. *Successful social media strategies never presuppose the use of social media.* In fact, we find that in many engagements social media are only a small part of the optimal program. Marketers are often delighted to discover that tactics that they know well, such as media relations, public speaking, and e-mail marketing, often have more utility in achieving their goals than social media. A blog is, after all, is only a tool, and tools are useless unless you know what to do with them.

This idea goes against the grain of American thinking, for we are a nation of gadget lovers. We like nothing better than to glom on to some new electronic bauble and then figure out what to do with it. Of course, a lot of these toys never turn out to have much value at all, unless, of course, you're eBay.

We can't run our businesses that way, though. There are far too many tools out there for anyone to comprehend. Mastering a few is better than being incompetent at many. Although social marketing tools themselves may be free to use, the resources required to use them properly aren't. The tools you choose to master should be the ones that will move you most quickly toward your business goals. Ask any good plumber to describe his toolkit, and he'll tell you in detail what every wrench, cutting tool, and tin of soldering flux is for. Plumbers can't afford to carry around stuff they don't need. Neither should marketers.

A Four-Step Process

Tool selection should be the natural outcome of a process that begins with goals and works backward to tactics and technologies. *The choice of tool should be one of the last decisions you make.* (See Figure 11.2.)

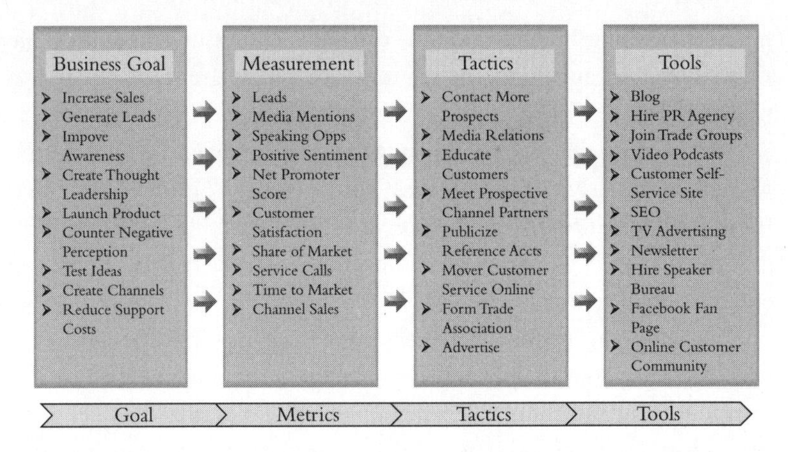

Figure 11.2 Four-Step Process for Social Media Selection.

Most companies we've encountered go about it the opposite way. They jump into blogging or Facebook with the hope that some magic will result. But as the social universe grows more and more crowded, the likelihood of succeeding with this unfocused approach becomes more remote. When you build a house, you start with a plan, create a process, and then choose the construction materials and tools. Doing it the other way around would be crazy. Marketing strategy works the same way.

Why Numbers Matter

A lot of marketers were English majors in college, which isn't surprising given that marketing is a communications-intensive discipline. Unfortunately, the people who allocate marketing budgets were usually accounting majors.

You don't need to know how to read a cash flow statement to succeed in marketing, but it sure helps these days. Too often, the objectives of marketing programs are expressed using vague terms like "improve" or "expand." Plug either of those terms into an Excel formula and you'll get an error message. You have a much better chance of getting budgeted if you can set measurable and achievable goals backed by agreed-upon assumptions about the steps needed to achieve them.

We believe that nearly everything can be measured, although sometimes you have to get creative about tactics. The mere fact that you're measuring results will make your chief financial officer (CFO) smile. In Chapter 14, we share some simple approaches to calculating return on investment.

The four-part process we outline here is big on numbers because that's the language that executive management speaks. It's also big on not letting numbers become a pair of handcuffs. Revise, iterate, and seek cause-and-effect relationships that help you improve future programs. Your CFO will give you credit for making the effort.

The process depicted here is one way to go at the task. Start with the business goal, choose metrics, define tactics, and then select tools at the very end. We've had good luck coaching our clients through this process because it forces them to make their decisions in context. Decisions are a lot less risky if you have a good reason for making them, and this model puts all the reasoning at the front. Let's look at it in more detail.

Business Goal

Start with an objective, and we don't necessarily mean revenue. Goals can range from improving brand awareness to correcting misinformation to generating leads to reducing costs. If achieving the goal involves some kind of communications, there's probably an online dimension to the process, but that may not be social media.

Be specific at this stage. Setting a goal like "increase sales" is too general because there are far too many ways to attack the task. A better goal is "increase sales of left-handed finambulators 50 percent by expanding distribution channels." The more specific you can get at the front, the easier the rest of the process will be. Apply metrics at this stage if you possibly can. Your goals aren't set in stone; they're merely guidelines to use as you work through the process and make adjustments.

Measurement

This is the ugly, contentious, blood-on-the-walls part of the process because it requires stakeholders to agree on what metrics will be used to determine success. Be disciplined; select three or four elements to measure, but no more than that. Remember, you can always change metrics later. The important thing isn't so much to pick the right yardsticks as to make sure everyone agrees on them.

People get unbelievably worked up about metrics, particularly if their job is to deliver leads. That's why it's important that all stakeholders agree on the metrics that matter. Many companies set goals arbitrarily by fiat. People are handed targets that they know they can't achieve, which makes them disillusioned and negative and thus less likely to achieve their goals. In contrast, people work harder to achieve goals that they've agreed are possible.

Don't set measurements by e-mail or wiki or other nonconfrontational tool. The best way to get the job done is to sit people down in a room (it's okay if a few are on a conference call) and let them talk it out. Write the agreed-upon standards on a whiteboard and then distribute the notes to everyone to reconfirm what they agreed to. It's helpful to have a good moderator involved in this process, someone who can see points of alignment and achieve compromises. Otherwise, you can waste a lot of time arguing over details. Also, remember that nothing is set in stone at this point. You can always adjust metrics later with everyone's agreement.

There are lots of great online metrics you can use. Many people still use traffic and page views, which have value, but keywords, bounce rate, time spent on site, pages per visit, and repeat visitors are all better indicators of audience engagement. This is particularly true for business-to-business (B2B) companies, many of which work in very focused industries. The niche company will never have big traffic numbers, so the goal should be to better engage the audience they do have.

Here are a few online metrics you can use, classified by the goals they represent:

Awareness	Engagement	Influence
Page views	Time spent on site	Sentiment analysis
Referring URLs	Bounce rate	Retweets/shares
Inbound links/ Trackbacks	Pages-per-visit	Bloglines/Blogpulse/ Technorati rankings
Unique visitors	RSS subscriptions	Compete/parody videos
Social bookmarks	Comments	Mainstream media endorsements
Search performance	Discussion group posts	Share of online mentions
Web visibility ratings (Compete, Alexa)	Contest entries	Inbound links/Trackbacks
Brand references	Friends/followers	Extended reach[1]
Video viewership	Insite search	Embeds
Mainstream media references	Return visits	Client recommendations

All of these indicators have value in different scenarios, and you should make an effort to understand that value before committing to them. We advise against relying too much on simple numbers like page views and visitors to assess performance. Our friend and colleague Shel Holtz has referred to the oldest web site metric—hits—as an acronym for "how idiots track success." It's easy to manipulate basic metrics to increase traffic temporarily. However, not all traffic is good traffic, and there are plenty of ways to attract "drive-by" visitors who are of no value to you. Third-party referrals and visits from people who spend time on your site and click through to a number of pages are better indicators that your message is hitting home.

Don't get stuck on using online measurements either. It's perfectly okay to count newspaper articles, seminar attendance, speaking invitations, and television impressions as indicators of progress. Remember that we're not seeking a way to apply the Internet; we're seeking a way to reach a business objective. Ultimately, the value of your online social community may be intangible, but it is not without value.

Tactics

This is the fun part. Once you've agreed on the metrics you want to use, it's time to map them to tactics. If you've done your homework on measurement, this stage should be pretty easy. Just remember to align your tactics clearly with the standards you'll use to measure success.

Here are some examples:

Metric	Tactic
Increase white paper downloads 50 percent	Add link to white paper on web site home page Promote download in monthly e-mail newsletter Promote to 10,000-name prospect list Promote through company and employee blogs Promote through Twitter use
Double volume of mainstream media references	Double public relations agencies retainer and targets Secure speaking engagements at four industry trade shows Follow and interact with top 25 targeted journalists on Twitter Launch topical blog in area of media interest
Decrease negative online mentions by 20 percent	Purchase and install conversation monitoring software Assign two staffers to respond to all online comments by e-mail and Twitter Track and report on all contacts with online influencers
Increase channel sales by 30 percent	Make courtesy call to each channel partner in first quarter Launch channel partner newsletter Lower volume discount thresholds Initiate channel blog Launch channel partner community

As you can see in these examples, social channels are only one of several ways to get the message across. Once you select tactics, you can then set priorities based on time, budget, staff resources, and likely impact. You can even create a project chart like the one that follows to help measure the impact of specific promotions on prospect response.

White Paper Promotion Timeline												
Task	**Jan**	**Feb**	**Mar**	**Apr**	**May**	**Jun**	**Jul**	**Aug**	**Sep**	**Oct**	**Nov**	**Dec**
Home page link												
E-mail newsletter												
Promotional e-mail blast												
Blog promotion												
Twitter messaging												

Tools

If you take care of the first three steps in this process, the final one should be obvious. In the last example, the company web site, e-mail newsletter, company blog, employee blogs, and Twitter are the key tools. The biggest questions are tactical: which weapons do you deploy first and how? In general, you want to start with the tactics that are the most familiar to you while coming up to speed on others. However, don't let that approach become an excuse for falling back only to what's comfortable. Every marketing organization should be ramping up with new tools these days, so be sure to work at least one social platform into the mix, if only for the purpose of educating your staff.

Experiment with the mix and deployment schedules of the tools you use. Stagger the rollout of some of the program elements so you can more clearly measure performance. For example, if an e-mail blast consistently triggers a 20 percent rise in visits to a landing page, you may want to schedule an e-mail to coincide with the addition of new content to see if that number changes. Or perhaps you find that combining an e-mail blast with a Twitter promotion yields a bigger boost to your key metrics than using those tools separately. E-mail service provider Infusionsoft has an innovative tactic: Marketers test two different headlines on the same blog entry and tweet each to a different Twitter list at different times of the day. This inexpensive form of A/B testing helps them write more compelling headlines and to identify topics that resonate with customers.

You can also use tools in combination with one another. For example, a new entry to the blog can also be cross-posted to Facebook, LinkedIn, and Twitter. Try staggering those incremental messaging tools as well by inserting a couple of days between each. In other words, post to Facebook on Tuesday, LinkedIn on Thursday, and Twitter the following Monday. This will give you an idea of the lift that each of these tools delivers. If you have multiple Twitter accounts, you can stagger those as well. Through this kind of experimentation, you'll learn what kind of lift you get from each channel. This enables you to make smarter decisions about combining them in the future.

This four-step process is by no means the only approach you can take to tools selection. A colleague of ours counsels his clients to switch the two steps in the middle so that tactics are selected before metrics. That's okay, too. What's critical is to always start with goals and make tool selection the final stage of a logical progression.

Process in Practice

Let's look at how the four-step process was used in a real-life scenario with a B2B client that sells parts used on large manufacturing lines. The company had recently introduced a new product to a market in which it had not previously been a major player. The product was selling slowly because of the company's poor name recognition in that industry. The product team was charged with increasing full-year sales of the product by 50 percent, but that goal was too broad to be actionable. We had to narrow the objective enough to permit us to select a limited domain of metrics.

Teasing out the opportunities, the product team settled on marketing to a group of influencers who don't actually buy the product but whose opinions can carry enormous influence. They are the process designers who work with manufacturing companies on setting up complex systems. These people are very knowledgeable about the technologies needed to implement their designs.

The team believed that the company's mind share with these designers was a weakness; they estimated that only about 10 percent of these professionals were even aware that the company had products in this market. If they could tap into this influential group, they could make significant progress toward the overall 50 percent growth goal.

Little was known about the target audience, but the team agreed that if it could double the size of its prospect list, it would consider the project a success. Remember that the goal at this stage was not to find the *perfect* metric, but to identify targets that the entire team could agree on.

Leads would be captured through white paper downloads, e-mail newsletter subscriptions, and "send me more information" appeals on the web site. Doubling the size of the existing mailing list of about 2,500 people would require attracting about 50,000 visitors to a web page over the course of the next year, assuming a 5 percent click-through rate to a registration form. Web traffic should grow steadily when backed by the right promotion and search optimization techniques, so the team estimated that a progression like the one depicted in Figure 11.3 was reasonable.

Creating awareness also meant building a presence in offline media, including trade publications and events. No hard metrics were available to correlate such activities to web traffic, but the team believed a goal of six mentions in prominent trade publications and four speaking appearances were achievable during the next year.

So now we have our three metrics in place:

1. 50,000 web site visitors in defined quarterly stages
2. 2,500 e-mail registrations
3. Six trade press mentions combined with four speaking opportunities

It was time for tactics.

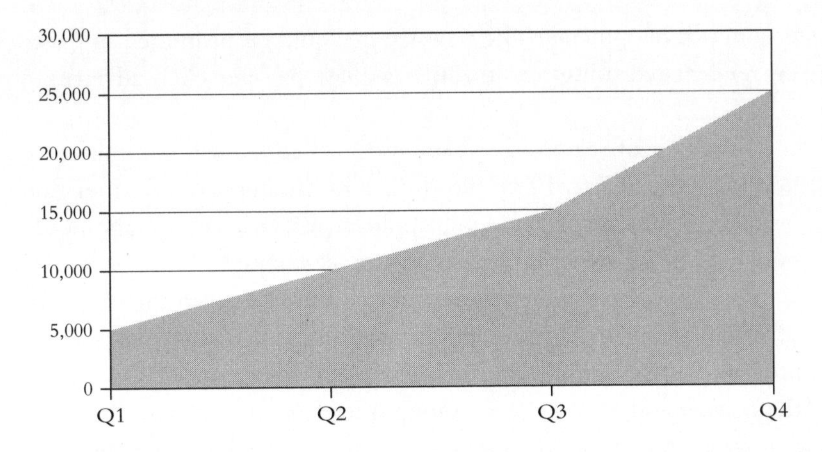

Figure 11.3 Projected Web Site Traffic Growth.

The company had little brand awareness with the target audience, so we came up with the idea of a survey. Research is a great multifaceted marketing tool, because it builds awareness with the audience being researched while also delivering insight on the group's interests and potentially even a few nuggets of news that could be shared with the media.

The first step would be to build a page on the corporate site that was targeted specifically to the designer audience. This would consist of helpful content provided by product developers and marketers, along with links to interesting information from other sources. The team resolved to reach out to bloggers who write about process control (yes, they are out there!) and ask to syndicate some content from their blogs. This would have the ancillary benefit of building awareness with that audience while creating inbound links that would drive search traffic. The team would also commission two white papers from freelance writers with expertise in this area and make those content assets available as free downloads to visitors who filled out a short registration form. Traffic would be driven by existing communications, word of mouth, and e-mail blasts to two 10,000-name mailing lists rented from a leading industry publication.

Finally, the company would launch a monthly newsletter aimed at the designer audience. Content would consist primarily of articles from employees and bloggers. It would also feature updates on new product developments. The newsletter would be promoted in existing print advertising and through a pilot pay-per-click advertising program.

Speaking of search, the team also created a small committee to develop a list of 7 to 10 keywords that would improve search engine visibility. These terms would be applied across the site to tags, headlines, and other areas that search engines care about.

Finally, the public relations agency would be given the objective of reaching out to industry publications with bylined articles about process control. This would help establish that the company was in the market and develop some thought leadership. The agency would also research and propose speakers at relevant industry conferences.

Now our four-step process was complete with a priority list that looks like Figure 11.4. It turned out that only a few social media tools were appropriate. Much of the work related to conventional web site development, public relations, and blogger outreach. The team planned to convene every three months to review progress. At those meetings, everything would be open for discussion. They could revise their goals, change their standards of measurement completely,

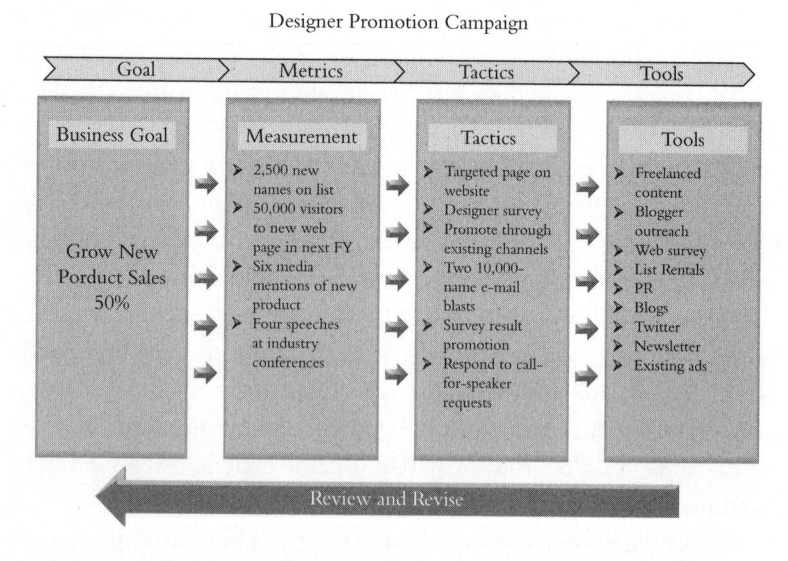

Figure 11.4 Designer Promotion.

or stay the course. As long as they agreed on goals and metrics, everything else should fall into place.

The four-step process may seem clumsy and time-consuming at first, but as you become comfortable with it, you will quickly learn to apply it to simplify selection of all the tools you use, whether or not they include social media. Just remember to start with the business goal. It makes the rest of the process much easier.

CHAPTER TWELVE

Lead Generation

Indium Corporation's web site proudly proclaims that the company is "Obsessed with Solder Paste." That statement links to a series of videos that show, among other things, a young girl receiving a can of flux from her adoring father as a Christmas present and unceremoniously tossing it into a box of similar gifts she has clearly received from dad in the past.

The father in these videos is Rick Short, Marcom Director at Indium, a maker of specialty alloys and solders based in Utica, New York. Audiences often snicker when they hear about Indium's business. What could be more prosaic than fusible alloy? But it's the specialized nature of Indium's business that makes the 500-employee company's market so lucrative. There aren't many people who care about dipping paste and wave solder, which are essential to the manufacture of the circuit boards that go in everything from cell phones to jet aircraft. Those who do care, though, buy it by the truckload. Rick Short's job is to find those major accounts.

In 2009, Indium came up with the innovative idea of using blogs to drive search visibility and generate leads. The strategy was, in Short's words, "Convert content to contacts to cash." Marketers assumed that problem solving these days usually starts with a search engine. By launching multiple blogs tuned to the search terms engineers were likely to use, Indium could quickly climb the Google ladder in topic areas where there was little competition.

Marketers and business executives narrowed the domain down to about 85 terms and began building blogs with titles like "Copper

Indium Gallium" and "Pop Solder Paste." The company enlisted staff volunteers to start writing entries about those topics using a defined set of keywords. In the end, Indium settled on 73 blogs crafted by 17 authors. Entries are cross-posted to multiple topical blogs as well as to a master corporate blog. The idea is to grab visitors' attention in a context in which they're most likely to make a buying decision.

The Indium bloggers, most of whom are engineers or product managers, deliver wisdom under the theme "From One Engineer to Another." Visitors can register to download related white papers or get customized answers to their questions from Indium experts. Those requests become leads, but they also yield insight about what brought the visitor to the web site in the first place. "When they download a white paper, they're ultra-specific and we know a ton about them," Short says.

The results: Between the second and third quarters of 2009, incoming contacts grew sixfold, with the majority of those referrals coming from the blogs. What's more, Indium's head of sales reported that blog-driven leads were better qualified prospects because the audience was focused and usually under pressure to solve a problem. In fact, prospects often welcomed the call from the Indium salesperson because it addressed an immediate concern.

Short isn't surprised by the program's success. Engineers like to engage with others who share their professional interests, and it's well known that an engineer's career success is enhanced by an active schedule of speaking and publishing. Blogs can be an easy way to build professional credibility. Engineers also like interacting directly with their peers. That's why Indium's strategy is to remove sales and marketing from the front of the conversation and to let business flow naturally from the knowledge-sharing process. "We strive to get engineers talking to engineers and get everyone else out of the middle," he says.

Get the Lead Out

Qualified lead generation is the most common business-to-business (B2B) marketing objective and the standard by which most attempts are measured. Lead generation has also spawned entire markets: vendors in the $10 billion+ global customer relationship management (CRM) industry compete over who can best manage leads, while B2B publishers, who are in desperate straits, are furiously repositioning themselves as lead-generation engines.

In sharp contrast to traditional outbound marketing tactics, U.S.-based B2B marketers say the most effective way to generate leads on social networks is by seeking out and participating in relevant conversations, according to a study by marketing automation vendor DemandGen. B2B marketers have always done this through trade shows, sales calls, and public relations. Those channels were expensive, however. Social networks and search can deliver much of the same benefit at far lower cost.

The art and science of lead generation has been transformed by search engines, which introduced the dynamic of self-selection. Traditional outbound marketing relied on scattershot techniques like advertising, direct mail, and events to attract prospects, but a new discipline that search marketer HubSpot calls "inbound marketing" aims to generate leads from actions that indicate a buyer is ready to make a decision. These can be in the form of search results, tweets, and other peer references. There is no need to interrupt buyers because they choose providers when they're ready to buy.

Savvy B2B marketers try to anticipate a prospect's needs and place messages that will reach people at each stage of the buying process (see Figure 12.1). The goal is to get in front of qualified buyers when they're making a purchasing decision. This approach can be far more productive than traditional advertising and direct mail, which rely on reach and frequency to hit the buyer at the right time. The Internet is persistent and always searchable. Success is more a function of actual product demand than chance.

Today, "It's entirely possible to build a community to draw those potential leads to you by having the right location, the right mix of tools and the right content to attract the right folks," wrote Paul Greenberg in *CRM at the Speed of Light,* Fourth Edition.

But this change of direction requires a change in mind-set, one that is far more dependent on listening than talking. Traditional marketing

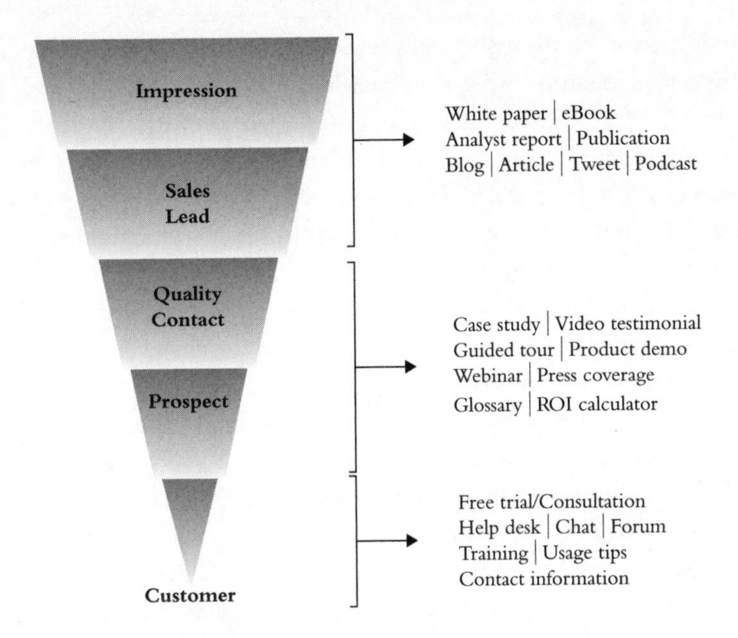

Figure 12.1 Content Along the Buying Cycle.
Source: Nowspeed Marketing, Inc.

presented a clear cause-and-effect scenario: a campaign delivered a measurable number of prospects within a defined period, which made performance reasonably easy to measure. Social marketing, though, builds on relationships and dialogs that may not generate results for months or even years. Search engines care less about time than they do about relevance, so the blog entry you posted back in 2007 may draw a qualified lead today if the content is still on the mark. This archival quality is one reason social marketing is difficult to measure. The impact is cumulative and effectiveness improves with time and persistence.

Despite these shortcomings, inbound marketing has yielded some notable lead-generation success stories. One of them is EmployeeScreen, a Cleveland-based services company that does employee background checks. Its market includes more than 1,000 competitors, many of them specialized boutiques. Gaining visibility is a constant challenge. EmployeeScreen has thrived, however, due in part to a diversified set of social media programs that deliver education and insight.

A section of the company's web site, dubbed "EmployeeScreen University," features scores of articles, white papers, and podcast interviews that step human resources (HR) pros through the legal and practical issues of hiring and employment law. The university actually began as a search optimization project. Managers were pleased to discover that they were able to climb into the top 10 Google results for some key terms within just a few months by posting topical articles on a company blog. A little creative packaging transformed posts into a curriculum.

Between 5,000 and 7,000 people visit EmployeeScreen University each month. One quarter of them click through to the business web site, delivering a constant stream of leads. The value of such organic traffic "is far greater than traditional advertising," says chief marketing officer (CMO) Nick Fishman.

The success has enabled EmployeeScreen to reduce its dependence on advertising and to engage with prospects at a deeper level. It's also demonstrated a greater truth, says Fishman. "One small guy can make very big waves."

The Social Funnel

Social marketing requires a complete inversion of conventional tactics. The focus must be on the buying process rather than the sales cycle. Traditional marketing is push; social marketing is pull. Traditional marketing is message; social marketing is conversation. Leads may come quickly, particularly when a buyer is toward the end of the buying process and a solution is matched to the right keywords, but they may also require lengthy cultivation and a lot of giving on the seller's part as he leads an early-stage buyer carefully toward a decision.

Social marketing also shifts more responsibility for managing leads up the funnel. "A lot of the sales cycle has moved back into marketing," observes Jeff Ogden, a technology marketing veteran who now runs Find New Customers, a lead-generation consultancy. He notes that the sales organization has traditionally played an important educational role in customer engagements, but "now prospects look up information online and avoid contact with sales people." Marketing is usually the department that curates that information. If you buy Ogden's premise, marketers should be growing their budgets at the expense of sales departments.

The B2B buying process is typically thought to consist of between five and nine stages, beginning with recognition of need and leading to conversion. Sellers need to start one step earlier than the recognition stage by first figuring out who has the need so that content can be pegged to individuals rather than the broad needs of an entire market. Each stage demands a different social marketing strategy. The traditional tools of marketing are still valid and effective, but they are being complemented of by a new breed of online channels that present new alternatives for engaging and sustaining relationships. Barbara Bix of BB Marketing Plus, a Massachusetts-based B2B marketing consulting firm, believes that the buying process and marketing strategy have not changed fundamentally but that the implementation has. Success depends on listening to small groups directly rather than segmenting large markets.

Stage in Buying Process	Traditional Media Tools	Social Media Tools
Has need	Database analysis Interview	Search analysis Twitter Online communities
Recognize need	Public relations (PR) Speaking placements Case studies	Blogging Word-of-mouth marketing Search analysis
Establish urgency	Direct marketing Offers Publicize competitors' activity	Twitter Postings to forums Blogging case studies Search marketing
Create company awareness	Advertising/PR/sponsorship	Blogging/Twitter Online product placements in YouTube and other venues "Share This" widgets
Create product awareness	Direct marketing	Blogging/Twitter Search engine optimization (SEO)

(*Continued*)

(*continued*)

Stage in Buying Process	Traditional Media Tools	Social Media Tools
Maintain visibility	Direct marketing PR White papers Reprints	Messaging to follower/friend lists Blogging Informational webcasts
Have the right product	Market research Focus groups Prototyping Usability testing	Social media monitoring Customer communities Crowdsourcing Open beta/usability testing
Make it easy to buy	Toll-free number One-click ordering	Twitter Widgets Affiliate marketing
Continue relationship	Newsletters Events	Blogging Twitter Customer communities Affiliate programs

Experts agree on a few key success factors that are common to every stage, which are discussed next.

Content is king.

The way to attract visitors and followers and to make connections is by providing useful information. That means resisting the urge to sell and focusing instead on delivering genuine value, even if it means recommending a lower-cost or competitive solution. It also means giving away expertise that you may have sold or kept secret in the past. There is really no choice, though. Buyers are flooded with information. They gravitate to those vendors that offer the most value before the sale is made. If scarcity is not an issue, they also freely share the advice they receive with each other. In the past, we might have called this stealing, but "Today's business model requires that people steal your content in order for you to be successful," says Maggie Fox, chief executive officer (CEO) of Toronto-based Social Media Group.

Quality content and search engine performance go hand in hand. Search engines are programmed to deliver results that their complex algorithms determine to be useful. That's why magazine articles, blogs, and Wikipedia entries float to the top of Google pages while product listings and catalogs sink. As of this writing, if you type "personal computer" into Google, the organic search results yield 19 definitions and news articles before the first vendor product page. Good content also tends to find audiences, which spread the word with very little intervention on the creator's part.

Sales-speak is death.

Useful content is that which addresses customer needs in as helpful and impartial a manner as possible. Sales pitches don't go over well online, particularly with knowledgeable B2B buyers. Customers are enjoying their new market influence and their freedom to associate with one another. They respond with disdain or even hostility to messages that are cloaked as advice. "An online interaction that morphs into a sales pitch is likely to send all but your latest-stage leads running in the other direction," writes Ardath Albee in *The Essential Marketing Automation Handbook*. People want to hear from others like themselves. Ask questions, but without the type of solicitous phrasing we've come to expect in advertising.

Span the buying cycle.

This step is particularly important for B2B marketers because prospects enter the funnel at different stages of the buying process. Share your expertise far and wide, using the keywords that customers use, and create a portfolio of content that meets the needs of different kinds of prospects. Build a library of content that matches buyer interests at each stage, and use intelligence gleaned from your web analytics to position individual items appropriately. For example, a visitor who arrives on your web site by searching for your company name is probably much farther down the sales funnel than one who arrives from searching a more general industry term. The content premiums they find on that landing page should match their stage in the funnel.

Success takes time.

Search visibility is unquestionably enhanced with age and volume. The more content you publish and the more frequently you publish it, the more search visibility you achieve. This means adopting new expectations of success. Your blogging "campaign" will pay few dividends during the first six months but will provide handsome returns after a year, if you post useful content frequently. Once you reach a critical mass of content and search performance, traffic becomes almost self-sustaining. In community settings, the tipping point arrives when participants begin creating and sustaining their own conversations without prompting.

Search Traffic

Search is the great equalizer of social marketing, and Google is the universal home page. If Google ranks your web site highly, it almost doesn't matter how big your competitor's marketing budget is. In fact, successful search marketing programs can quickly pay for themselves through cost savings on traditional channels. "Our hope of competing in any way with SAP and Oracle depends on our keyword performance," says Kirsten Watson, director of corporate marketing at Kinaxis, a small software company that has used social programs to gain a foothold in what many people thought was an inaccessible market.

Search engine optimization (SEO) is a huge topic that fills books larger than this one. It involves the strategic use of keywords, page titles, tags, headlines, and other textual components combined with inbound links from credible sources. We provided a quick primer on this topic in Chapter 7. If you want to know more, pick up *Inbound Marketing* by Brian Halligan and Dharmesh Shah for an introduction and *Search Engine Marketing, Inc.* by Mike Moran and Bill Hunt for a deeper dive. Search engines typically deliver 20 to 40 percent of a business web site's traffic, which can be of high quality if the terms are matched to a buying decision.

You'll want to handle incoming traffic differently, depending on whether it's driven by search or links. In the case of search results, there are three important pieces of information you need to know: search terms, entry pages, and bounce rates.

The *search term* tells you what keywords are bringing people to your site. Chances are that a small number of keywords are driving most of your traffic. Double down on these words. Make sure you use them on every relevant page (and we stress relevant; inserting successful keywords into places they don't belong frustrates visitors), include them in page titles, and list them in meta tags. Also look for opportunities to include them in press releases, product names and other official company information. Maximize the visibility of your site to the search engines for these important terms.

Most people don't arrive at your site via the home page. They search Google and come to whatever page has the information for which they're looking. The point of entry is called the *entry page,* and your web statistics will show you which ones are most popular. Study your top entry pages carefully because they're the ones that are working. Use them as indicators of what type of content is pulling best with your audience. Apply what you learn to your other pages, but more importantly, maximize the opportunity of these high-traffic web pages to establish a persistent connection with the visitor through e-mail, RSS, Twitter, or Facebook. Offer invitations to subscribe to newsletters, attend webcasts, download white papers, and follow you on Twitter. Use content premiums like white papers and sample downloads to match the likely stage of the visitor in the buying cycle.

Bounce rate is the percentage of visitors that land on a page and leave without exploring further. While a high bounce rate is fine in some situations, you want this number to be as low as possible for lead gen purposes because this is the percentage of people who are probably unfulfilled by your web site. Whatever it is they think they're going there for, they don't seem to be finding it.

Experiment with tactics like links to related content or downloads to draw visitors deeper into your site. Duplicate whatever works to other popular entry pages.

Link Traffic

For links coming in from other sources, you need a different strategy because you're trying to understand motivations of a human who posted the link rather than of a machine. Look at these factors:

A *referral link* is a link that sends traffic to you from somewhere else on the Internet. You want to know where this link lives and why it's linking to you. The author may be a potential ally or adversary. Find out by looking at the *anchor text,* or the blue underlined text that contains the link. It tells you why people are visiting and the reasons can very greatly. For example, the anchor text "world's greatest tool company" will bring a completely different kind of visitor than "avoid this tool company." Knowing why a visitor arrives is critical to knowing what message to craft.

Another metric to understand is *bounce rate.* This can be a tricky factor in evaluating inbound links because if the link describes your content incorrectly, your bounce rate may be high, and there's little you can do about it. You want to know of any terms that yield a low bounce rate, though. These are the ones that engage visitors and keep them clicking through to other areas of your site. They're probably important to your search optimization strategy. At the very least, they tell you how others describe you.

What's the Diff?

The difference between search and web site links is that you must build influence with web site owners to see results. People who generate a lot of inbound traffic to your site may be as valuable as paying customers, even if they buy nothing. Companies in the building trades will tell you that even though architects don't buy their products, they are more important than the contractors who pay the bills because architects specify vendors and brands. Many companies are now incorporating influencer relations programs into their marketing and public relations efforts. SAP, for example, has an active program to nurture relationships with technology and business bloggers. The software giant even hosts an annual conference for them. Research determined that "the combined channels that the industry and influencer relations team manages has a $40 billion impact on purchase decisions worldwide," says Don Bullmer, vice president of global communications at the software giant. As the information technology (IT) trade media has waned, influencers have acquired even more weight at SAP.

Influencer programs attempt to build awareness by encouraging referrals from people who are respected authorities in their communities. You can't control what these people say, of course, but you can bring them into the loop, which almost always improves relationships. The currency of influencer programs is information, not money. By conferring insider status on these influential people, you give them the opportunity to raise their status and visibility in their own communities. Although we believe online influencers should be treated the same as media contacts, the nature of the engagement is more along the lines of grassroots community relations than press relations. They may not know an "exclusive" from an "embargo," but bloggers are more likely than reporters to be experts in your product or category and to have a deep level of technical knowledge. They're also more likely to be collegial than competitive. While reporters tend to be driven by scoops, bloggers are motivated by understanding. They're more inclined to share with each other so that everyone understands an issue better. Be prepared to marshal your internal domain experts to respond to their challenging questions.

Of course, you can also generate your own inbound links. Traffic from LinkedIn Groups to which you belong, comments on other blog posts, visual essays on SlideShare, and links posted on Facebook can be useful resources for testing messages and building traffic. Apply the same discipline to your own links that you would to those created by others.

Test different variations of anchor text to see what performs best. Use this insight to fine-tune all the links you post on external sources.

Lead Management

Once a prospect is in your sales funnel, the task turns to qualifying, scoring, and nurturing the lead. The first two processes involve assessing each person's ability to buy and the urgency of the decision. Nurturing is about guiding prospects down the decision path so that they reach their own conclusions and are more invested.

All three tasks can be tackled together. If you nurture leads properly with content premiums like worksheets, white papers, and webcasts that match their stage in the buying cycle, you can qualify and score them at the same time. For example, a visitor who downloads a white paper about your industry is at an earlier stage in the cycle than one who uses your return on investment (ROI) calculator. This yields important insight into the buyer's interests and the urgency of his or her decision.

The tools that marketers have at their disposal during the nurturing process have changed little over the past few years. They include webcasts, white papers, free trials, analyst reports, specification sheets, ROI calculators, and case studies. What has changed is our ability to self publish this content and match it to buyer profiles.

Just 5 years ago, marketers had limited capacity to match content to intent and thus were forced to resort to long qualification forms to understand their prospects. We all hate filling out those multiscreen web forms. The historically high abandonment rates for webinar registrations testifies to their inefficiency. Today, you can learn much about prospective customers from the type of content that they consume and, in turn, avoid annoying them with questions. However, this requires you to understand content and integrate information about prospecting it into back-end CRM systems. It also means communicating this information to your sales force.

Figure 12.2 shows an example of what a content-driven interaction might look like.

We can safely assume that this person should go to the top of your prospect list. Without giving us anything more than an e-mail address

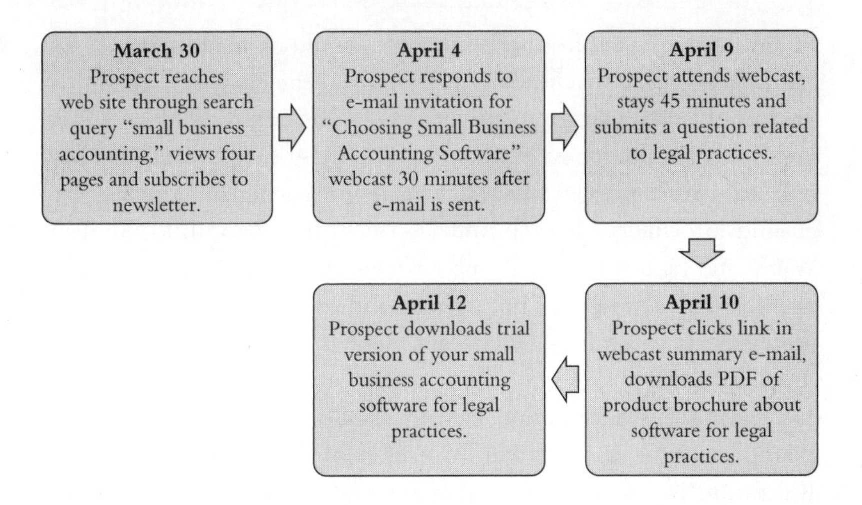

Figure 12.2 Prospect Flow Chart.

(we assume the user's browser accepts cookies so we can track activity beyond the first visit), the prospect has told us that he or she:

- Probably works for a law firm.
- Is highly interested in the topic and feels some urgency about making a decision. This is indicated by the speed of response to the webcast promotion, attentiveness during the webinar, and frequency of web site visits.
- Is late in the buying cycle, judging by post-webcast activity.
- Has a high level of interest in your product, judging by the large amount of information collected and the download of the free trial.

If you were able to capture any more information, perhaps during the webinar registration, you could research this prospect even further. For example, a personal or company name might unearth a web site or Twitter account with valuable background information. It may also point to the prospect's profile on LinkedIn. If you use LinkedIn's premium services, you can generate leads by sending messages directly to other users. Following that reasoning a little further, you may discover that the person heads the Denver chapter of a professional association. This makes the prospect a particularly valuable lead, because a group leaders is in a position to influence others.

Whoever is sent in to close the sale should be made aware of this information. But that doesn't necessarily mean that the rep should disclose that knowledge to the prospect. The creepiness factor is an important consideration in sales contacts these days because it's possible to scare a prospect away if you reveal having too much background knowledge. People-finder services like ZoomInfo, Spokeo, Wink, and Jigsaw, which assemble background and contact information through a variety of both public and private means, enable sales professionals to compile an unprecedented amount of information about prospects.

Having this information in your back pocket can be useful. For example, if you discover that a member of the Denver professional association is one of your customers, you could use that information to drop a name during a conversation with the prospect. If the prospect is active online, postings in blogs and forums might give you insight into other opportunities in the company. LinkedIn company profiles reveal common connections you may have or names of other prospects within the company.

However, be judicious in how much of this information you reveal. There can be a fine line between prospecting and stalking, and most customers don't want to be isolated in making a decision. "One-to-one marketing was supposed to be the holy grail of customer relationship management. The problem is that we are hyper-social beings who prefer to operate within our tribes," write Francois Gossieaux and Ed Moran in their 2010 book *The Hyper-Social Organization*. "We do not want to be isolated from our group so that salespeople who know more about us than we feel comfortable with can give us the hard sell."

Prospecting 2.0

Up until now we've focused mainly on inbound prospecting, which is about building content that attracts people who are looking for solutions. However, social media has also revolutionized traditional prospecting. People use online channels to post requests for information or share frustrations with products they're now using. These mini–requests for information are a veritable treasure trove of new business.

The tools and tactics you use for outbound marketing are very different from the ones we just discussed. Primarily, they consist of listening. In Chapter 6, we provided guidance on how to build a listening dashboard.

Blogs are considered the most effective social network for B2B prospecting, followed by LinkedIn, then Facebook, then Twitter, with YouTube coming in last, according to a *B-to-B* magazine survey. (Figure 12.3).

On a cost-per-interaction basis, Twitter is definitely the the mother lode of prospecting because it is so easy to use. Create a complex search query at search.twitter.com along the lines of a Google query, but also search for additional terms like "anybody know," "looking for," and "recommend," which match the type of casual terms people use to tweet for advice. We tried a Twitter search on the phrase "does anyone know" followed by an assortment of product categories and found requests for advice on printers, e-mail service providers, consultants, trainers, and accounting software packages.

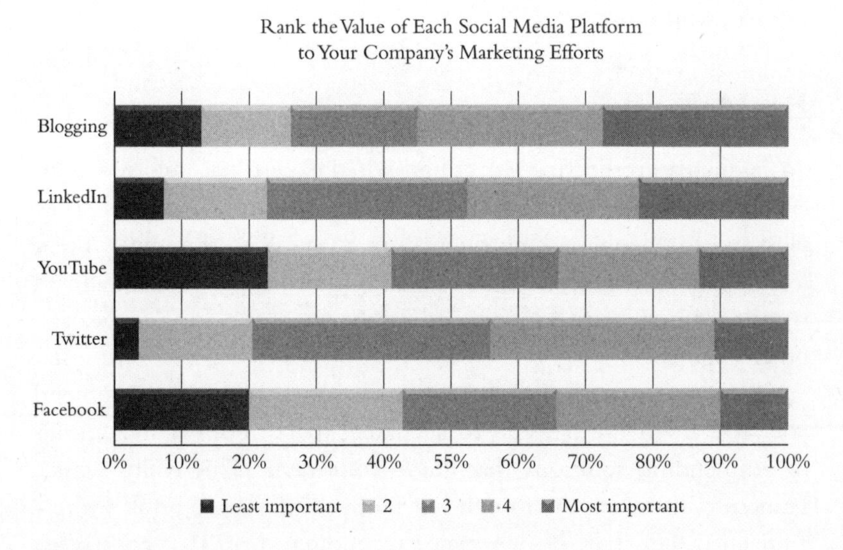

Figure 12.3 Rank the Value of Each Platform.

Source: B-to-B magazine.

Save your searches as RSS feeds so that every time you open your feed reader, they're updated with the latest information. You can also try a Twitter list site like Listorious or TweepML to look for people in industries or professions that matter to you. There are hundreds of lists of tweeting lawyers, for example.

LinkedIn groups, LinkedIn Answers, discussion boards, and Yahoo! Answers can also yield prospects. We tried searching the Boardreader forum search engine for the phrase "does anyone know" followed by "lawyer" and came up with nearly 750 requests over the past 3 months.

Reaching out to questioners requires a light touch. Often it's best simply to answer the question, create a follower, and lay the groundwork for further conversation. If you think the solution is your product, follow that user and invite him or her to send you a direct message so you can set up a phone call. Keep your public persona helpful and save the sales pitch for the one-on-one. "LinkedIn Answers are a great way for you to demonstrate your interests, expertise and problem-solving capabilities to entire networks of people, which can indirectly drive interest in your company and new business," wrote marketing automation firm Marketo in its "Definitive Guide to B2B Social Media" workbook.

Be Helpful

Social media prospecting works best when experts get involved. This is particularly true in technical areas where questions are often complex and the people asking them want to speak to the gurus. Look for the natural communicators in the ranks of your technical staff and recruit them to help. As we noted earlier, engineers love to speak to other engineers.

Experts are your best brand ambassadors, but we recommend you give them the latitude to act like experts, even if that means recommending solutions that aren't your own. This really works. Francois Gossieaux, the founder of Human 1.0 whose book we referenced earlier, tells of one major technology firm that contracted with two database management experts to monitor online forums and help solve problems. The experts were instructed to recommend any products they thought were right for the job, even if the products came from competitors. It didn't matter that other companies may have picked up some incremental business from this activity; within 3 months, the two experts had built so much credibility that they were the single largest generator of new leads for the contractor.

Marketo, a marketing automation software company founded in 2006, does this really well. In growing from a few founders to a staff of more than 100 in a generally abysmal business climate, it has demonstrated the power of being helpful. "Content is how you market in today's B2B world," says Jon Miller, a Marketo co-founder. Marketo practices what it preaches and it packages creatively. For example, the company partnered with JellyVision, maker of the popular "You Don't Know Jack" trivia game, for "You Don't Know Jack About Online Marketing," a fast-paced and fun takeoff that gently reminds players of what they still need to learn about their discipline. And, by the way, Marketo can help.

It favors easy-to-read e-books over often ponderous white papers. Multifaceted resources called "kits" combine already available content like blog entries and checklists into one downloadable unit. "Cheat sheets" are tip lists that the company prints and laminates for distribution at trade shows. "They go like hotcakes," Miller says. The B2B Sales and Marketing Book Club is a minor stroke of genius. Authors donate sample chapters for free download in exchange for visibility. "We probably have more people dedicated to content than any other company of our size," Miller says.

Another of our favorite examples of a "be-helpful" strategy is Clickable, a New York–based search engine marketing firm. Facing a crowded market and a weak economy in 2008, the fledgling company recruited several of its experts to go forth and answer questions posted online by the company's target audience of search advertisers, small and mid-sized business owners and agencies. They did so in the communities and forums those prospects were already using, inviting people back to the Clickable site only when appropriate. This group, which came to be known as the Clickable Gurus, was given nine core principles to uphold. Note that none of them mention selling:

Clickable Gurus' Core Principles

1. Be a trusted advisor.
2. Engage authentically.
3. Maintain a steady rhythm of good deeds.
4. Help marketers at all skill levels.
5. Offer simple solutions and objective advice.
6. Use real, personal profiles.
7. Always disclose affiliation with Clickable.
8. Never shill, but welcome newcomers to Clickable when appropriate.
9. Channel learning to help improve Clickable.

Clickable used the information these experts gathered and dispensed in several ways. Their advice was used to populate discussion topics in the company's forums and captured in regular blog entries. The Gurus also became valuable internal sources of advice on Clickable's products and strategy. The experts clearly identified their company affiliation in public forums, both to promote transparency and to drive brand awareness.

For Clickable, the program was a gusher of new business. Within a year, the Gurus and the community platform were generating more than half of all new customers, leading to a 400 percent increase in new monthly billable advertising. Monthly visitors to Clickable.com jumped from less than 5,000 in July 2008 to nearly 100,000 a year later.

The idea of giving away expertise for free may sound counter-intuitive, but in the information-saturated world of web 2.0, it's the only way to attract attention. In their 2009 book *Trust Agents,* Chris Brogan and Julien Smith repeatedly emphasize this point. "Being helpful in full view of others helps guide you into being a trust agent, and that gives you the opportunity to do more business," they wrote. "Unlike conspicuously making an effort to be nice because other people will see, the Web just displays it naturally, because everything is in public view. Being helpful becomes not only a great thing to do, but also a good strategic move." The social web just naturally rewards generosity. It turns customer service into public relations.

When you think of it, being helpful is the essence of good human relationships. A couple of years ago, Paul needed repairs to a clothes dryer that wasn't drying. He called a local sales and service organization ready to write a check for $300 but was surprised when the technician on the phone offered to walk him through the process of fixing the machine himself. That small business has since received every dollar Paul has spent on appliances. It seems that trust isn't just common sense; it's pretty good business practice, too.

PROSPECTING WITH TWEETS

Boutique digital marketing agency Soweb Inc. has an innovative approach to using Twitter to generate sales leads. The Ft. Lauderdale–based firm treats new Twitter followers as prospects and applies an informal discovery process to qualify them. Sales reps examine the profiles of new followers and conduct web searches to see if they are potential clients. If so, their activity is monitored in a special tweet stream.

When prospects tweet about topics that could generate business for Soweb, sales reps respond with links to helpful advice. The agency follows the Twitter guideline known as the "70:20:10 rule"; 70 percent of its tweets link to external sources unrelated to the company, 20 percent are about personal or nonbusiness issues, and the other 10 percent are promotional. It's considered obnoxious to aggressively promote yourself on Twitter.

"Companies don't like to be sold to," says principal Ernesto Sosa. "We deliver value with the goal of encouraging followers to seek more information and contact us directly." As relationships grow, so does Soweb's opportunity to pitch for new business at the appropriate time. The company generates 15 percent of its new business through Twitter, so the strategy is working.

The firm also takes advantage of an optional Twitter feature that enables users to reveal their location. Prospects in southern Florida are considered especially attractive, so nearby followers get special attention.

Soweb's Twitter following is a modest 1,400, but Sosa says lead generation on Twitter doesn't have to be a numbers game. "You need clearly defined goals, processes, responsibilities and metrics," he says. "Have tight collaboration between your marketing and sales people. And be patient."

CHAPTER THIRTEEN

Profiting from Communities

Spiceworks is very good at managing business-to-business (B2B) communities online. It has to be; community is central to its business.

Spiceworks is a media company that acts like a technology company. Its namesake product is a sophisticated network management suite for small and medium businesses (SMB) that it gives away for free. The SMB market is coveted by technology firms, and many of them pay Spiceworks for the chance to interact with its audience of more than 1 million information technology (IT) professionals for programs ranging from market research to product design.

Spiceworks sells advertising space on its software console, which members use to monitor their networks. IT professionals share tips and tricks, review products, and upload video tutorials. As the community grows, so does the value of the social network as a resource to all involved. Members have posted more than 20,000 product reviews and created hundreds of discussion groups. Their technical questions are now routinely answered within minutes. More than 400 people recently self-organized a buyer's group to get better deals on backup software.

The Spiceworks community spreads beyond the web site. As of this writing, nearly 20 regional user groups called SpiceCorps have sprung up around the North America and others are forming overseas. An annual user conference attracts thousands. Conversations long ago expanded beyond troubleshooting and now encompass product reviews, career advice, and swap meets for software utilities. There's even a long-running thread called "What Is the Funniest Thing a User Has Asked You?" It started in October 2008 and has attracted more than 700 contributions 18 months later.

Essential Utility

Spiceworks represents the best of what B2B communities can accomplish. The community is built into every facet of its operations; the company even asks members to vote on proposed enhancements to its software. The social network is so essential to the company's business that member-generated content like the most popular posts and product reviews overflow onto the corporate home page. Spiceworks staffers have a vested interest in optimizing member engagement because the company profits from it. The bigger and more active its member base is, the more it can monetize the community through advertising and other sponsored programs. In the process, Spiceworks has learned much about what makes communities work.

It has learned, for example, that professional development is a huge motivator for community participation and that members will give generously of their time with no reward other than visibility among their peers. It has also learned about the "1:9:90 rule," which states that the vast majority of content is generated by a small percentage of its visitors. And it's learned the truth of Metcalfe's law: the value of a network increases as a square of the number of members.

Online communities are a bit of a paradox. They are both the oldest form of social media and also the newest. Forums and discussion groups date back to the late 1960s and have been a staple of customer support operations at technology companies for 30 years. Internet newsgroups, CompuServe, The Well, and other early communities had memberships in the hundreds of thousands a decade before the web browser was invented.

Those early online outposts looked little like Facebook or LinkedIn, though. The modern features that have made social networks the fastest-growing consumer phenomenon in history have created all kinds of new use scenarios, including some compelling B2B examples. When used effectively by B2B marketers, social networks can be the convention centers of social media. They are flexible gathering halls that can fill a wide variety of purposes, ranging from client services to product development to lead generation. But the key is to get members to want to participate.

Friends and Fame

The great innovation in online communities came in 1998, when Classmates.com introduced the concept of personal profiles and friends. Those metaphors are now a staple feature of every social network and provide powerful incentive for participation. Profiles are members' custom home pages. Everything the member contributes, from establishing contacts with others to joining groups to posting status updates, is captured in the profile. The more active the member is, the higher the visibility and the greater the value of the network to his or her personal success.

"Friends" or contacts are a virtual version of their real-world equivalent. When people decide to connect on a social network, they can exchange information publicly or privately. They form persistent connections based on trust. That's how relationships work in real life, too. Online connections on social networks are an efficient way to stay up to date with your professional contacts. Once connected, you can more effortlessly keep the contact information and employer status of everyone in your network current. A social network is like a rolodex, except it updates itself automatically.

In B2B communities, personal profiles are a way to register areas of expertise that others may find useful, and in the process, be seen as a thought leader in your business segment. For example, a member of LinkedIn can look up other members in the Dallas area who specialize in sales automation. The level of activity a member of a social network maintains also serves as a validation point. It's one thing for people to say they're experts in something like direct marketing, but it's more powerful when they can prove it by solving real-world problems facing other direct marketers in full view of an online social networking community. That proof is stored in the person's profile, is discoverable after the fact, and serves as a sort of public badge of credibility for all to see.

Online friendships also translate fluidly into real-world connections. "Community isn't just about discussing products, but about getting to know each other and making friendships," says Nicholas Tolstoshev, a Spiceworks community manager.

Online contacts in B2B communities frequently arrange impromptu gatherings at trade shows and events. Successful community managers we spoke to invariably augment their online worlds with physical events to meet and thank their most active members and to cement those relationships in the physical world. Because it's so easy to make virtual connections on social networks, deepening those relationships with real-world encounters is a great way for B2B marketers to motivate their members to invest more time in their online customer communities.

Before the introduction of personal profiles, it was difficult for participants in online networks to build visibility. Particularly in western cultures, we now know that visibility is the single most powerful driver of participation. That's one reason social networks have soared in popularity. Many communities use a recognition system that ties a member's status to contributions. A few, like SAP, even celebrate their most active members at physical events.

SAP works with an elite group of about 85 "mentors" chosen by its community. These well-connected, active participants reflect the geographic, industry and even gender diversity of the company's desired customer base. Most mentors work at system integrators—firms that install and customize SAP software for clients—and are in touch with a wide variety of SAP customers. Others are independent consultants or customer employees, with a few pundits (bloggers and analysts) and SAP employees also in the mix.

That insight is invaluable to SAP developers. Mentors get exposure within the community, which benefits their companies. They also have access to top officials at SAP, which gives them insights others don't have. SAP uses the input and perspective of the mentors to guide the company's actions on products, policies, and projects, so the mentors wield special influence. SAP even uses the mentors as information agents to help spread news to the company's customers. By demonstrating their domain expertise online, the mentors are rewarded with RFIs and RFPs from potential clients, who consult the SAP community to research their purchasing needs. Instead of an auto-updating rolodex, SAP gets a self-educating marketplace.

Spiceworks awards points to members who post well-regarded answers to other members' questions. Valued members of the community are invited to participate in conference calls with Spiceworks developers. Their contributions are rewarded with inside information. Community managers also publish occasional interviews with featured members, highlighting their contributions and career accomplishments. "Online status drives a huge amount of activity without our sending money out the door," says Tolstoshev. In B2B social networks, it's the ability to elevate your professional status that sustains momentum and drives interactions among peers.

National Instruments (NI) has the NI LabVIEW Champions program to recognize "leadership, expertise and unparalleled contributions to the technical and product communities." This ultra-elite group of about 25 contributors is treated to product previews, recognition on the NI web site, and a direct channel to the company's leadership, among other perks. They earn it: champions typically contribute several thousand support posts annually to support forums, lead local user groups, share hundreds of example code programs, or even run their own LabVIEW communities and blogs. There's one LabVIEW Champion who has even answered more than 15,000 support questions since 1999.

FohBoh.com, a social network for restaurant owners and food service professionals, highlights new contributions from its members on its home page and invites others to congratulate them on their contributions. TopCoder, a contract software developer that hosts programming competitions and licenses the best solutions to commercial customers, applies an elaborate algorithm to the code submitted by its members to determine the quality of their work. Lists of top contributors are maintained for major competitions and quality ratings are reflected in individual profiles. Top coders win money and also visibility that leads to job promotions and lucrative new business contracts.

You can give to get on LinkedIn as well. The most prolific contributor to LinkedIn's "Answers" forum is Dave Maskin, a New York–based event marketing specialist who has answered an incredible 25,000 questions. Maskin refers to himself as "Mr. Lead Generator," indicating that by delivering value to his community, he generates a steady stream on new business opportunities.

Hosting Conversations

Back-and-forth discussions were the first "killer app" of B2B communities and continue to be the most popular activity. Forums are particularly useful in B2B scenarios because they enable customers to solve pressing problems quickly. Forums are the simplest type of social network, consisting of a single threaded discussion emanating from a root topic. For less competitive complex queries, text-based discussion forums perform exceptionally well in search results because of their precise labeling and keywords. Active communities can save considerable customer support costs. In their 2008 book *Groundswell,* Charlene Li and Josh Bernoff cited the example of a Dell customer who saved the company an estimated $1 million per year by answering technical questions that would otherwise require Dell resources. He educates Dell's customers for free.

For the purposes of this chapter, we define a "community" as a public or private online destination that includes, at the minimum, registration and member discussion. Many of the principles we discuss here work perfectly well on Facebook or LinkedIn groups, but most of our examples are from niche or branded sites.

Sometimes, it's the niche subject-matter that provides the spark. AuntMinnie.com is a 150,000-strong social network for radiology professionals. The turning point for member participation came when medical students who aspire to become radiologists began to flock to the site to exchange academic advice. "They didn't have a place on the Web to talk about training to be a radiologist," says the social network's editor-in-chief Brian Casey. "They had questions about what schools other members liked and what others thought of schools they were considering attending. That drove participation." An added benefit is that those students will emerge from medical school already familiar with the online network.

Before starting a community, survey the landscape. You may find that active online communities already exist. That's increasingly likely these days because support communities are so easy to create on Facebook, LinkedIn, WetPaint, and other services, they have unleashed "the power of organizing without organizations," as Clay Shirky wrote in his breakthrough book *Here Comes Everybody*. If a niche social network in your business category already exists, you could work with the administrators of those forums to offer support in exchange for access to their members. It's best if you can have unfettered access to all the content and the member list, however, so your ultimate goal should be to support an independent, self-sustaining community, rather than one owned and operated by another product or service provider, if you can. Otherwise, using Facebook or some other low-maintenance option may be a reasonable option. You have a natural advantage because you are by default the most trusted source of official information about how to use and support your own products, and in the case of Facebook, the community is large enough to sustain momentum.[1]

Customer support communities have practical value across your business. They are a simple way to identify problems and new product opportunities. They save money on telephone support, build searchable libraries of solutions that your client support organization can use and turn customer service into public relations. They can help you spot enthusiastic customers who can assist in product development and word-of-mouth marketing. They can even be a recruiting source.

"We know some of our members so well that when we need feedback we call them directly," says Wyatt Kilmartin of RIDGID Branding, operator of the RidgidForum community for professional tradespeople. "They give us insight on our business that we're happy to use."

As RidgidForum grew in popularity and member value, the most active participants took responsibility for raising awareness by encouraging colleagues to join and even organizing a field trip to visit RIDGID's Elyria, Ohio, headquarters. About 50 plumbers, electricians, HVAC specialists, and woodworkers traveled at their own expense to spend the day engaging in demos, competitions, and discussions hosted by the RIDGID Tool Company. RIDGID now considers these enthusiasts a valuable resource for all sorts of advice.

2 Million Friends

One of the most successful B2B social networks is SAP's Community Network, with more than 2 million members and 1 million monthly unique visitors. Each day, about 6,000 items are posted to more than 350 discussion forums. The site also features 5,000 bloggers, of which two thirds are the company's customers, partners, and other non-SAP member entities. In fact, only about 2 percent of the SAP community's members work for SAP.

The community has value to SAP on almost every level of its business. For one thing, it enhances SAP's appeal to prospects. "If we can make our customers more successful than our competitors' customers, then our competitors' customers are going to come to us," says Mark Yolton, senior vice president of the SAP Community Network. "With higher levels of success and satisfaction, our customers are going to buy more, upgrade faster, extend their capabilities, and so forth."

There's also practical value for SAP in making customers more efficient. "If customers can reduce some of the burden of day-to-day operations, adopt best practices and overcome challenges faster, they're going to have budget left over, and they can buy more stuff," Yolton adds. That "stuff" means more SAP software, services, tools, templates, and middleware, and more from SAP's ecosystem of software, services, and technology partners as well.

Members get value from the community on multiple levels. Yolton ticks off a few:

- **Speed**. The ability to get fast answers makes members more valuable to their companies.
- **Professional networking**. The community is the most efficient way for members to build a worldwide contact network that can pay off in many ways.

- **Recognition**. Prestige within a professional community is a ticket to promotions and salary increases.
- **Access**. Top contributors get the inside scoop on SAP activities in advance, giving them a professional edge.
- **Education**. Members are one another's best source of training, so the SAP marketplace self-educates.
- **Insight**. In much the same way that people use the activity stream in Twitter and Facebook to track news recommended by their peers, members can use the SAP online community to follow links shared by others who have similar interests. That, in turn, gives them an early view into emerging trends or cutting-edge solutions that have not yet gone mainstream.

Other Uses of Communities

Support is the low-hanging fruit of B2B online communities, but it's far from the only value they deliver. Communities organized around topics of professional interest can generate brand awareness, thought leadership, and leads if perceived as a genuinely useful resource to the industries they serve.

An outstanding example of this in the B2B world is the RSA Conference, which has been running annually since 1991 and is widely regarded as one of the world's premier information security events. The annual gatherings are managed by RSA Security, a unit of EMC Corporation, and bring together more than 1,000 security professionals every year in San Francisco and to similarly sized events in Europe and Japan. The events are supported year-round by online communities, blogs, podcasts, and other social media.

One of the reasons the RSA Conference has been so successful is that it's a neutral forum. Competitors share the stage with the sponsor, and the program is designed by a committee of industry experts, of whom only a few work for RSA. It would be easy for RSA to turn the event into a marketing platform, but the company knows that its thought leadership equity is far too valuable to squander on a sales pitch.

Professional development is another powerful motivator for customers to join communities, particularly in B2B markets. In Chapter 12, we told you how EmployeeScreen uses education to generate a constant lead stream. HR.com is a B2B social network that has turned that concept into a business.

The community of more than 200,000 human resources (HR) professionals hosts about 30 webcasts each month devoted to topics like recruitment strategies, goal management, legal issues, and workforce development. Each seminar draws an average of 400 human resources professionals to hear advice from sponsors, who pay thousands of dollars for the privilege of speaking to the audience. About 300 experts regularly provide content in exchange for leads.

Through a partnership with the Human Resource Certification Institute, HR.com gives members the chance to earn credits toward professional certifications. They also have access to a library of documents from the Society for Human Resource Management that carry a charge for non-members.

For the first four years of its existence, HR.com employed a traditional editorial model with a staff of editors and paid contributors. In 2005, the company became one of the first B2B communities to shift entirely to a social network model. Today, all the content is generated by members, sponsors, and partnerships with third-party providers. It doesn't matter if the material has already been posted elsewhere. What counts is that it's valuable to the members. "I suspect that a lot of our content is not unique, but that's okay with us," says McGrath.

The value isn't in the uniqueness of the information as much as its place in a collection of contextually relevant content. Members can seek one another out for advice and job opportunities, browse the webcast archive, and network in the active online communities. The more active the members are, the greater the value to everyone.

Community sponsors can also learn a lot just by listening. Monitoring sessions to identify pockets of activity and trending keywords can yield insight about where customer sentiment is headed. You can even test new ideas by launching discussion topics around them to see where the conversations form. Active topics can identify problem areas or new market opportunities. When AuntMinnie's Brian Casey is looking for ideas for editorial content, "I can just drop someone a message," he says. "I have 150,000 experts at my fingertips at any time."

Crowdsourcing

One of the most exciting new uses of communities that B2B companies are discovering is their value in the product development and enhancement cycle. Nearly all of the community organizers we interviewed consult their members for ideas on how to improve their products or address new markets; a few have formalized the process in online exchanges called "innovation communities."

The poster child for this approach is Dell's IdeaStorm, a communal suggestion box that anyone can use to recommend improvements to the tech company's products and services. Launched in early 2007, IdeaStorm gathered more than 14,000 suggestions during its first three years, of which Dell implemented 400.

IdeaStorm is a sophisticated customer feedback loop that incorporates community voting and a ranking system. Dell also recognizes the 20 most valuable contributors by enshrining them in a "top 20" list and displaying their point totals as awarded by votes from their peers.

Your own approach can be simpler. Many B2B companies already maintain customer councils; adding an online version is as simple as tapping a few influential members on the shoulder and asking them to join an exclusive club. People love to contribute to the success of businesses in which they have a significant professional stake, and this is particularly true in B2B communities. Contributors' rewards need be nothing more than access and recognition.

A few words of advice: Acknowledge and follow up on the ideas your constituents contribute. That doesn't mean you have to implement them, but if contributors think their suggestions are going into a black hole, they will quickly stop participating. Acknowledgment and follow-up can be a chore, but they are essential to stimulating activity. Also, consult legal experts to be sure you have coverage when asking outsiders for ideas. Make sure today's contribution doesn't become tomorrow's intellectual property lawsuit.

Crowdsourcing product development ideas are catching on elsewhere. Other branded forums include Procter & Gamble's

Connect + Develop, Best Buy's IdeaX, and Starbucks' My Starbucks Idea. UserVoice is one of the emerging class of service providers that host innovation forums for customers that include Sun Microsystems and Nokia.

National Instruments, a developer of test and measurement automation software and hardware for use by design engineers and scientists, has an online forum called LabVIEW Idea Exchange where customers can submit ideas directly to the company's product developers. The firm also hosts private communities to seek focused feedback on specific products.

"It's helped R&D prioritize," says Deirdre Walsh, community and social media manager at National Instruments. "We used to have a lot of debates on which features to develop next. This streamlines the process." She adds that 14 new features in a recent new version of a National Instruments product were suggested by the community.

Salesforce.com's IdeaExchange is an online community where its customers can suggest new products and enhancements, interact with product managers and other customers, and preview upcoming product releases. Rather than trying to prescribe solutions, Salesforce .com listens for what customers want and provides those products first. New product development is based on actual market demand.

There are also commercial services that broker innovation exchanges between businesses with problems and contributors' solutions. The most successful of these is InnoCentive, a Massachusetts-based firm that hosts a social network it calls the Open Innovation Marketplace. Businesses, academic institutions, and organizations submit thorny problems to the network, where more than 200,000 registered problem solvers offer ideas in exchange for cash rewards. The company has successfully completed more than 1,000 engagements. Cash prizes can run to the tens of thousands of dollars, but money is one of the least important reasons innovators contribute, says chief executive officer (CEO) Dwayne Spradlin.

"Solvers want to work on problems that matter," Spradlin says. "They also want to be a top solver. Money is perhaps the third most important incentive." Organizations that seek crowdsourced solutions are also motivated by factors other than cost savings. "The vast majority of our customers come to us for better and faster innovation, not cheaper innovation," Spradlin says. "They want to get products to market before the competition, but they don't know how to manufacture them quickly enough."

In 2007, the Oil Spill Recovery Institute used InnoCentive to seek a solution to a problem that had long bedeviled oil spill cleanups in frigid environments: the oil/water mix freezes to a viscous mass that sinks to the bottom of the water and is almost impossible to recover. The winning solution was submitted by John Davis, an engineer in the concrete industry. Davis suggested adapting a tool used in his industry that sets up a constant vibration to keep cement from hardening while it's being poured. The technique worked perfectly, winning Davis $20,000 and a trip to Alaska to assist in a cleanup.

"Most innovation comes from the margins," Spradlin says. "Somebody who's doing work in one field realizes that what they're doing can be applied somewhere else." A few years ago, it was difficult and expensive to find expertise outside of one's immediate network. Today, the market is booming. SmartSheet.com has assembled a list of more than 50 public crowdsourcing services, and that roster doesn't include the hundreds of private and semipublic communities.[2]

Community Essentials

In the process of interviewing more than a dozen community managers, we found ourselves frequently revisiting several issues. Here's the advice we got from the experts about what organizers should consider.

Public or private?

This is a big decision usually made at the front end (although not necessarily), and it should be driven by your strategy for the community. If marketing or customer support considerations are driving the decision—and scale and visibility are important—then public communities are the way to go.

The advantage of public communities is that they can grow quickly and, if successful, can generate a lot of search traffic. Search is an important consideration, because visitors to a community support forum, for example, may be well-qualified prospects. For that reason, consider adding promotions contextually on highly trafficked forum pages. Large communities are terrific for listening, enhancing customer relationships, and testing ideas and messages. They can quickly become self-sustaining. Public communities are also a good platform for word-of-mouth marketing programs, promotions, and incentives.

But there are significant downsides, too. Membership in public communities tends to be of lower quality than that of private communities, and a lot of unused accounts can accumulate as visitors register once and don't come back. Lower-quality membership also tends to create lower-quality content, which tend to dissuade elite professionals from participating. There are also limitations on a business' ability to float or test new ideas because the network is effectively open for all to see, including competitors.

Private communities are popular in B2B settings because members value efficient, focused communication with professional peers. "Privately branded communities enable a company to zero in on a more targeted audience and engage in deeper conversations to create long-lasting relationships and drive measurable business results," wrote Christine Banning, vice president of marketing at SCORE, a nonprofit small business mentoring and training association, in a submission to *BtoB* magazine's 2010 Social Media Marketing Awards.

SCORE joined with PartnerUp, an online community for small businesses, to create a resource where members of both organizations could get answers to questions about running their companies. The collaboration drove membership from 100,000 to 165,000 in one year and increased the total audience for SCORE's newsletters to more than 200,000. By keeping the community private, SCORE made sure that members knew whom they were talking to. That improved the quality of interactions and also the value of SCORE to existing and prospective members.

Hybrid approaches are increasingly available through integration with popular public networks. For example, LinkedIn publishes a set of programming interfaces that lets members link their profiles and networks to third-party sites. American Express adopted the LinkedIn integration in its OPEN Forum network for small business owners to drive up participation without sacrificing the service's focused membership.

Private communities are usually smaller than public ones, but that's often a virtue. The point is to build a quality audience. Members may be granted access to privileged company plans or consulted for feedback on issues of high importance. A private community may even be a spur off a public gathering place with access limited to top customers or the most valued members of the public community.

The biggest downside of private communities is that they require a lot more effort to manage than public ones. Administrators may be required to take an active role in approving members, responding to questions, planting seeds for discussion, and weeding out off-topic subject matter. The smaller the community, the less likely it is to become self-sustaining, so be prepared to spend some time there. How much is difficult to estimate. AuntiMinnie's Casey spends 10 to 15 percent of his time administering just one of the site's more than 15 topics that collectively generate 200 to 300 comments per day. SAP has 30 to 50 people engaged in managing the communities, which total 2 million members. However, only three to five of those employees are full-time community managers. The rest contribute or serve the members on an as-needed basis. If you plan to share privileged information with members, be sure you have the IT tools in place to prevent unauthorized distribution, such as password-protected documents.

Know the 1:9:90 rule.

This nearly universal trait of public communities has baffled organizers for years. In almost every case, a small percentage of members contribute nearly all of the content, while the vast majority listen or do nothing. In reality, the population of contributors is more than 10 percent. In *Groundswell,* Bernoff and Li cite Forrester Research's Social Technographics profile that segments online adults into six categories: creators, critics, collectors, joiners, spectators, and inactives. They estimate that creators made up about 18 percent of the U.S.

population and critics, about 25 percent. That means that 57 percent of members of online communities in the United States don't actively participate.

These ratios seem to apply regardless of the focus of the community. For example, the profile of owners of Hewlett-Packard computers matches that of U.S. adults in almost every category, according to *Groundswell*. There are some significant variations correlated with age and location, however. For example, 41 percent of young males are creators, compared with just 8 percent of people older than age 52. Interestingly, Asian countries have a much higher percentage of creators, ranging from 22 percent in Japan to 38 percent in South Korea. By contrast, in most of Europe, the figure is 10 percent or less.

This phenomenon appears to be a matter of human nature, and there is very little you can do to change it in unrestricted communities. Our best advice is to cultivate the loyalty of the most active members and encourage them to be your eyes and ears in the lurking majority. You can energize passive members to some degree through incentives or simply by urging them to speak, but you're not going to change their nature.

The right content.

If it's easy to get to, content is still king. But useful content that anticipates and solves your potential customer's problem is what B2B marketers should be focused on creating. Any kind of information is technically content, but what drives people to register and participate is information which helps them do their work more effectively and efficiently.

Nearly every community organizer ultimately encounters conflict between the urge to market and the need to serve. Resist this temptation. B2B customers are some of the most cynical buyers in the world. Many are barraged by marketing pitches every day and have learned every dodge and trick in the book.

"Content feeds the social media beast," wrote sales automation company Marketo in its *Definitive Guide to Social Media* e-book. "Audit your existing marketing assets and identify the educational pieces; these perform much better in social media than traditional sales collateral."

Businesses today have an unprecedented opportunity to become trusted sources of advice. With traditional media in a precipitous decline, professionals are turning to one another for advice on where to find information. You can play in this game if you're willing to set aside your marketing agenda and simply help your customers be more successful. Give to get.

The best content creators for a B2B community are the people who build your products and your customers. Seek out enthusiasts who want to engage with your customers and give them a profile and a forum to spread their expertise. Look for experts at different layers of the organization. Your chief engineer or technology officer is going to appeal to a different type of purchasing stakeholder than your developers. Look for opportunities to spotlight these experts in special events, such as a blogger round table or tweet chat with your chief technology officer (CTO) or a daylong off-site brainstorm with your product engineers.

You'll probably be pleasantly surprised to find that topics sell better than speakers. This is a reversal of the star-driven paradigm of professional conferences. "There's no relationship between speakers and attendance" at the webinars produced by HR.com, according to founder Debbie McGrath. Her company used to pay thousands of dollars for prominent experts to anchor events but found that attendees responded no better to stars than to unknowns. The topic was what mattered.

If you don't have the resources to produce much original content, consider curating content produced by others. The web has become an albatross of spam blogs and twitbots. Serve your customers by editing and pointing to the best content with a link blog, in Linkedin Groups or on Twitter. Curators gather, vet, and highlight information from a variety of sources. Curation is a powerful new concept in an information-saturated world. People don't have time to seek out all the information they need, so they gravitate to resources that aggregate content along special interest lines.

According to a May 2010 Pew Internet report by Kristen Purcell, aggregators are the second most popular news sites on the Internet, among those who have a favorite. In the consumer realm, Google News, Digg and Drudge Report are just three examples of successful aggregators. A B2B example is Sphinn.com, a web site that accepts links submitted by members and then rates the information of greatest interest to marketers.

A prior 2009 survey of 2,787 U.S. news consumers by the research firm Outsell found that news consumers are more likely to turn to an aggregator (31 percent) than to a newspaper site (8 percent) or other site (18 percent) for information. "A full 44% of visitors to Google News scan headlines without accessing newspapers' individual sites," Outsell wrote.[3] There is no reason to believe the information-consuming habits of busy businesspeople are any different.

The Economic Development Council of Western Massachusetts (EDC), a non-profit that supports businesses in several Massachusetts counties, posts 25-30 headlines and summaries of articles from regional publications and blogs to its news page each week. It has reaped the benefits of word-of-mouth marketing and better performance on search engines, which favor relevancy and frequency. Visits to WesternMassEDC.com were up 40 percent in the year after the experiment began, with nearly all of the growth coming from visits to the news page, which is now the site's second most popular entry page. Regional publishers actually court the organization to have their headlines featured on the site and the service has improved member affinity, according to Mike Graney, senior VP of business development. You can even make aggregation the core theme of your service. British electronics distributor Premier Farnell plc launched element14 in 2008 to serve as a kind of Facebook for the voracious information appetites of its audience of electronic design engineers.

Members can see and comment on each other's activities, participate in discussions, and share documents. The latter feature is a distinctive service of element14, which has amassed a library of thousands of manuals, research papers, how-tos, and schematics. Any registered member can upload documents and rate the ones he or she has read.

The company's partners are a key constituency, because they can get their content assets in front of a highly desirable audience. The more Premier Farnell's suppliers participate, the better their reputation with the community. Partners can also apply to become featured experts who field tough questions from members and share the answers with everyone. However, being a business partner does not qualify anyone for inclusion. "They have to demonstrate significant expertise in their area," says Jeff Hamilton, director of design engineer marketing. "This is not about advertising."

Divide and conquer.

As your community grows, activity will tend to cluster around certain areas while other topics may peter out. Consider moving the active threads into their own area. This makes it easier for members to find others with similar interests and also for you to monitor the ebb and flow of activity by topic.

Creating topical discussion areas is a particularly valuable service to your most active members because it makes it easy for those valued participants to hang out in and contribute to their areas of expertise. Segmentation also indulges members' desire to be with their peers. Veteran engineering pros, for example, don't want to be bothered with questions from college sophomores.

Having the flexibility to prune and graft areas of special interest is an important consideration when choosing a platform for your community. At the very least, you should be able to aggregate discussions from multiple areas and consolidate them under a new heading. But the issues go beyond simply moving around threads. Certain interest groups within your community may merit special features, such as online events, downloads, chat rooms, or even transaction services.

For example, Serena Software supports online storefronts where its partners can sell applications or "mashups" built with the company's software development tools. Partners get access to a set of services, such as sales support and accounting, that other community members doesn't see. The same might be true for your customers. Certain active groups may gravitate toward interactive events or document sharing, for example, while other groups don't care. You should be able to selectively target these features.

Relax.

Business professionals are people too, so make your community a place where they can build deeper professional relationships through entertainment and shared personal interests. Here are a few examples:

- HR.com devotes a portion of its home page to "HR Humor." Those links lead to cartoons, jokes, and thematic crossword puzzles submitted by members. There's also a clever video of kids describing why they aspire to do the dirty work of HR. The video has amassed more than half a million views.
- Kinaxis' Supply Chain Expert Community bills itself as a place where supply chain pros can "learn, laugh, share, connect." The site features comedy videos produced by Second City, a spoof of the *Late Late Show*, a video comedy series called "Married to the Job" and more. "In supply chain, laughter really is the best medicine," says Kirsten Watson, director of corporate marketing.
- SAP has a "coffee corner" in its community, which reflects the company's European heritage and cultural appreciation for the casual conversations that typically occur around an espresso machine. Hobbies, sports, families, and other topics are discussed, including a special section devoted to "ranting," where members can just let off steam about life's little frustrations.
- AuntMinnie.com has a section called "Off Topic," where members discuss everything from politics to the Super Bowl. Casey says that politics is actually one of the most popular subjects on the site.

NERD HEAVEN

National Instruments is a test and measurement automation company that's sometimes called "Home Depot for engineers." Social networks, wikis, and discussion forums support vibrant online discussions among its core engineering customers. Engineers are natural tinkerers, and National Instruments' culture reflects that. "People here are always buzzing about new technologies," says community and social media manager Deirdre Walsh.

A discussion-based community provides first-level technical support to more than 100,000 members. Customers can search a database of nearly 1 million messages that have been gathered over the past decade. The community answers about half of all support questions, saving National Instruments a significant amount of money. "It was essential to embrace social communities early because it was impossible for us to become experts in every area in which our customers were using our technologies. No industry represents more than 15 percent of our revenue, so it was essential for us to connect like-minded, domain experts," says Walsh.

In 2008, the company launched the NI Developer Zone Community, a rich collaborative environment that enables engineers at 25,000 companies to swap code, share documents, and upload video, among other things.

National Instruments has five major objectives for its communities:

1. **Ensure customer success through fast and accurate support.** Any question that isn't answered by the community within 24 hours escalates to an NI applications engineer. With the addition of code and document exchanges, customers can share their own innovations with one another.
2. **Get product feedback.** The LabVIEW Idea Exchange is an innovation forum where customers can submit ideas for enhancing the company's flagship LabVIEW software directly to developers. There are also private communities for focused feedback for other products, including a new one devoted to robotics that is also open to high school students.
3. **Increase awareness and loyalty.** There's a LabVIEW page on nearly every social network you can imagine, including MySpace, Squidoo, and Meetup. The social listening posts are used to track what Walsh calls "actionable conversations," or discussions that indicate opportunity or a problem that needs attention.

4. **Drive new and repeat business.** Issues that draw lots of interest may spawn their own communities. For example, National Instruments has online groups for each of its annual user conferences. Members can see key demonstrations and download a customized parts list to build the demo themselves. "It's a way to carry the conference along after the event," says Walsh.

   The community is also used for prospecting. Trade show visitors who express interest in a product area are often invited to join the relevant online forum.
5. **Grow the size and health of the community.** With members from more than 25,000 companies and 1 million entries in its support forums, this goal seems to be taking care of itself.

THE CUSTOMERS ARE REVOLTING

David van Toor arrived at Sage Software in 2007 in the middle of a crisis. The new general manager of Sage's customer relationship management group was facing an open revolt by users of its ACT! small business software over an upgrade that had introduced unexpected problems to some customers. Van Toor opted to use a community to capture and guide the discussions. Here's what happened in his own words:

> In 2006, we rewrote the product and called it an upgrade. That had the effect of not so much moving the cheese as changing the food group. It was very favorable for larger companies of 10–20 users, but it completely changed the user metaphor for the small client.
>
> When I arrived in 2007, we were facing a lot of negative posts on message boards, the worst being Amazon, where raving negative fanatics were posting negative reviews. Prospects were getting form letters from our competitors pointing to these comments. Amazon was responsible for significant sales. I landed in the middle of that problem.
>
> Our philosophy was that if people are going to complain, let them complain in our kitchen rather than over our fence. We created our own community. It turned out many of these customers just wanted to talk. We had to get into one-to-one conversations with 800,000 customers.

(*continued*)

(*continued*)

The first thing I did was create an "Ask David" e-mail address on the website. I would review the posts and respond directly when appropriate. I'd also blog about some of the more common issues.

Support was all paid at the time and a large group of customers was largely unsupported. I wanted every customer to have some level of support based upon how much they wanted to pay, even if that was nothing. We carved off some support people to monitor the posts on the forum and to resolve them quickly. I posted on the blog what progress we were making.

We had an advisory board of 80 customers, and they were more than happy to spread the word. The organic growth was huge. There were hundreds of thousands of posts within a month. We had a lot of fans who wanted things to work out. When they heard there was a way they could talk to us, they came in droves.

Initially, half the responses were positive and half told me I was an idiot. We welcomed them all. Whenever we had a very negative post, we'd call the person directly. In most cases, we were able to convert that person into a positive user through a rational discussion that addressed their needs and let them know we were listening. There were 200–300 people we were able to convert from negative to positive, and that accounted for nearly all the outspoken complainers. Many more people who weren't so negative were converted through competent product support.

Sometimes people were unreasonable, but most of them just wanted to vent to someone who could do something. Giving a free upgrade or waiving a fee usually made a positive difference. In a world where customer service is public relations, it becomes a marketing expense. Mainly it was just a matter of being honest and giving credence to the fact that they had a problem. I listened to their concerns, gave credibility to them and didn't pass judgment on whether they were wrong or right. It was important to listen, be honest and not speak in a marketing voice.

There was one customer in Canada who'd had a horrible experience. We couldn't unravel the mess by phone, so we flew three engineers from Phoenix to work with him. We spent more on the trip than the customer spent with us, but it was worth every cent. If we hadn't resolved his problems, he would continue to post his tirades and I would lose sales.

Some of our most negative customers became our strongest references. Others became our best product testers. We measured customer loyalty with Net Promoter Score. One year later, the increase in the score was twice what would be regarded as excellent. Our customer loyalty scores had improved 20% and the number of participants in our beta program tripled.

The community grew in importance inside the organization. Our beta program shifted from a traditional model to one that included the community. It was so efficient that we were able to add more features to the product than we could before because we got immediate feedback.

I think what stops a lot of companies from embracing online communities is the CEO saying, 'What's the ROI?' To that I say, 'What's the ROI of bringing your wife flowers on your anniversary?' Even if there's no positive ROI, there can be a negative one for not taking action.

People buy stuff from people. They gravitate to business relationships that mirror personal relationships. If the CEO responds to me in 10 minutes, I want to do business with a company like that.

CHAPTER FOURTEEN

Return on Investment

We've told you about a few companies that have achieved a notable return on investment (ROI) from their social marketing initiatives. They include Indium Corporation, whose blog-driven search strategy yielded a sixfold increase in leads in just one quarter, and Clickable, whose Gurus drove a 400 percent 1-year growth in billings.

These numbers are impressive, but in our experience, they're more the exception than the rule. In conversations with hundreds of marketers over the past few years, we've observed that few of them closely track the ROI of their social marketing programs. In fact, many of the most successful marketers we've met aren't that concerned with ROI at all. Rather, they invest in social marketing because they believe that the intangible benefits—customer engagement, market awareness, continuous feedback, and professional development—are good for any company, regardless of the financial impact. They measure like crazy, and some of the most common criteria they use are referenced in Figure 14.1, but they rarely translate the benefits of engagement into hard dollar figures.

Most of these early adopters work for companies with adaptive, change-oriented management. That's good if you can get it, but the reality is that most top executives are still wary about social marketing.

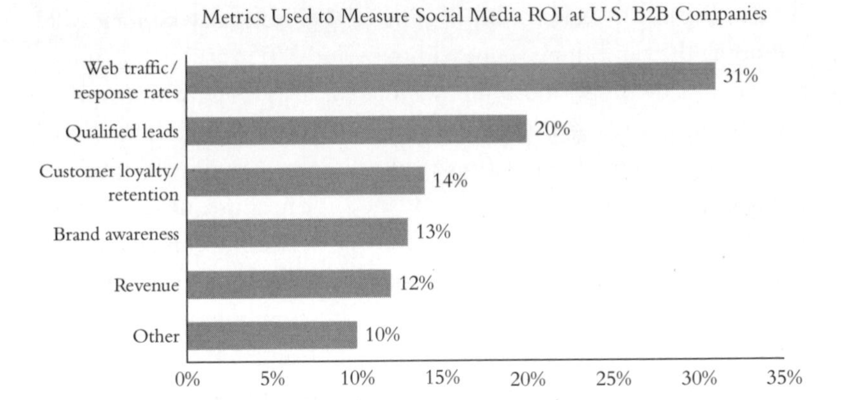

Figure 14.1 Metrics Used to Measure Social Media ROI.
Source: Visible Technologies & Sirius Decisions via eMarketer.

ROI is typically the number one or two most cited concern we hear from the people who work for these companies.

We're conflicted about the whole ROI debate. On one hand, we believe that businesses should make decisions based on sound reasoning rather than vague promises or impulse. ROI analysis enforces rigor that leads to better decisions. On the other hand, we believe ROI objections are often used to *avoid* decisions that executives don't want to make for other reasons, such as fear of losing control. Few people want to admit that they're afraid, so they fall back on convenient stalling tactics, of which ROI is a primary one.

The reality is that businesses make decisions without applying hard ROI criteria all the time. What's the return on landscaping, an expensive conference room table, or free bagels on Fridays? It may be possible to calculate a payback through extensive customer perception or employee satisfaction analysis, but why bother? We know these investments make people feel better. If your employees feel better, they do a better job and your customers have a better experience doing business with you.

In his book *How*, author Dov Seidman argues that in a world where information flows freely and technology connects us instantly around the globe, success no longer lies in what we do. Now, it's "how we do what we do" that matters most. "Sustainable advantage," Seidman writes "lies in the realm of how." The ROI of how may be intangible, but doing the right thing is not without value. "Transparent and honest practices" is the single most important factor in assessing your corporate reputation, according to the 2010 Edelman Trust Barometer. For public companies, corporate reputation results in positive goodwill, expressed as a line item on the balance sheet. By the same measure, negative goodwill is recognized as a liability. If your social marketing exploits are successful, the resulting goodwill will increase your stock price and even serve as a justification for your firm to demand premium pricing. Still, many managers struggle to connect the dots. Caught in the weeds, they look for short term ways to measure their marketing investments.

Furthermore, much of the money that business-to-business (B2B) marketers have poured into direct-mail campaigns, trade show exhibitions, and trade print advertising for the past 50 years have shown questionable returns. The only reason we make these investments is that these practices are established and businesses are accustomed to them. "ROI calculations don't work well for social media, and they don't work well for marketing in general," says Benjamin Ellis, a serial entrepreneur based in the United Kingdom who now specializes in social marketing.

What's the ROI of a satisfied customer who may or may not pay more for your product or sing your praises to others? It's hard to say, but that doesn't stop some world-class companies from spending lavishly on customer satisfaction. EMC Corporation has been known to charter jets to fly technicians across the country in the middle of the night to take care of a customer whose computers are down. Do you suppose the storage giant conducts an ROI analysis before making the decision to fly commercial versus private? Of course not. EMC is a premium-priced provider whose philosophy is to always go the extra mile to take care of the customer. In the aggregate, the company may be able to justify its practices in the form of higher customer satisfaction and repeat sales, but we doubt the support manager who charters the midnight express is required to justify each added expense in the short term.

That said, we understand the ROI justification is a hurdle many marketers must clear to get their social programs off the ground. We believe that many social marketing programs *can* be justified, but the process requires discipline and careful documentation. After all, the

Internet is the most measurable medium ever invented. If you can isolate variables, establish correlations, and apply a little creativity, it's remarkable what you can do. In this chapter, we suggest some approaches.

Defining ROI

A lot of marketers would probably like to be in Susan Popper's shoes. The vice president of marketing communications at SAP was recently asked by *BtoB* magazine how she is measuring ROI on marketing efforts. Her response: "When [our target audiences come] to our site, they watch the videos and they are engaging with the content on the site. Our impression-to-visit ratio (as measured by click-through rates) doubled this year versus last year." That's an impressive *result*, but it isn't a *return*. To compute ROI, you need to think in financial terms.

According to Wikipedia, ROI is "the ratio of money gained or lost (whether realized or unrealized) on an investment relative to the amount of money invested." There are two important variables in this equation: return and investment. There's also a third vital term: money.

Return is payoff as measured in revenue generated or costs avoided. There are other ways to measure results (for example, improvement in customer satisfaction scores), but unless those outputs can be measured financially, they really don't qualify as considerations in ROI. We believe many of these intangibles actually can be translated into financial terms, and we'll cover that later in this chapter.

But for now, let's look at a couple of basic examples. A simple one is an ROI analysis of the impact of hiring a new sales representative. Let's say the new rep carries a fully loaded cost of $100,000 and delivers $2 million in incremental annual sales revenue at a 10 percent net profit. In that case, the first-year ROI of hiring the salesperson is 100 percent, expressed as profit divided by investment:

Cost of sales rep	$100,000
Revenue generated by rep	$2,000,000
Profit margin	10 percent
Net profit	$200,000
ROI [(net profit − cost)/cost]	100 percent

We can apply the same type of analysis to cost avoidance. That's what Pitney Bowes did when a 2007 postal service rate increase prompted 430,000 calls from customers. The mailing service provider launched an online forum to deflect some of the most common questions and tracked 40,000 visits in 6 weeks. Pitney Bowes was able to correlate savings in call center costs and estimate that the forum more than paid for its first-year costs in just a short time.

Let's say we implement a customer self-service portal as a way to reduce support costs. We assume that the portal will require half of one full-time equivalent (FTE) employee to administer, that the fully loaded cost of that employee is $70,000 and that the portal will enable the company to eliminate one support position at a fully loaded cost of $70,000. Let's further assume that efficiencies will enable us to reduce administrative support costs to one-quarter an FTE the second year and 10 percent the third year. At the same time, the value generated by the community will enable us to cut an additional one-half customer support position each year.

Here's what the analysis would look like:

Year	Item	Annual	Cumulative
1	Administrative costs	$35,000	$35,000
	Savings	$70,000	$70,000
	ROI	100 percent	100 percent
2	Administrative costs	$17,500	$52,500
	Savings	$105,000	$175,000
	ROI	500 percent	233 percent
3	Administrative costs	$7,000	$59,500
	Savings	$140,000	$315,000
	ROI	1900 percent	429 percent

The portal looks like a good investment, yielding a positive first-year ROI and blowout value in the third year. The cumulative value is also very strong. Even if our annual savings estimates are off by 50 percent, we'd still get nearly a 10-fold return on operating costs in year 3.

These are two simple examples, but they both require confident forecasting based on accurate historical data. For many companies, that's far from simple. In the case of the sales rep, we must be able to predict with reasonable certainty that the person can generate $2 million in incremental business in year 1. There are a lot of factors underlying that assumption. For example, we assume predictable growth in the overall market and in our growth rate relative to the market. We must be confident that there is $2 million in new business out there to find. In niche B2B markets with a small number of potential customers, that assumption may be optimistic. And then there are unforeseen circumstances: the bankruptcy of a major competitor could move that revenue goal higher, whereas the emergence of new competition might force us to trim our forecasts.

There are also nuances of calculating net present value, inflation, opportunity cost, return on capital, and other fine points of finance that we won't try to cover here for the sake of simplicity. ROI calculations are rarely a precise science to begin with.

Good ROI analysis almost always requires accurate historical information, which few companies have, in our experience. Capturing and analyzing historical data requires time and discipline. It's easy to cast aside analytical tasks when everyone is focused on generating revenue. However, you can't forecast the future without understanding the past. Historical data also sets a baseline for measuring change. That change can then be measured and compared against actions that may have caused it. If you can correlate action to impact, then you can calculate ROI.

In Figure 14.2, lead activity appears to correlate positively with traffic to a company blog. The positive correlation is indicated by the change from baseline, which appears to correspond with the upward movement in blog traffic. Even then, a definitive correlation can't be established until other factors are eliminated from consideration, such as a promotion or a new advertising campaign, but in many scenarios, these indefinite correlations are sufficient.

Identifying correlations can be a time-consuming process, requiring new variables to be introduced independently of one another so that change can be isolated. However, you don't necessarily have to test only one variable at a time. With split testing, you can try two different experiments, each targeting a different segment of your customer base.

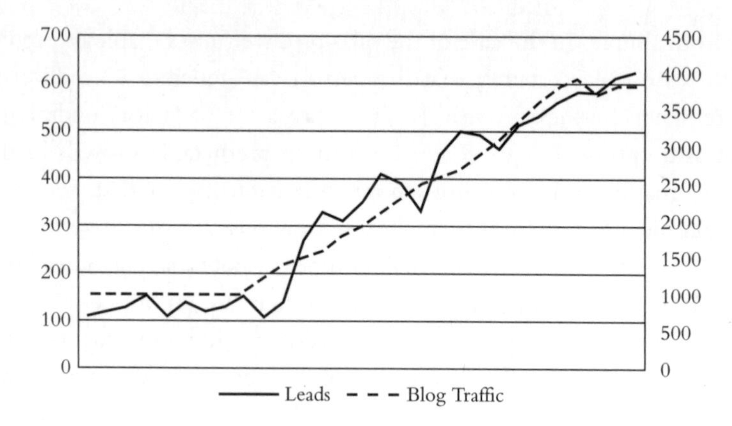

Figure 14.2 Positive Correlation.

Suppose you license e-mail marketing services to customers on a subscription basis. For the past three years, your renewal rate has been about 40 percent annually, so you can reasonably expect that trend to continue. This gives you a baseline from which to test new tactics.

You're going to try out two new incentives this year to increase renewal rates. One provides a 10 percent discount on the annual fee to each customer that renews more than one month ahead of deadline. The other provides access to six customer-only educational webcasts during the next 12 months for all customers who renew, regardless of timing. Each eligible customer gets one incentive or the other. This should give you a sound indication of ROI because you can compare your results against historical data.

It turns out that both programs are equally successful in boosting renewal rates, but the webcast promotion has a better ROI (see table on the next page). That's because 40 percent of the renewing customers who were offered the discount renewed before the one-month deadline, which incurred a higher discount obligation. Not only was the webcast promotion more cost-effective, but it carried a predictable cost of about $1,500 per webcast, compared with the variable cost of the discount. The webcast is probably the smarter incentive to offer.

This example presupposes that the company has good data about past renewals, but many companies lack the systems to capture complete data in the first place. A good customer relationship management (CRM) system is essential. Many excellent solutions are now

	Historic	With 10 percent discount	With webcast
Expiring customers	100	100	100
Average annual revenue per customer	$5,000	$5,000	$5,000
Renewal rate	40 percent	60 percent	60 percent
Profit margin	20 percent	20 percent	20 percent
Profit from renewing customers	$40,000	$60,000	$60,000
Incremental profit from incentive	N/A	$20,000	$20,000
Cost of incentive	N/A	$12,000	$9,000
ROI	N/A	67 percent	122 percent

available on a software-as-a-service basis today, including Salesforce .com, RightNow Technologies, and NetSuite. You can find a complete directory at Saas-showplace.com. But choosing the tool isn't nearly as important as knowing how to put it to work.

Effective CRM requires discipline to capture every customer contact from initial web site visit through sale and continuing with ongoing support. That means involving more than just the sales force in the process. To calculate the ROI on social marketing, you need to understand every dimension of the customer relationship, beginning with the action that creates the first contact. It's not enough to begin tracking when the lead is generated. Marketing should have the systems in place to identify the action that created the lead, whether that's a search query, e-mail link, customer referral, or some other event. Most CRM systems are good at tracking customer activity after leads come in. The difficult job for marketing is figuring out the sequence of events that brought them there.

We can't emphasize this enough: being able to predict the future means knowing a lot about the past. If you can't establish effective baseline expectations, then your forecasts are little more than educated guesses. To do ROI right, you need to track every customer contact, not just interactions with the sales force.

Metrics

Web analytics today deliver unprecedented insight about online interactions. The basic features of the free Google Analytics service match the capabilities of products that cost thousands of dollars just a few years ago. Premium services like Webtrends build in sophisticated behavioral analysis and sentiment analysis and can track offsite activity such as a prospect's comments on Twitter or use of a mobile application. They can even trigger customized e-mails or tweets when a person's behavior matches certain predefined patterns.

With all this rich data now available, it's remarkable how many marketers still use only the basic metrics of traffic and unique visitors to measure success. We're not big fans of these measurements; it's easy to generate spikes of valueless traffic by posting celebrity photos or top 10 lists, for example. In Chapter 11, we listed some common metrics you can use and how they relate to different business goals. We think richer measures such as referring keywords, top content, bounce rate, average time spent on site, pages per visit, and content analysis yield more actionable insight that will only get better.

The best way to select relevant metrics is to work backward. Start with sales trends, match them to web activity, and look for the metrics that correlate most closely. Those are the metrics that are most meaningful to you. For example, if an increase in session time spent on the site appears to correlate with registrations for a webcast, then that indicates that webcasts resonate with the audience.

You also shouldn't confine metrics to those that can be measured online. One of the most popular indications of customer satisfaction is the Net Promoter Score (NPS), introduced in 2003 by Fred Reichheld of Bain & Company. Obtaining an NPS requires asking customers a single question on a 0-to-10 rating scale: "How likely is it that you would recommend our company to a friend or colleague?" This simple tactic has been adopted by big B2B companies like General Electric and American Express as a key performance indicator. While the score doesn't relate directly to revenue, it appears to have a positive correlation.

You can also choose to monitor classic metrics that have nothing to do with the Internet. These include press mentions, speaking invitations, and performance on customer satisfaction surveys. Metrics also vary by objective. For example, the success of a blog set up to generate leads may be measured by inquiries, time spent on the site, and repeat visitors, whereas one targeted at search optimization may be evaluated based on keyword rankings and inbound links.

Whether a correlation to revenue can be clearly established is unimportant. What matters is that the stakeholders at the company agree that a correlation exists and that values can be assigned to it. In other words, if everyone can agree that page views indicate a desired financial outcome, then that's a good starting metric for evaluating ROI. One thing you absolutely need to know, however, is how people reach your site. Unique URLs are a way to measure that. We're astonished at how many e-mails we still get from brand-name companies that don't make use of this simple tactic, which enables a marketer to specify a web address that is unique to the e-mail, tweet, wall post, or any other message. Unique URLs use a simple server redirect function to identify the source of an incoming click. They look like this: http://mycompany.23.com/public/?q=ulink&fn=Link&ssid=5155. Everything after the question mark is a unique tracking code that tells where the visitor came from. The URL Builder tool within Google Analytics can be used to easily generate unique tracking codes.

Unique URLs enable your analytics software to track inbound traffic from each source separately so you can determine the ROI of each social marketing channel. Without unique URLs, visits are simply classified as "direct traffic," meaning that the source could be a forwarded e-mail, bookmark, or an address typed into the browser. There isn't much you can do with that.

A simple example of how you might use this information is to measure traffic to a landing page and analyze the number of visitors who fill out a registration form according to the referring source. This would show you, for example, that registration rates are twice as high from a newsletter as from a tweet. The value of those registrants divided by the cost of the newsletter is an ROI metric. Unique URLs are also valuable for split testing; you can try out two different invitation messages in the same e-mail and use a different URL for each to measure response to different messages.

Putting It All Together

Let's apply all the factors we've described to two social marketing scenarios. First, we'll compare the ROI of webcasts to that of white papers. Start with historical data. What is the conversion rate of webcast viewers versus people who download a white paper? What is the lifetime value of an average customer? Compare the outputs and divide by costs to assess ROI:

$$\text{ROI} = \frac{(((\text{audience} \times \text{conversion rate}) \times \text{average lifetime value}) \times \text{profit margin}) - \text{cost of acquisition}}{\text{cost of acquisition}}$$

Let's assume the following:

- The average lifetime value of a customer is $50,000 at a 10 percent profit margin.
- The average cost of delivering a webcast to 100 registered viewers is $3,000; viewers convert at a 2 percent rate.
- The average cost of delivering a white paper to 500 registrants is $10,000; registrants convert at a 1 percent rate.

Our ROI analysis looks like this:

	Webcast	White paper
Audience size	100	500
Conversion rate	2 percent	1 percent
Lifetime profitability	$10,000	$25,000
Cost of acquisition	$3,000	$10,000
ROI	233 percent	150 percent

The webcast ROI is superior, but not by much. Armed with this data, we might choose to promote the webcast more aggressively to leverage its stronger ROI. However, another option would be to focus on improving the white paper's conversion rate. In fact, doubling the rate would drive ROI to 400 percent, making this a potentially higher return action.

Let's look at one more example in which we use a blog for lead generation. We know that performance will be slow during the first few quarters until search engine traffic kicks in. Based on the experience of others, we believe that lead growth will improve steadily as traffic builds. We expect to be at 50 leads per month by the end of the first year and 160 leads per month by the end of the second year. Our historical data tells us that a lead is worth $100. We further estimate our editorial costs at $2,000 per quarter during the first year, doubling to $4,000 during the second. Here's our analysis of quarterly and cumulative ROI.

Quarter	Leads	Total Lead value	Cost	Quarterly ROI	Cumulative ROI
Y1Q1	10	$1,000	$2,000	−50 percent	−50 percent
Y1Q2	25	$2,500	$2,000	25 percent	−13 percent
Y1Q3	35	$3,500	$2,000	75 percent	17 percent
Y1Q4	50	$5,000	$2,000	150 percent	50 percent
Y2Q1	75	$7,500	$4,000	88 percent	63 percent
Y2Q2	100	$10,000	$4,000	150 percent	84 percent
Y2Q3	130	$13,000	$4,000	225 percent	113 percent
Y2Q4	160	$16,000	$4,000	300 percent	144 percent

This gives us a firm foundation to make the case for investing in the blog. If leads aren't coming in as quickly as we had estimated, we can adjust costs downward to improve ROI by setting up content-sharing arrangements.

Measuring Intangibles

The trickiest aspect of ROI analysis is accounting for intangibles. These include factors such as customer satisfaction, customer loyalty, brand reputation, and market influence. Many social marketing projects are justified for these reasons, but the outputs are never measured, either because it's not worth the effort or because the measurements aren't in place.

In fact, all of these outputs can be measured and have been for years using some of the following tests:

Value	Measurement
Customer satisfaction	Customer surveys, renewal rates, referrals, incremental business, testimonials, Net Promoter Score
Customer loyalty	Renewal rates, incremental business, response rates, event attendance, testimonials, Net Promoter Score
Customer engagement	Newsletter subscriptions, online community activity, response rates, event attendance, testimonials, feedback volume
Reputation	Market share research, awareness research, media citations, analyst research
Market influence	Market share research, lift studies, media/social media citations, speaking invitations, analyst research
Leadership	Attitudinal research, growth rate, media citations, copycat competitors

However, research statistics aren't sufficient. You have to find a way to translate these measurements into dollars and cents. That's where creativity comes in handy. Many of the metrics on the right can be mapped to business outcomes, but only if historical data are available to correlate with those changes.

For example, you can calculate the business value of customer loyalty by comparing the revenue derived from customers at different longevity levels, such as more than five years, three to five years, and less than three years. Then look at the support and sales costs allocated to these same customers. You'll probably find that long-term customers are cheaper to support and have lower sales costs than newer customers. Comparing the ratio of revenue to expense for each longevity segment should give you an idea of where to invest.

What is the business value of reputation? There's a lot of research to support the notion that B2B customers weigh this factor heavily when making buying decisions. A simple telephone survey can identify which customers value reputation the most. You can then see where they rank in order of value to your business. If they are near the top (and we believe they will be), then that is compelling evidence that investment in reputation pays off. You can also compare the average profitability of these customers versus those who don't value reputation as highly and see which has more investment upside.

You can even quantify, to some degree, factors that are almost impossible to measure. For example, suppose that a publicity campaign results in 5 million impressions in mainstream media. By conducting pre- and post-campaign "lift" studies, you can measure changes in awareness. Then drag out the record books or published industry averages to compare previous increases in awareness to corresponding changes in the business, such as lead quality and conversion times. You can quantify the value of those outputs to calculate ROI.

Once again, these analyses require accurate historical data. If you can't segment your customers according to criteria like these, the justification process is far more difficult. That doesn't mean it's impossible, though. Analyst estimates, industry averages, and ratios derived from analyzing your competitors and those in other industries may yield similar insights.

How does this all relate to social marketing? We believe it's critical. The ROI objection is the roadblock you're most likely to encounter in selling a social marketing initiative. You need to speak the language of your inquisitors. Social marketing has also introduced new cost variables into the business. For example, press tours used to be a standard tactic for increasing market awareness, but today a blog may do the same thing at a much lower cost. To understand the true value of these new tools, you need to have a baseline for comparing them against past practices. Get your Excel skills in order, because you're going to have some explaining to do.

THE VALUE OF FOLLOWERS

When marketers get up on stage to describe their social marketing successes these days, they invariably refer to follower and fan totals. On Twitter, follower counts have become a sort of merit badge, despite the fact that anyone can quickly run up that number by simply following people

(*continued*)

(*continued*)

who automatically follow back. There are even paid services that help inflate follower totals.

What is the true value of a Twitter follower? There is no industry standard to calculate that number, but if you have the right metrics in place, you can do that for your own organization. Here's how:

Look at the total number of clicks to your site from Twitter in any given month and divide that by the number of tweets you posted that linked to your site. Using tracking codes makes this easier. The result gives you the average visits per tweet and retweet. Once you have this number in hand, you can look at the behavior of visitors who arrive from Twitter and compare it against those who find you from other sources. Look at page views per visit, time spent on the site, and visitor paths to identify what percentage of Twitter visitors become leads or customers. Using your standard qualifying metrics, you should be able to determine the average value of a Twitter visitor.

For example, if 1,000 visitors arrived from Twitter in a given month as a result of 20 tweets, that yields an average of 50 visits per tweet. If you know that 5 percent of Twitter visitors register for a download or newsletter and that the value of an average registrant is $50, then you can calculate that Twitter delivers $2,500 in business value, or an average of $125 per tweet. If you have 5,000 followers, then you can also calculate that an average follower is worth 2.5 cents.

This formula is overly simplistic, of course. Not all Twitter followers are created equal. If you want to dive deeper into the mechanics of influence, services like TweetReach.com and Twinfluence.com can calculate the total reach of your followers or tweets according to so-called second-order followers, or those who follow the people who follow you. These metrics can also be used to estimate the value of retweets by certain popular members.

This same approach may also be applied to finding the value of Facebook fans, LinkedIn connections, SlideShare followers, and the like. When they launched the 2011 Ford Explorer, the Ford Motor Company ran online display ads giving users the choice to click through to a Facebook Page or a destination landing page. According to Scott Monty, the automaker's digital and multimedia communications manager, unique visitors coming from the Facebook page were 30 percent more likely to take the intended on the landing page than visitors who clicked through from the display ad. Of course they were. They were more engaged. How's that for social marketing ROI?

CHAPTER FIFTEEN

What's Next for B2B Social Media?

"There's a sucker born every minute," declared David Hannum, a nineteenth-century showman and rival of circus impresario P.T. Barnum. That statement may have been true when Hannum was perpetuating the Cardiff Giant hoax in the 1860s,[1] but it doesn't hold water today.

"Wait a minute," you object. "I thought Barnum uttered that famous quote."

Nope. Google it. As Casey Stengel (not Yogi Berra) once said, "You could look it up." (Not "You can look it up," as many people misstate that quote as well.)

We've just shown you two examples of why the half-life of misinformation is becoming perilously short in the days of social media. Today, we are just a few clicks away from the truth, or at least popular opinion, about almost anything. As barriers to information sharing have fallen away, our ability to be misinformed has diminished. The consequences of this change on businesses and institutions is nothing short of revolutionary.

There are still suckers in the world, but today they're also informants. Experiences are quickly shared online, and those who try to obfuscate or deceive are rapidly unmasked. Transparency happens. Opacity is death.

Social media is not a strategy or tactic. It's a channel that no one controls. Customers can use it to talk about you as easily as you can use it to talk about yourself. Now that anyone can publish and search, buyers and sellers can easily discover one another. Sharing insulates people from repeating others' mistakes.

To succeed with social marketing, a company must surrender ultimate control of the message. Social media will instantly fact-check claims against a global encyclopedia of customer experience. Business marketers will learn to promote positive customer interactions, invite feedback, and participate in existing conversations. They will also learn that social media impacts every corner of the operation, not just the marketing department.

Social marketing is a team sport. To win, companies must convince their advocates to engage and devote resources to listening. "You can just broadcast company news, but I don't think that's too interesting," says Adam Ostrow, editor-in-chief of Mashable.com, a social media news site. "The way we use social media as a brand, and the way businesses we like are using it, is to interact."

In *The World Is Flat,* Thomas Friedman observed that the Internet is neutralizing historical and geographical divisions and creating a field in which competitors half a world away can play as easily as if they were next door. This will force businesses to reassess their value propositions. Proximity and exclusivity will be less important. Businesses that thrived in the past because they were the only game in town will find themselves suddenly marginalized. Differentiators like customer service, innovation, and relationships will become critical. B2B companies will have a somewhat easier time with this transformation because their customers are more likely to value relationships than people who buy consumer products. But almost no one will be untouched by this redistribution of priorities.

Five years ago, Paul paid a professional designer $1,000 to create a business logo in a process that consumed over a month of time. Two years ago, he farmed out a comparable job to an Indian designer he had never met who finished the job in three days. Price: $47.

Lesson: If you're in the graphic design business these days, you'd better be scrambling to find a niche.

Crowdsourcing—or outsourcing projects to freelancers through an online work exchange network like Elance, Guru.com, or Amazon's Mechanical Turk—is undermining the value of proximity. These networks provide access to a global marketplace of talent from every desktop. They are massively disrupting some markets, but enabling others, as in the case of the Oil Spill Recovery Institute, which solved an intractable problem by asking the world for help (see Chapter 13).

"Ecosystems around platforms like Mechanical Turk and new entrant LiveWork will likely exceed $100 million per year, as will offerings from mature services like Elance and Guru.com as they continue to perfect the user experience across a wide range of work categories," concluded a study conducted by SmartSheet.com.[2]

Inside-Out Marketing

Social media is forcing companies to look beyond external communications and take stock of their internal practices as well. The fresh crop of young recruits now arriving on the scene will expect to use the same tools in business that they use at home. Employers who continue to restrict access to Facebook, YouTube, and other tools of communication will find themselves increasingly isolated. Whether people are using Twitter or something else a decade from now doesn't matter; they will never give up the freedom it brings. "Letting people do what they do and socialize in a way that supports their work is going to be critically important," says Chris Messina, open web advocate at Google.

Social media shifts the balance of power from employer to employee. Glassdoor.com is a social network where people share inside information about the places they work, including salary data. On Unvarnished.com, members rate the performance of their colleagues. Hiring managers at listed companies have far less flexibility to dicker on salary or candy-coat workplace conditions. Employees no longer need to accept a new position at a company to see if it's a good fit.

Businesses that want to hire the best and the brightest need to create an environment that employees will recommend to their peers.

The business of public relations is changing, too. Press releases, although often necessary, are highly inefficient. While organizations struggle to approve them, unofficial voices fill the void with opinions. The chain of command simply cannot keep pace with the speed of the crowd. Just ask BP LLC.

Examine your internal and external business practices. Try to learn how you can communicate more openly and rationalize what you're saying with what others are saying about you. It's the only way to have any control over the message.

Secrets of the River

People love to watch rivers, even if they're online. In Facebook, the newsfeed captivates our attention. In Twitter, it's the continuously updated tweet stream. In Google Analytics, it's the ability to visualize the behavior of our visitors over time. These are activity streams—digestible, bite-size chunks of information that keep us continuously informed about people, projects, and topics. They may just be the killer application of B2B social technology.

Sourceforge.org is a web site where software developers share and improve freely shared source code. The community solves problems more quickly than any individual member could because no one has control. Github.com is an alternative to Sourceforge that has a built-in activity stream. "I can friend or follow that code," says Google's Messina. "If any improvements are made, they appear in my activity stream."

Employees can use activity streams to keep abreast of deadlines and monitor the work of their colleagues. Project dependencies and milestones can trigger alerts that contributions are needed. If a project participant is reassigned or calls in sick, everyone who monitors the stream is informed. Being "in the loop" is no longer a matter of being on the right e-mail list. Anyone who's interested in an activity can subscribe to it.

Chatter is Salesforce.com's enterprise collaboration platform. It automatically pushes status reports and details to everyone who follows a project. Participants can update the activity stream and recipients can define sophisticated rules to filter the information they see. Instead of digging through e-mail inboxes choked with irrelevant information, people subscribe to what they need to know and unsubscribe when they're no longer interested.

Activity streams will revolutionize web analytics and replace project reports. Why spend the time creating a status report, when you can simply archive your status updates? In the future, we'll be able to watch activity on our web sites like we watch a movie. We'll rewind and zoom in on important events and members will opt in to tell us what content they shared and with whom. Businesses will gain insight into visitor motivations, not just entry pages and session lengths. Correlating content with activity streams will give us a much better gauge of how people react to our content.

The commercial Internet started life as a collection of static pages. In the future, it will be more like a river. But the rapids, eddies, and meanders will emerge and disappear with stunning speed. The challenge for businesses will be to anticipate them and react in anticipation.

Seven Habits of Highly Effective B2B Social Marketers

Altimeter Group analyst Jeremiah Owyang has said, "For business, real-time is no longer fast enough." As scary as that sounds, there's a lot of truth to it. In Chapter 1, we suggested that businesses must learn to get comfortable with making mistakes because markets no longer permit the luxury of taking the time to avoid them. Rapid response is replacing risk analysis. The most essential skill of the B2B marketer has become the ability to listen.

We wrap up our short look forward with a list of what we believe will be the essential attributes of successful B2B social marketers:

1. They will trust people to do the right thing.
   In *The Starfish and The Spider,* Ori Brafman and Rod Beckman argue that the top-down, militaristic hierarchies of the

industrial age are far more vulnerable to failure than self-healing decentralized systems. If you crush the head of a spider, its legs are useless. But if you cut off the leg of a starfish, it grows a new one. If your company is regenerative, then people and jobs can adapt more quickly at less cost. To get there, "you have to push more responsibility and control to the edges of the org chart," says Google's Messina.

2. They will think like customers.

   Rather than focus on what internal advocates think is important, marketers will learn to focus on what's important to customers. They will also learn to listen for implicit as well as explicit needs, understanding that customers often articulate problems better than solutions.

   Dell and Salesforce.com are two of the leaders in this area.

   Rather than guess what new products to develop, they listen to what customers say in online communities or they simply ask what customers want.

3. They will be interactive.

   Facebook's appeal is in its ability to connect people. In contrast, most web sites are still one-way channels. Engagement is an e-mail address, a web form, or a "request a quote" button. Static sites are far less interesting than social ones. Successful social marketers will leverage the technology of connection.

4. They won't get eaten.

   The Internet is chewing up entire industries. "The rule of cannibalization is you either cannibalize yourself, or someone else does it for you," says Pete Cashmore, chief executive officer (CEO) of Mashable.com. There is opportunity in destruction. Apple changed the music industry by making it easier for people to buy the song instead the album. While the old guard tried to rescue a dying business model, Apple invented a new one. Successful marketers will recognize when customer behavior is changing and anticipate opportunities these changes create.

This won't be easy or painless. The Internet is removing inefficiencies from many business processes with stunning speed. A lot of large and profitable industries—like mainstream media—are structurally inefficient. They and the people who work for them are suffering terribly as these institutions are torn down. Efficiency can be painful. The Industrial Revolution gutted the livelihoods of many blacksmiths, cobblers and woodworkers, but a half-century later, it would have been hard to argue that our economy wasn't better off for the productivity gains.

5. They will be action-oriented.
   Setting up a council to draft a report on the potential impact of social media to be reviewed by upper management is a stall tactic. By the time a strategy is in place, competitors have moved on to something else. Planning cycles will be much shorter and action much quicker in the future. Successful companies will understand that speed creates the risk of error, but they'll tolerate that downside in exchange for more agility.
6. They will understand their unique value proposition.
   Businesses should be thinking about how the Internet changes their value proposition and move to where the puck is going to be. They will constantly look for sources of sustainable competitive advantage. Here are three B2B examples:

   Discount Provider. VistaPrint, a provider of low-cost, short-run printing and online marketing tools, stays on top of a cost-sensitive business by giving small business owners all sorts of free educational content about how to market with their products and services. The company maintains a comprehensive online marketing center and ongoing calendar of webinars that cover everything from social media marketing to writing compelling copy. It provides access to valuable content in exchange for the right to market to those who consume it.

   Specialized Provider. Indium Corporation addresses a highly specialized market by putting engineers in direct contact with customers. "Engineers think a certain way and speak certain languages. We get everyone else out of the middle," says Indium's Rick Short. Adds Mark Drapeau, online public diplomacy director at Microsoft, "If you're a marketing or PR person, you're just a conduit. Use social media to expose expertise to a broader audience."

High-End Provider. Korn/Ferry International is the world's largest executive recruiting firm. It places only those executives who earn $250,000 per year or more. "The process of finding candidates is becoming commoditized," says Korn/Ferry executive vice president Don Spetner. "The real value comes in helping clients assess the fit of a candidate and providing services to help them retain and maximize their performance." To reinforce that value, Korn/Ferry developed a proprietary online assessment tool that analyzes how candidates think.

7. They will fly without a net.
   At Facebook, employees develop new features on the live site. There is no replicated development database because that would delay the deployment of new features. That gives Facebook the ability to deploy new features very quickly. Google tests many of its innovations in public, acknowledging all the while that features may not work the way they're intended.

   These companies are learning, in the words of author Mike Moran, to *Do It Wrong Quickly*. They understand that customers can be remarkably forgiving if they know that the company is testing uncharted waters, particularly if those customers can see the people behind the effort.

The new world of B2B marketing is fraught with chaos, peril, uncertainty, and unprecedented opportunity. How lucky you are to be part of it!

APPENDIX

Elements of a Social Media Policy

Chapter 5 outlined the basic principles of social media policy and recommended procedures for preparing your own document. Here we offer specific topics that your policy should address and recommend language to use. There is a large database of downloadable policies at SocialMediaGovernance.com. We recommend looking up documents created by other companies similar to yours and using them as a guide.

Policy Statement

Begin with an official policy statement. This is the place to manage your company's reputation. You may want to involve the marketing or public relations department in drafting this language. If the policy is going to be publicly available, this is the section that will get read most.

Here are some of points you'll want to consider for this section:

1. Your company recognizes that its employees have the right to use social media if they choose.

2. Your company understands and appreciates that social media is fundamentally changing the way people communicate.
3. The same principles that apply to the activities of employees in your company's existing policies apply to social media as well.
4. Your company respects the legal rights of its employees.
5. This policy applies to activities both at work and outside of work if those activities affect job performance or any business interests.

Objectives

Before you circulate a draft for review, make sure you have consensus on the objective of the policy. Negotiating edits among your stakeholders is pointless unless everyone is working toward the same goals. If your goal is to empower employees to leverage social media and the information technology (IT) department's goal is to limit access (if it is, you've got some educating to do), these conflicts need to be ironed out first. Draft the policy to reinforce, not reform, the organization's existing personality.

Your objectives should look something like this:

1. Establish practical, reasonable, and enforceable guidelines by which <ORGANIZATION NAME> employees can conduct responsible, constructive social media engagement in both official and unofficial capacities.
2. Prepare <ORGANIZATION NAME> and its employees to utilize social media channels to help each other and the communities <ORGANIZATION NAME> serves, particularly in the event of a crisis, disaster, or emergency.
3. Protect <ORGANIZATION NAME> and its employees from violating municipal, state, or federal rules, regulations, or laws through social media channels.

If you live in the United States, you don't have the right to deny employees' right to free speech. But you can impose certain restrictions to protect your organization's reputation if employees' social media disclosures occur in a public forum. You cannot restrict employees from participating in a secure online social network, no matter how distasteful the purpose of that network may be.

Guiding Principles

Before diving into situational guidance, establish the overarching principles on which your organization's social media policy is founded.

For example, if your organization "trusts and expects employees to exercise personal responsibility whenever they use social media, which includes not violating the trust of those with whom they are engaged,"[1] then say so. If you believe that employees should "never use social media for covert advocacy, marketing, or public relations," and that they should "clearly identify themselves as employees when communicating on behalf of the organization," give them boilerplate disclaimers to include with any social media disclosures for which they have a potential conflict of interest or that could adversely affect your corporate reputation. For example:

1. "I work for <ORGANIZATION NAME>, and this is my personal opinion."[2]
2. "I am not an official <ORGANIZATION NAME> spokesperson but my personal opinion is . . ."
3. "The postings on this site are my own and don't necessarily represent <ORGANIZATION NAME>'s positions, strategies, or opinions."[3]

Disclaimers belong on employee profile pages. A disclaimer inside a blog post or status update is insufficient. It also may be a good idea to include a second disclaimer in specific updates or comments if they could be easily misunderstood as official company statements.

Social media disclosures shouldn't be required for information that doesn't mention the company or relate to the company's business.

More guiding principles to consider:

1. Only designated spokespeople can make public disclosures on behalf of the company in an official capacity, but all

employees may use social media to make public disclosures for themselves individually.

2. All employees may use their personal social media accounts to refute false or misleading information online, but only if they comply with the terms of the policy. [The idea here is that all employees are encouraged to carry the company message into their online interactions, so long as they include the standard disclaimer, so their disclosures are not seen as representative of the official company line.]
3. While the company respects the rights of employees to use social media, it is every employee's responsibility to ensure it does not interfere with his or her ability to get the job done.

You may also wish to consider extending the policy to your company's contractors, vendors, and agencies.

In September 2009, Fleishman-Hillard senior vice president Seth Bloom appeared in a YouTube video to respond to criticism about client AT&T's delayed multimedia messaging service for iPhones.[4] The video did a pretty good job of explaining the reasons for the delay, but Bloom ambiguously identified himself as "the blogger guy with AT&T." In fact, he was the blogger relations point person on the account at Fleischman-Hillard. The issue here was one of attribution. Bloom presented himself as an AT&T employee, when he was not. The incident prompted embarrassing coverage in *Advertising Age* and charges of deceptive practices. Had AT&T had a social media policy that extended to outside service providers, perhaps this incident could have been avoided.

Disclosure and Transparency

Good reputations are built on trust. If you want people to trust you, you have be straight with them about who you are and any affiliations that may shape your opinion. Potential conflicts of interest can be handled by requiring employees to disclose their real identity and employment status when discussing company-related topics in public channels. If an employee has a vested interest in any topic being discussed, we recommend that employee be the one to point that out. Frankly, we can't imagine a context in which you would want your employees to represent themselves as anything other than who they are, but we think you should say so in your policy.

We also recommend requiring employees to be consistent across all their public-facing social media profile pages. Conflicting information from one social media account to the next can damage an individual's credibility, and that may reflect badly on the employer. As a rule of thumb, particularly at large organizations, you should have human resources (HR) remind new employees in their welcome materials or orientation that if they intend to refer to their job or employer in social media, they should include a standard disclosure. Make sure the social media policy discourages ambiguity along these lines. When using Twitter, the profile and/or user name can fulfill this function (for example, @Richard_at_Dell).

Advise employees also to provide a functional means by which they can be contacted in a timely manner. If an employee starts a heated debate on a social media channel, you want to make sure he or she doesn't abandon those conversations without resolution. Employees who choose to engage in social media channels about issues related to their employer should be required to monitor feedback and respond to questions or comments in a timely manner or to notify someone else in the company to finish unresolved conversations.

One of the reasons traditional corporate gatekeepers often resist empowering unofficial spokespersons is that they've seen firsthand how the news media gets things wrong, and they fret that employees with no media relations experience will be sitting ducks for misinformation. One way to deal with this fear is to ask employees to only talk about company news or information that can be linked to on the official web site.

More disclosure and transparency issues to consider include:

1. Require that employees engage in company-related conversations only with other parties who also identify their affiliations.

2. Prohibit employees from masking their online identities.
3. Prohibit the bulk posting of messages, an unethical practice known as comment spam.
4. Insist that employees take special care when engaging directly with minors or avoid engaging with minors at all.

Not all social media disclosures are alike. The posting of a link to a press release on a branded company web site demands different disclosures than an expression of opinion.

Kodak does a particularly good job of disclosing all its business activity on Twitter through a simple web page that lists its various line-of-business and employee accounts (see Figure A.1).

Toyota, although not a B2B company, uses a custom JPEG background image on Twitter that lists the names of employees tweeting under that account, their subject matter expertise, and their individual Twitter IDs (see Figure A.2).

When objective information, such as links to press materials or other official company news is broadcast over the branded Toyota account, the tweets are left unsigned. But if any of these team members engages in conversations on the branded Twitter account, he or she assumes responsibility for what is said by signing initials. Extensive back-and-forth conversations can be transitioned to their individual accounts at the employee's discretion.

Compensation and Incentives

In 2009, the Federal Trade Commission (FTC) passed laws that make it illegal to pay a blogger, or anyone else outside of an organization, to write endorsements or other social media disclosures without publicly acknowledging the financial arrangement. We believe paying bloggers or individuals to write reviews or endorsements is a form of bribery, an unethical practice, and to be avoided. Nevertheless, in some cases it may be necessary to provide bloggers with accommodations, products for review, or other promotional materials so they can evaluate and opine on your products or services. In those instances, limit the value, and require that, if exceeded, it must be disclosed on the company's web site.

Connect with Kodak on Twitter

Follow the Kodak Corporate landscape

KodakCB

KodakCL

Keep up with Kodak community and events

KodakEvents

KodakChallenge

KodakCommunity

Watch for Consumer news and deals

KodakDeals

KodakConnect

KodakPrinters

GalleryExposure

Explore the latest trends in Graphic Communications

kodakidigiprint

Follow our International tweeters

Kodak_DE

Kodak_UK

Kodak_FR

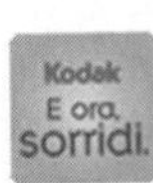

Kodak_IT

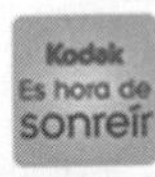

Kodak_ES

Kodak_RU

Kodak_AU

flickr

YouTube

Figure A.1 Kodak Social Media Presence.

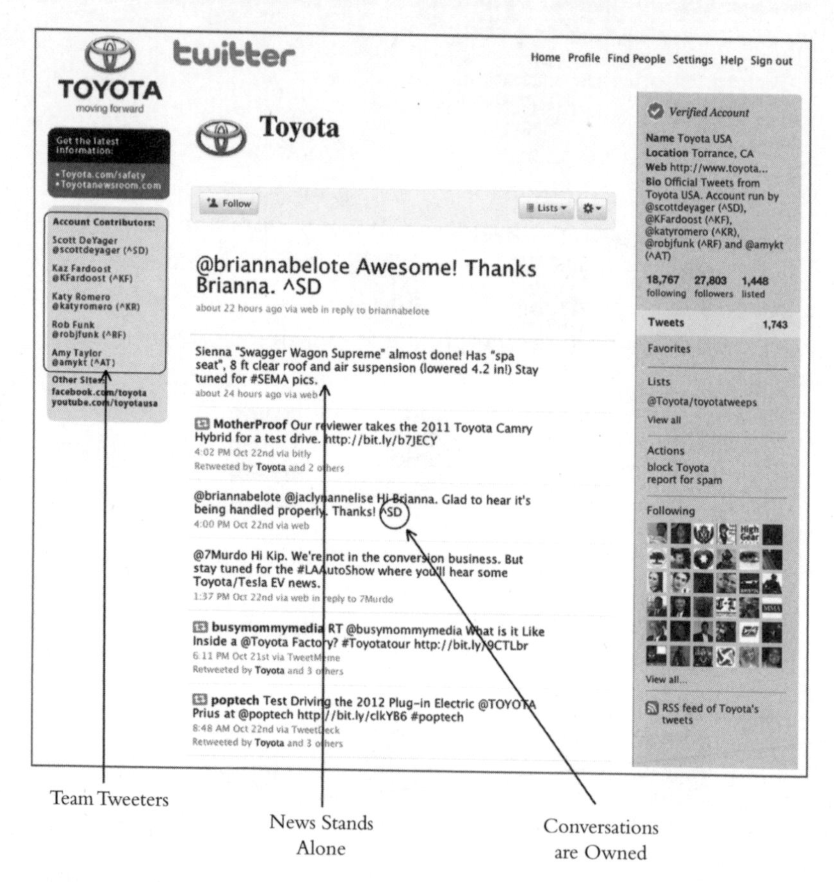

Figure A.2 Toyota on Twitter.

To help companies comply with the new FTC guidelines, the Word of Mouth Marketing Association (WOMMA) has a "Social Media Marketing Disclosure Guide" that suggests disclosure language such as, "I received <item> from <company>," "I received <item> from <company> to review," "I was paid by <company> to review," and "I am an employee or representative of <company>." In the case of Twitter, WOMMA recommends using hash tag notations like #spon (sponsored), #paid (paid), or #samp (sample).

Respectfulness

Encourage employees to be mindful of your company's core values in their social media disclosures. Of all the factors that could contribute to an unflattering representation of your organization by an employee, lack of respectfulness or intolerance is the most common cause.

Disrespectful behavior like harassing others, using ethnic slurs, making personal insults, and exhibiting racial or religious intolerance is probably already restricted by your company's code of conduct policy. Extending that to you social media policy is easy enough.

Encourage employees to demonstrate respect by striving to advance conversations in a constructive, meaningful way. Solicitous product pitches that don't answer a question are disrespectful, as are tweeted links to landing pages that have nothing to do with the conversation, or loading tweets with irrelevant hashtags.

Privacy

As an employer, your policy needs to protect your employees' rights to personal privacy and to keep their personal beliefs, thoughts, opinions, and emotions private. Prohibit employees from sharing anything via social media that could compromise the personal privacy of their colleagues.

Employees have the right to privacy of their physical likeness as well. That means your policy should preclude employees from sharing pictures or video of their colleagues without obtaining their permission. Disclosure of private facts about others based on speculation or unreasonable intrusion should also be off limits.

Confidentiality

Employees should be restricted from referencing project details or customers, partners, and suppliers by name in all external social media channels without explicit permission. These channels should also never be used to conduct internal company business, resolve internal disputes, or discuss confidential business dealings with outside contacts. As a rule of thumb, when in doubt, leave it out.

Security

If you work at a company or organization whose facilities are possible targets for acts of terrorism or armed robbery, prohibit the use of cameras or other visual recording devices, the creation of text messages, text descriptions, e-mails, photographs, sketches, pictures, drawings, maps, graphical representations, or explanations of your facility or complex without obtaining approval of the external communications department or executive management. Social media communications are semiprivate at best. Employees should never share any information that could compromise the security of any company-owned or company-operated facility.

Diplomacy

Remind employees that people with different political views, religious backgrounds, and sexual orientations may read their social media disclosures. Ask them in your policy to think long and hard before releasing a status update that could negatively impact intangibles such as corporate reputation and morale. Again, when in doubt, leave it out.

If yours is the type of company that prefers to take the high road, you may also want to discourage employees from making negative references to competitors unless the claims can be attributed to a neutral, nonpartisan third-party source by means of a hyperlink. Even then, we believe accentuating the positive is just good business sense.

Legal Matters

To protect your company and employees from infringing on the copyright claims of others, you should establish guidelines for exactly how and how not to share.

These guidelines, which were inspired by the Associated Press Stylebook 2009 "Briefing on Media Law," can help shed light on how you might structure parameters around intellectual property ownership:

1. Employees may share links that transit users to works hosted by rightful copyright owners or their resellers without obtaining permission first.
2. Employees may share an excerpt of up to 140 characters without obtaining the copyright holder's permission, as long as the work being shared is publicly available on a rightful copyright holder's web site and provided the sharing is not being done to undermine the financial objectives of the copyright owner.
3. Employees may embed copyrighted content in social media channels without obtaining the permission of the copyright owner, as long as the embed code has been provided by a rightful copyright owner.
4. In unusual circumstances such as disasters or emergencies, where the public's right to know outweighs the financial objectives of the rightful copyright owner, employees may share copyrighted works without the permission of the copyright owner. Examples include images of a rapidly advancing wildfire, a natural disaster, or an act of terrorism.

To circumvent acts of libel, employees should be restricted from using social media to evaluate the performance of their co-workers, vendors, or partners or to criticize or complain about the behavior or actions of customers.

Employees should also be restricted from using social media channels to discuss or comment on their employer's financial performance (a critical factor at U.S.-based public companies), legal matters, or litigation.

During Emergencies

Social media tools are becoming increasingly important in emergency management communications. Even in times of crisis, though, only employees with the authority to speak on behalf of your company should be authorized to do so in an official capacity.

It's fine to encourage all employees to share official company information via social media channels during a crisis, disaster, or emergency, but be sure they limit communications to official company information. In an emergency, it's better to link to official information at the source than to try to summarize.

If an employee who isn't authorized to speak for the organization has valuable information that could benefit those affected by the emergency, require that they post a disclaimer.

If an employee decides to endorse or republish someone else's social media disclosure about your company, or a company-related topic, make sure he or she verifies that the social media disclosure being republished was, in fact, distributed by the attributed source. For example, before retweeting someone else's tweet, verify that the user cited did, in fact, distribute that tweet by visiting their Twitter account to check its origin. There have been numerous cases in which false tweets attributed to news sources were redistributed by others to promote misinformation and confusion. Anyone can make up a retweet.

Penalties

Make it clear that the failure to comply with your company's social media policy may result in withdrawal, without notice, of access to company information, disciplinary action up to termination, and civil or criminal penalties as provided by law. For vendors, contractors, and agencies, state that penalties may, at the company's discretion, be enforced against the company, or the company's primary point of contact, and the company employee to which that person reports.

Definitions

Company policies often include a glossary of terms. Given that everyone needs to have the same understanding of where the boundaries lie and that the mechanics of emerging technologies may not be understood be all parties, we recommend you include a set of definitions on your social media policy as well.

Here are a few to consider. Expect them to change and be updated over time.

1. **Social media channels.** Blogs, microblogs, wikis, social networks, social bookmarking services, user rating services, and any other online collaboration, sharing, or publishing platform, whether accessed through the web, a mobile device, text messaging, e-mail, or any other existing or emerging participatory communications platform.
2. **Social media account.** A personalized presence inside a social networking channel, initiated at will. YouTube, Twitter, Facebook, and other social networking channels allow users to sign up for their own social media account, which they can use to collaborate, interact, and share content and status updates. When users communicate through a social media account, their disclosures are identified as coming from the user ID they specify when they sign up for the social media account.
3. **Profile page.** Social media account holders can customize the information about themselves that is available to others on their profile page.
4. **Hosted content.** Text, pictures, audio, video, and other information in digital form that is uploaded and available for publication. If you download content from the Internet and then upload it to your social media account, you are hosting that content. This distinction is important because it is generally illegal to host copyrighted content publicly on the Internet without first obtaining the permission of the copyright owner.
5. **Social media disclosures.** These include blog posts, blog comments, status updates, text messages, posts via e-mail, images, audio recordings, video recordings, and any other information made available through a social media channel. Social media disclosures are the actual communications a

user distributes through a social media channel, usually by means of an account.

6. **External vs. internal social media channels.** External social media channels are services that are not hosted by the company, such as Facebook. Internal social media channels are hosted by the company, reside behind a firewall, and are visible only to company employees and other approved individuals.
7. **Copyrights.** Copyrights protect the right of an author to control the reproduction and use of any creative expression that has been fixed in tangible form, such as literary, graphical, photographic, audiovisual, electronic, and musical works.
8. **Embed codes.** Unique codes that are provided to entice others to share online content without requiring the sharer to host that content. By means of an embed code, it is possible to display a YouTube user's video in someone else's social media space without requiring that person to host the source video file. Embed codes are often used by copyright owners to encourage others to share their content via social media channels.
9. **Company or company-related topics.** Examples include news and information about your industry, businesses, employees, customers, trading partners, products, and services.
10. **Official company information.** Publicly available online content created by the company, verified by virtue of the fact that it is accessible through a company-owned and company-operated domain.
11. **Links and inbound links.** A link transits a user from one domain to another. A hyperlink that transits from an external domain to your own domain is referred to as an inbound link.
12. **Tweets and retweets.** A tweet is a 140-character social media disclosure distributed on the Twitter microblogging service. Retweets are tweets from one Twitter user that are redistributed by another Twitter user. Retweets are how information propagates on Twitter.

There may be other terms you would want to include based on the social media aptitude of the community your policy is intended to serve. In our experience, the 12 terms noted here are the major areas that need to be addressed.

Social Etiquette Online

Everything you need to know about social media participation, you learned in preschool: no biting, stealing, kicking, scratching, lying, or cheating. The customs and social norms we accept as appropriate in the physical world apply in cyberspace, too. In the name of specificity, spell them out.

A solid social media policy establishes guidelines for effective social media engagement enterprise-wide. Social skills are much more important than technical skills, and a social media policy needs to clearly articulate those intangible, personality-specific skills that determine an individual's strength as a team player or a community member.

NOTES

Preface

1. "Google Sites Account for Two-Thirds of 131 Billion Searches Conducted Worldwide in December," New Media Institute, Jan. 22, 2010. http://bit.ly/B2BSearch.
2. "Building Effective Landing Pages," Marketo, 2009, http://bit.ly/B2BMarketo.
3. "The Rise of the Digital C-Suite: How Executives Locate and Filter Business Information," *Forbes Insights,* http://bit.ly/B2BForbes.
4. Alan E. Webber, Eric G. Brown, and Robert Muhlhausen, *How to Take B2B Relationships from Indifferent to Engaged* (Cambridge, MA: Forrester Research, 2009), http://bit.ly/B2BForrester.

Chapter 1

1. "B2B Online Marketing in the United States: Assessment and Forecast to 2013," AMR International, 2010, http://bit.ly/B2BAMR.
2. "Business.com's B2B Social Media Benchmarking Study," December 2009, http://bit.ly/B2BBenchmark.

Chapter 2

1. "Paid Crowdsourcing, Current State & Progress Toward Mainstream Business Use," SmartSheet.com, September 2009, http://bit.ly/B2BCrowd.

Chapter 3

1. Software executive and former analyst Peter Kim has amassed a list of nearly 1,500 social media marketing examples at http://wiki.beingpeterkim.com/.
2. Robert Half Technology, "Whistle—But Don't Tweet—While You Work," March 2010, http://bit.ly/B2BSMMHalf.
3. Cision, "National Survey Finds Majority of Journalists Now Depend on Social Media for Story Research," January 20, 2010. http://bit.ly/B2BCision.
4. Jeffrey Tomich, "Monsanto Planting Cyber Seeds," *St. Louis Post-Dispatch,* March 29, 2009, http://bit.ly/B2BMonsanto.
5. "The Living Company: Habits for Survival in a Turbulent Business Environment," *BusinessWeek,* www.businessweek.com/chapter/degeus.htm.

Chapter 5

1. http://bit.ly/B2BPolicies.
2. http://bit.ly/B2BAltPolicies.

Chapter 6

1. Doug Ngo, "Blogging Declines among Teens, Young Adults," CNET, Feb. 3, 2010, http://bit.ly/B2BBlogging.
2. Michael Krigsman, "Blogger Relations at SAP," ZDNet, Jan. 5, 2010, http://bit.ly/B2BSAP.

Chapter 7

1. "The State of Inbound Lead Generation: Analysis of Lead Generation Best Practices Used by Over 1,400 Small- and Medium-Sized Businesses," HubSpot, March 2010, http://bit.ly/B2BHubSpot.

Chapter 8

1. "Twitter Usage In America: 2010," Edison Research, April, 2010. http://bit.ly/B2BTwitterUse.

Chapter 9

1. http://bit.ly/B2BTrust.

Chapter 11

1. Number of fans/followers multiplied by fan/followers of people who follow you.

Chapter 13

1. That isn't always the case, as makers of some technology products have learned. For example, many underground forums tell how to hack everything from an iPod to a Toyota Prius. That isn't the kind of value the company support form should provide, however.
2. http://www.smartsheet.com/paid-crowdsourcing-current-state-and-progress.
3. http://www.outsellinc.com/press/press_releases/news_users_2009.

Chapter 15

1. Google it.
2. "Paid Crowdsourcing: Current State & Progress toward Mainstream Business Use," Smartsheet.com, September 2009, http://bit.ly/B2BCrowd.

Appendix

1. IBM Social Computing Guidelines, http://bit.ly/B2BSMMIBM.
2. Social Media Business Council, Disclosure Best Practices Checklist 2, http://www.socialmedia.org/disclosure/personalunofficial/.
3. IBM Social Computing Guidelines.
4. PR Newser, http://bit.ly/B2BSMMATT.

ABOUT THE AUTHORS

Paul Gillin is an award-winning technology journalist who caught the social media bug in 2005 and has never looked back. He advises marketers and business executives on how to optimize their use of social media, search, and other online channels. His clients have included the Walt Disney Company; Turner Broadcasting; Mars, Inc.; Volvo; Qualcomm; and Corning. He is a popular speaker who is known for his ability to simplify complex concepts using plain talk, anecdotes, and humor.

This is Paul's fourth book about online communities. His other works are *The New Influencers* (2007), *Secrets of Social Media Marketing* (2008), and *The Joy of Geocaching* (2010), which he co-authored with his wife, Dana.

Paul was previously founding editor of online publisher Tech Target and editor-in-chief of the technology weekly *Computerworld*. He is a regular contributor to *BtoB* magazine and the author of two blogs: PaulGillin.com and NewspaperDeathWatch.com. He is also a popular media commentator who has been quoted in hundreds of news and radio reports since the early 1990s.

Paul is also a senior research fellow at the Society for New Communications Research and co-chair of the social media cluster for the Massachusetts Technology Leadership Council. He holds Red Sox season tickets and can often be found scuba diving during his all-too-infrequent tropical getaways. E-mail him at paul@gillin.com or follow @pgillin on Twitter.

Eric Schwartzman is a strategic corporate communications, public affairs, and public relations consultant whose clients have included AARP, Boeing, Cirque du Soleil, Johnson & Johnson, Lucasfilm, MGM Grand Casinos & Resorts, NORAD, Southern California Edison, the U.S. Department of State, the United States Marine Corps, and the Pussycat Dolls.

He helps assists with strategic communication strategy, policies, media audits, pilot programs, and training. He is a frequenter speaker at professional conferences and the creator of the SocialMediaBoot Camp.com training seminar. His award-winning podcast "On the Record . . . Online" (@ontherecord) about technology's impact on corporate communications has delivered more than 250 interviews with major figures in journalism and communications.

Eric started his career as a business-to-business marketer in entertainment and interactive gaming. He is the founder of iPressroom, an online newsroom software as a service provider, which was acquired in 2009 by private investors. E-mail him at eric@ericschwartzman .com or find him on Twitter at @ericschwartzman.

INDEX